## Lay This Body Down

CLYDE MANNING, Defendant's statement.

Gentlemen of the jury, and Judge, your Honor, I am not guilty of murder. The crime what I have done, I done it to save my own life. When these crimes was started, one day when they first started, that week, him and his three boys had been to Monticello. He was fixing to send them off. He knowed the men had been down there talking to the men on the farm and he was fixing to send them off. He come home after they come from town, and he says, "Clyde, we are going to do away with these boys and I want you to help." I knowed about them other men being killed on the place and I knowed what he was going to do. I says, "Mr. Johnny, I don't want to do that, I don't want to do it." And he says, "Well, by God, it is all right with me, if you don't want to, it means your neck or theirs; If you think more of their necks than you do of your own it is all right, if you do, it is yours. I have nobody to speak to or nobody to tell or have to help me or save me and I have to go to do it." I had to go with him that night. After these killings started, he would call me all through the night. He would call me during the night to see if the cows were in the wheat or in the oats and he would say he heard a noise with the mules and for me to see if any of them were hung, and I figured it he was calling me to see if I was off the place. If I had been off the place he would have found me and he would have brought me back there, and would have killed me. He would have put the dog on me and caught me.

If I had had any chance to get away I would have tried it.

I didn't do what I done of my own free will. I had to do it, and I will tell you gentlemen, before God if

# LAY THIS BODY DOWN

## The 1921 Murders of Eleven Plantation Slaves

GREGORY A. FREEMAN

Lawrence Hill Books

**Library of Congress Cataloging-in-Publication Data**

Freeman, Gregory A.
　　Lay this body down: the 1921 murder of eleven plantation slaves /
Gregory A. Freeman. — 1st ed.
　　　　p.　　cm.
　　Includes bibliographical references.
　　ISBN 1-55652-357-2
　　1. Manning, Clyde. 2. Williams, John S. 3. Murder — Georgia —
Jasper County Case studies. 4. Afro-Americans — Crimes against —
Georgia — Jasper County Case studies. 5. Plantation workers — Crimes
against — Georgia — Jasper County Case studies. 6. Trials (Murder) —
Georgia — Jasper County Case studies. 7. Peonage — Georgia — Jasper
County. I. Title
HV6534.J36F74　　　1999
364.15'23'09758583 — dc21　　　　　　　　　　　　　　　99-23182
　　　　　　　　　　　　　　　　　　　　　　　　　　　　　　　　CIP

© 1999 by Gregory A. Freeman
All rights reserved
First edition
Published by Chicago Review Press, Incorporated
814 North Franklin Street
Chicago, Illinois 60610
Printed in the United States of America
ISBN 1-55652-354-8
5 4 3 2 1

"Also worthy of emphasis are the peculiar characteristics of Williams and Manning, as disclosed by Williams's nonchalance and utter disregard for the life of a negro, although otherwise he was a law-abiding, prosperous farmer who was kind to his family and neighbors; while Manning was noted for his simplicity and lack of criminal impulses, but was absolute clay in the hands of his lord and master."

*Excerpt from report of the federal Bureau of Investigation, 1932*

# Contents

# Acknowledgments

Writing this book was a deeply personal experience, but one that inevitably drew in those around me. I must thank a few people who played significant roles in the completion of this book.

First and foremost, I would like to thank my dear friend Wesley Hardegree, a man who knows a good story when he sees it. Without Wes bringing the story of Clyde Manning and John S. Williams to my attention, *Lay This Body Down* would not have been written.

Others made their own contributions, large and small, along the way. To all my good friends and family, I want to express my great appreciation for your enthusiastic support. Your confidence and expressions of interest inspired me to press forward with the project, assuring me that others would see the significance of this story. A great many of my friends deserve notice, but I must mention Todd Maki, Dana Hasbrouck, Leslie Gray, Maureen Hardegree, Laura Bryant, Scott Moore, and John Buschman.

My publisher, Linda H. Matthews, provided valuable perspective, and, finally, I am eager to thank my editor, Yuval Taylor. Yuval was with me on this project practically from the beginning to the end, and his important contributions can be found throughout the book.

I thank you all.

# Introduction

From the moment of birth, we Southerners are immersed in the history of our homeland, and the focal point is always the Civil War. We can't travel ten miles without running across a battlefield, a marker commemorating a historic Civil War event, or a monument to fallen Confederate soldiers. The Civil War is seen as the defining moment in our history, a moment that abruptly shifted the region from one way of life to another.

But within all the history there is a lie. The lie, told to Southerners and everyone else, is that slavery disappeared after Appomattox. It did not. Slavery existed well into the twentieth century in America, in the form of peonage, whereby blacks were fined for vagrancy or other supposed crimes and then forced to work off the debt on local farms for what often became a lifetime of brutal conditions. For those trapped in peonage, the technical distinction between themselves and the slaves of a previous generation was meaningless.

Most of the participants in peonage, both perpetrators and victims, faded quickly into the dark night of history, never to be seen or spoken of again. But two of the last players in the South's struggle with slavery, a white farmer named John S. Williams and his black field hand, Clyde Manning, must not be forgotten. Their story shows that slavery, even fifty years after the Emancipation Proclamation, remained an insidious cruelty that robbed men of their humanity, free will, and, some would say, even their souls. As the victims of slavery became just a bad childhood memory in the Southern psyche, Clyde Manning lingers before taking that final step and fading away, lingering only because his tragic story has not yet been told.

Manning's story is unique. Not only was he a victim, he was a perpetrator. Though not a peon, he was a slave to Williams. Yet he was in charge of the other slaves on the plantation—locking them up at night, issuing work orders in the day, and holding men down as they were whipped. When Williams decided to rid himself of eleven black men, most of the dirty work was done by Manning. Men were chained and thrown off bridges as they begged for their lives, one was ordered to dig his own grave, and others were executed with an axe. Manning performed the killings with little protest because he knew the hopelessness of his own situation. Nevertheless, his compliance may be difficult, at this late date, to understand. Was Manning so completely controlled by the white farmer that he could not resist such terrible instructions, or had his servitude made him as cold and heartless as his master? Was he the twelfth victim or the second killer? This book hopes to at least suggest some answers to those questions.

The story of Manning and Williams is one of despondency and hopelessness for the individuals involved, but of transition and partial redemption for the region. It is a story of contradictions and surprises, a story that helps us redefine the South. Manning was caught in the last throes of American slavery, but he would benefit from some of the first efforts, however modest, to treat the black man as a human being. He was compelled to act as a Judas goat toward his fellow men but would finally help bring an end to the system that made his betrayal possible.

When it comes to the idea of blacks and whites existing as equals, side by side, the post–Civil War South has been caught in transition. In little more than a hundred years, it has moved from a time of undeniable cruelty to one of tolerance and hope, but the process has been painful, especially for blacks. The most obvious steps in this evolution were visible even to those watching from afar; the more subtle steps, however, were seen only by Southerners, and some only by the blacks and whites who actually lived through them.

This true story exemplifies this struggle. The deaths that occurred on a middle Georgia plantation in 1921 became an important step in the evolution of the South. All at once they bore witness to the almost unbelievable cruelty of whites who still saw blacks as belongings to be used and discarded, and the evolving attitude of a society and a justice system that no longer accepted that notion as a certainty. In 1921, Georgia was on the cusp of understanding. John S. Williams was being left behind, and he didn't even know it.

For Williams, the American South was still the land he grew up in. A South in which the black man was free, but just barely. A South in which the white man was in control, totally. A South in which there was no question that a white man's word would be taken over that of a black man.

But for Clyde Manning, the American South was simply the two thousand acres of the Williams plantation. Clyde Manning was an anachronism, a black overseer of slaves nearly sixty years after the Civil War. While the rest of the world moved forward, Manning lived a life almost exactly like that of his ancestors in bondage.

And now, many years later, this chapter of American history is almost lost, unknown even to those living on the very land where the events took place, unknown even to Southerners who acknowledge the many dark points in the region's history. And it is a story that is certainly unknown to anyone who has never touched the red clay of Georgia.

For those of us who grew up on that red clay, this story is difficult to hear. I first learned of it in the middle of the 1996 Summer Olympic Games in the city I am proud to call my home. As the entire world focused attention on Atlanta, which was in turn doing its very best to dispel any stereotypes about a backward, racist South, I stumbled across a story that made me feel ashamed to be a Southerner. A friend had been looking through some historical material on his family in the area of middle Georgia where these events took place, and he found a brief account of the killings in a local history book. As we prepared to go to an Olympic event one morning, he tossed the book in my lap and said, "You won't believe this."

My first reaction was utter shock. Antebellum slavery is well known, of course, and I knew that it had taken more than a hundred years after the war for Southern blacks to achieve anything close to true equality. But I did not know that there had been an interim period in which slavery quietly persisted while Southerners allowed the world to believe that they had done away with it.

The existence of slavery in 1921 was shocking enough, but I also was disturbed that I had never heard about this episode in my home's history. It was so terrible, so important, yet it was news to me. As I discussed it, I realized that my circle of well-educated friends and colleagues were just as surprised as I was. This was not a matter of one Southerner having overlooked a crucial part of his history. This was a gross oversight by our homeland, if not an outright effort to obliterate the history of what happened to Clyde Manning and the many thousands of men and women like him.

I knew that I had to tell this story. But I was reluctant to focus attention on such a disgraceful episode, because I knew that it would inevitably reinforce every negative stereotype about my home. The story was true, but, as a white man living in the South, I was ashamed to tell it.

But then I realized that there is more to it than a series of shocking murders and two gripping courtroom dramas. The story of Clyde Manning and John S. Williams runs much deeper than the horror on the surface. What begins as a tale of murder on a single plantation becomes increasingly significant as it unfolds. We see that the killings were only the defining events of an epic tale involving federal investigators who unwittingly prompted the murders of eleven innocent men, a state governor faced with an opportunity to correct his own past misdeeds, the nation's press in search of the seminal definition of Southern racism, and wealthy Atlanta socialites who astounded everyone by attempting to rescue a black man who admitted to eleven murders.

This story may be discouraging for any Southerner who tries to focus on what is good about the region, for it is a terribly tragic one. But in the end, there is solace in knowing that the white community did not fulfill all the negative expectations of a nation that expected to find rabid racists running the court system. The community that allowed slavery to exist is the same community that came through and tried to do the right thing in the end. I choose to believe that this is the essence of the South.

In writing this book, I felt very strongly that I must provide a reliable, historical account, since there is no other complete one available. But I also wanted to provide insight into the mind of Manning and tell the story in a compelling way. With those goals in view, I provide here an entirely factual exposition of the events while also providing some modest assessments of Manning's mindset at critical points. While unprovable, these assessments are based on my understanding of Manning from his own statements and actions.

Nothing in this book is fictionalized. Everything happened as it is depicted here. All of the dialogue is based on statements documented during the investigation and trials. Extremely detailed information is available: the testimony in two murder trials, reports from a federal investigation lasting several years, and extensive newspaper coverage from the days when readers relied on a highly descriptive printed account to set the scene. The descriptions of a person's demeanor, appearance, or precisely what sort of action took place are all based on reports of the time and the recollections of those involved. In the few instances in which the records are unclear or contradictory, I provide the most likely scenario based on the overall situation and characteristics of those involved.

The title of this book is taken from an old slave song. Just as they had a hundred years earlier, sorrowful spirituals often rang through the night on the Williams plantation, the mournful words helping to ease the pain of those caught in a world they could not imagine escaping. On the death of a black man or woman, the song often was "Lay This Body Down," a melancholy madrigal in which one singer would begin and the rest would follow in unison, repeating the refrain around an all-night campfire. More than just a song of mourning, it was a longing for peace, release, and freedom. Its lyrics describe the hopelessness of a life in slavery and a bittersweet yearning for the peace that would come only with death.

On the Williams plantation, sadly, there often was occasion to sing such a sorrowful song. One can imagine Clyde Manning singing it as if he knew the truth in every word:

*O graveyard, O graveyard, walkin' troo de graveyard; lay this body down.*
*I know moonlight, I know starlight, I'm walking troo de starlight; lay this body down.*
*I know de graveyard, I know de graveyard, when I lay this body down.*
*I lay in de grave an' stretch out my arms; I lay this body down.*
*I go to de judgment in de evenin' of de day, when I lay this body down.*
*And my soul and your soul will meet in de day, when we lay this body down.*

# Participants

## On the plantation

John S. Williams—*white plantation owner in Jasper County, Georgia*

Huland Williams, Leroy Williams, Marvin Williams—*adult sons living on the plantation with their father*

Gus Williams—*another son, a physician, living elsewhere in Georgia*

Clyde Manning—*black worker on the Williams plantation, acting as farm boss over the other men*

Rena Manning—*his wife*

Gladys (or Gladdis) Manning, Julius Manning—*his brothers*

Grace Napier—*his sister*

Emma (or Indie) Manning—*his mother*

Rufus Manning—*his uncle*

Clyde Freeman—*black worker on the Williams plantation, Clyde Manning's third cousin*

Claude Freeman (aka Shorty)—*black worker on the Williams plantation, brother of Clyde Freeman, also acted as farm boss over some of the other workers*

## Other black workers (a partial list)

Johnny Benson (aka Johnny Benford, Little Bit)

John Brown (aka Big Red, Red)

Gus Chapman

Charlie Chisolm

Frank Dozier

June Dunning

Fred Favers

Emma Freeman

John Will Gaither (aka Big John)

Willie Givens

Will Goosby

Johnny Green

Iron John (aka Long John, Iron Jaw) (not the same as Big John)
Will Napier (married to Grace Napier, Clyde Manning's sister)
Lindsey Peterson
Willie Preston
Harry Price (aka Foots)
John Singleton
Fletcher Smith
James Strickland
Nathaniel Wade (aka Blackstrap)
Johnnie Williams (not to be confused with John S. Williams)

## Off the plantation

Eberhardt Crawford—*black resident of Covington, Georgia, in Newton County*

A. J. Wismer and George W. Brown—*agents of the federal Bureau of Investigation (later known as the FBI)*

Hugh Dorsey—*Governor of the State of Georgia, 1917–1921*

John B. Hutcheson—*Judge of the Stone Mountain circuit in Georgia, presiding over the trials of Williams and Manning*

B. L. Johnson—*Sheriff of Newton County*

B. B. Bohannon—*Chief of Police in Covington, the seat of Newton County*

Dr. C. T. Hardeman—*Newton County physician who examined the bodies of the murdered men*

A. M. Brand—*Newton County solicitor, chief prosecutor in the trials of Williams and Manning*

Graham Wright—*Assistant Attorney General for the State of Georgia, assisting the prosecution*

W. M. Howard—*special state's attorney, assisting the prosecution*

Greene F. Johnson—*Williams's defense attorney*

E. Marvin Underwood—*Manning's defense attorney*

A. D. Meadows—*Covington judge assisting in Manning's defense*

W. Woods White, Dr. C. B. Wilmer, Dr. M. Ashby Jones—*white Atlantans who helped fund Manning's defense and the prosecution of Williams*

# 1

---

# "Don't Throw Me Over"

Jasper and Newton Counties in central Georgia are not all that different from the way they were in 1921, at least as far as the more pleasant aspects of Southern culture are concerned. More than three-quarters of a century after the murder trials of John S. Williams and Clyde Manning, they, like many Southern communities, have changed for the better in terms of racial equality and integration while retaining much of their old Southern-style charm.

Pick any small Southern town and you can see a study in the conflicts that have shaped the region over the past century. Blacks and whites still mainly keep to themselves when it comes to churches, civic groups, and social gatherings, but the rest of their lives overlap in an easy, routine way. The vestiges of segregation are still there, as is plenty of overt racism, but the American South is not what many outsiders think it is. And quite possibly, it never was.

Jasper and Newton Counties are typical examples of small Southern communities that have held on to their local identities even as nearby towns have been swallowed by urbanization and robbed of commerce and population. On a typical afternoon, the county seats, Covington in Newton County and Monticello in Jasper County, are still alive with the flow of local residents, both of them far enough away from the sprawling Atlanta metropolis to retain their small-town independence.

And Covington and Monticello are still deeply Southern. Atlanta is Southern only in comparison to other big American cities; in many ways it has become a generic big city without the personality that defines a Southern community. A great many residents of Atlanta were not born in the South, and, even if they have decided that they really do like grits, there is no connection to the land on which they live. But in Covington and Monticello, the people know that they are Southerners, and they are proud of it. Their towns are slow and peaceful, seemingly content to idle quietly as the world around them picks up speed.

Monticello is the smaller of the two, consisting almost entirely of a town square surrounded by old brick storefronts, not all of them occupied. Monticello is holding on, but just as in 1921, it is only the front door to a rural community. Nearby Covington is much more alive. While still a pleasant little spot where the hours stroll by with no hurry, there is business to do and people to see. Both towns look traditional, with green, parklike town squares surrounded by brick-front stores; the highest points are the old courthouses with clocks on their towers. Monticello has only a smattering of businesses downtown, but Covington is still a commercial center for both counties. Around the city square, stores offer hardware, furniture, insurance, real estate, drugs, and one even offers Web pages. At Smiley's Restaurant, a country cookin' buffet, you can "catch a good meal at a good price," and the sign touting the new Sunday dinner hours ends with a hearty "God Bless You!" Inside, blacks and whites enjoy fried chicken and banana pudding together while listening to old-fashioned gospel music.

Just beyond the town squares are dozens of beautiful neoclassical Southern mansions with tall white columns, wide wraparound porches, brilliant white paint, and little signs indicating how soon after the Civil War destroyed most homes of that type they were built. Because it is still so picturesque, so typically Southern, Covington was used for the opening montage of the popular television series *In the Heat of the Night*, with the Newton County Courthouse featured prominently.

These are communities where people still wave at each other as they pass on the street whether they know each other or not, and the occasional out-of-towner is spotted on the sidewalk right away. Every other vehicle is a pickup truck, but a fair number of minivans also slowly circle the town square. The county sheriff still provides an escort to funeral processions, and drivers traveling in both directions still pull over to the side of the road as a sign of respect while the procession passes. The occasional honking horn on the streets means someone has spotted a friend and wants to say hello; it couldn't mean that anyone had been so rude as to honk in anger. And on a Saturday afternoon outing to the library, a twelve-year-old boy with an accent like sweet molasses can openly dote over his aging grandmother, calling her "Honey" and making sure she has everything she needs.

In both towns, the focal point of the town square is the local courthouse. Both are traditional structures, the Monticello courthouse a bit more typically Southern with its Ionic columns and beige brick. The Covington courthouse is red brick with white trim and a soaring clock tower. Both buildings have been beautifully maintained. But the Covington courthouse has a richer history because the murder trials of John S. Williams and Clyde Manning were both held there. In 1921, all of Georgia and indeed much of the country was focused on the second-floor courtroom in that red brick building.

The actual physical center of both town squares, however, is a memorial to the Confederate soldiers. These memorials are an almost obligatory centerpiece of any Southern town. Usually consisting of a tall stone pedestal supporting a statue of a proud soldier leaning on his rifle, the memorial always includes a passage or two paying tribute to the fallen soldiers of the Confederacy, praising their valor in their struggle against overwhelming odds.

The Confederate memorial in Covington, however, includes another passage of a type not often seen. Resembling a disclaimer, the inscription on one side of the monument—the side visible when facing the courthouse —notes that "No sordid or mercenary spirit animated the cause espoused by those to whom this monument is erected or inspired the men who bravely fought and the women who freely suffered for it. Its final failure could not dishonor it, nor did defeat estrange its devotees."

That oddly defensive inscription says much about the way many Southerners see their history—not only the history of the Civil War but also everything that has happened since. There is a strong urge to honor the good people who came before you, and, for many white Southerners, there is a compulsion to defend them from accusations that they were just slaveholders or segregationists.

Even today, the people of Newton and Jasper Counties are much like those who would have witnessed the trials of John S. Williams and Clyde Manning. Neither uniformly good nor uniformly bad, they are normal folk who happen to live in a region whose history is tightly woven with slavery and racism, whose history is inescapable no matter how they try to move forward. There is no doubt that the community is progressing, but to truly succeed, it may be necessary to look back.

When one looks back at the case of Williams and Manning, one's eyes inevitably fall on the bridges spanning the shallow waters of Jackson Lake and its surrounding rivers. The lake is a focal point for life in Jasper and Newton Counties, just as it was in 1921. Most local residents find some everyday tie to Jackson Lake though it is not a source of livelihood or even much recreation —you live on the lake, you live on this side or that side of the lake, or you cross the lake to get from here to there.

The construction of Lloyd Shoals Dam in 1910 caused three rivers to pool at the bottom of Newton County: the South River, running down from the western border of the county; the Alcovy River, running down the eastern side; and the Yellow River, which meanders down the middle. The result was a Y-shaped lake dividing three counties, with Newton County to the north, Jasper to the southeast, and Butts to the southwest. The two bridges connecting Jasper and Newton Counties, and another within Jasper County, are now modern concrete structures, sleek and sturdy, entirely suited to their task. They look like any other bridges on country roads, and there is no lasting reminder of the tragedies that occurred there. They are not the same bridges that served as the killing sites for some of the men who had become a liability for John S. Williams, yet they span the same waters, and the remnants of the original wood and steel structures can still be seen in the dark waters below.

On a cold night in February 1921, Lindsey Peterson, Willie Preston, and Harry Price plunged from these bridges. Their deaths are an appropriate introduction to the Williams plantation murders, not because they were the first, but because they were perhaps the most horrifying. Their experience speaks volumes about Williams, about Manning, and about the time they lived in.

John S. William's car moved swiftly along the rough Georgia road, the three men in the back seat talking softly among themselves. There was no conversation between the twenty-six-year-old Clyde Manning, a handsome young man with coal-black skin, and the other two men in the front: Charlie Chisolm, another black worker from the farm, and John S. Williams, the white farmer at the wheel.

Manning may have dreaded what was to come, but Mr. Johnny had made it clear that he could not say no. "It's your neck or theirs, Clyde. Whichever you think the most of." So he stared straight ahead, watching the car's headlights faintly penetrate the damp night air. He could barely hear the struggles of the three men in the back, pulling in vain against the wires that bound their hands and feet and trying not to strangle each other with the chains that tied two of them together by the neck.

Lindsey Peterson and Willie Preston were scared, but not yet terrified. They spoke quietly to each other: Where were they going? What was going to happen to them? It was not unusual for Mr. Johnny and his sons to put his workers in chains, and it certainly was not unusual for them to be left wondering what was next. All they knew for certain was that they must not ask and they must not protest. No matter the destination, that could only make things worse.

Harry Price, on the other hand, was terrified. He was sweating furiously in the chilly, wet Georgia night, and he could be heard praying hard.

All three must have wondered what they had done to deserve this. Had they not worked hard enough on Mr. Johnny's farm? Had they made trouble in some way? Punishment was expected on the plantation, but the men usually had some idea what they were being punished for. They must have realized, of course, that they were not being taken to the train station as promised. Mr. Johnny and his sons regularly shared their workers among their own farms, so perhaps they hoped that Mr. Johnny was sending them to a neighbor's land. But that would not have explained the rocks.

The car stopped in the middle of Allen's Bridge on the Yellow River. Mr. Johnny stepped to the road, told Peterson and Preston to get out, but told Price to stay put. Manning came around to the driver's side and urged the two men, "Y'all get on out and do what Mr. Johnny say. We can't put up with no foolishness."

The men struggled with the chains and weights that tied them, and Manning reached in to lend a hand. Mr. Johnny helped lift the hundred pounds of rocks in the sack tied to the trace chains that bound the men, supporting the weight enough so that the men could get out of the car. The men moved slowly, straining under the weight, the chains causing them to bump into each other and stumble.

Price sat in the backseat with his own bag of rocks hanging from his neck and resting on his lap. He watched as his friends were led to the edge of the bridge by Manning, Mr. Johnny, and Chisolm. He heard Mr. Johnny say only one thing: "Throw them over."

5

Manning and Chisolm grabbed the two men firmly and started pushing, but Peterson and Preston panicked, shuffling about, trying to run, even with the chains binding them and the rocks weighing them down. Manning would later recall that their look of fear was a horrible thing, and he did his best to avoid looking them in the face. They were young and strong, but the chains made them easy to handle.

Without saying anything to Mr. Johnny, Manning and Chisolm did their best to follow his orders. They grappled with Peterson and Preston and forced them against the bridge railing as the two chained men pleaded not to be thrown over. They called Manning and Chisolm by their first names, screaming and crying helplessly. It was clear they knew not only that they were about to die, but exactly how—and how horribly.

In a short moment it was over. As the chained men were pushed over the railing, the rocks tied to their necks made them top-heavy, and their legs flipped over quickly. There was a soft splash, and in an instant they were gone. Manning turned around to see Mr. Johnny already walking back to the car.

Manning and Chisolm climbed in without a word to Price. Manning wondered why Mr. Johnny didn't want Price thrown off the bridge too, but he wasn't about to ask. Within moments, he had an idea where they were going. Price probably figured it out just as quickly. Mann's bridge, over the South River, was only about a mile away.

As before, the car came to a halt in the middle of the bridge and Mr. Johnny stepped out. "All right, boys, get out," he said. "Hurry up and get it over with." Manning and Chisolm helped Price out of the back seat, with Manning lifting the heavy bag of rocks so that Price could walk. Mr. Johnny didn't say anything this time. Chisolm began to push Price toward the railing while Manning, with his eyes downcast and avoiding Price's face, supported the rocks.

Manning was surprised when Price shook himself free of Chisolm's grip and in a low, quavering voice said, "Don't throw me over. I'll get over." Apparently not knowing what else to do, Chisolm let Price shuffle slowly toward the railing on his own. Manning walked alongside, carrying the bag of rocks that Price could not support without help. When he got to the railing, Price turned his back to the river and faced Mr. Johnny, standing near the car. He pulled himself up on the railing and balanced himself there, with Manning still holding the bag of rocks for him.

He sat there for a long moment, tears streaming down his dark cheeks and his whole body trembling. No one said anything. Manning stared downward, his gaze passing through the rusted metal bridge railing and into the blackness of the river. Price looked from Manning to Chisolm as if he were trying to think of something that would help him, but nothing came.

"Don't throw me over," he said once again, calmly. And, after another long pause, "Lord have mercy."

With those final words, Price leaned back and disappeared into the darkness.

# 2

---

# "When I First Remember Myself, I Was in Jasper County"

The deaths of Peterson, Preston, and Price certainly were not the first Clyde Manning had witnessed. Many of his friends had been abused and killed on the Williams farm, and more often than not he had had a hand in it. He had lived there from the age of thirteen or fourteen, when his father was killed by a shotgun blast from someone lying in ambush. Williams took in Manning, his mother, and his siblings in their time of desperate need and in some ways acted as Manning's tutor and surrogate father. The depth of their relationship was illustrated by the many occasions on which Williams gave Manning instructions that it seemed no man could follow, and Manning obeyed with a diligence that is hard to ascribe solely to fear or blind obedience.

The Williams property was located in central Georgia, about forty miles from Atlanta, and the boy never strayed far from it. Even as an adult, Manning never traveled and knew very little of the surrounding counties, much less anything farther away. Like most of his fellow laborers, he never learned to read. Illiteracy tends to encourage a strong memory for places, dates, names, and other details, and Manning would demonstrate that skill later, when called on to recount his experiences.

But he remembered little of life before or beyond the Williams plantation. When asked during the murder trials about his childhood, he replied that he did not know where he was born. "When I first remember myself, I was in Jasper County," he said.

Manning grew into a good-looking young man, very dark skinned, about 150 pounds and strongly built. The Williams family entrusted him with far more responsibility than the other laborers on the farm. The plantation owner allowed him to drive the family cars—or at least attempt to. On his first try, he wove crazily all over the farm and eventually ran over the Williams family mailbox—a scene that always would be recalled with some humor.

Manning and Williams had a special relationship that was obvious to the other plantation residents. While certainly not loving or indulgent toward Manning, Williams apparently had some affection for the young man, springing from his earlier tutelage of him. That small feeling was encouraged by Manning's obedience, his eagerness to make Williams happy. The white man came to appreciate Manning the way one appreciates an obedient and trustworthy dog.

Manning's eagerness to please no doubt had several origins, but the overriding motivation was fear. When Manning married in 1913, protecting his family took on increased importance. Not only were his aging mother and siblings at risk if he tried to leave or defy the Williams family, but so were his new wife and children.

The thought of leaving the Williams plantation crossed Manning's mind every now and then, but most of the time, leaving the farm was not his goal. He had come to trust John S. Williams in a way, with an uneasy trust born of the certainty that the white man was powerful, fearsome, and firmly in control of Manning's destiny. One might conclude that the young Manning came to look at Williams in the same way a child would look at a fearsome father, clinging to the only protector he knows, for better or worse.

John S. Williams was a classic example of the Southern gentleman farmer. By 1920 he had become successful in his home state, well known and respected. His huge plantation sprawled across much of the county, and his big white house perched on a high hill—a typical country home but with many "city" conveniences—was the envy of his fellow farmers. There was a rose garden out front, tended by Mrs. Williams, and a generous planting of shrubbery and vines. A visitor's eye would be drawn to the most obvious sign of Williams's prosperity—three cars parked in three garages.

Always well dressed when going to town in his recently purchased Chandler touring car, Williams carried himself with a calm, dignified confidence. He was a tall, thin man with a sharply cut jawline, a neatly trimmed mustache, and penetrating eyes. By the age of fifty-four, he had fathered twelve children—sons Huland, Gus, Marvin, Leroy, Luke, J.S., Curtis, Robert, and Edward; and daughters Mary, Iva Sue, and Tillie. The youngest child, Edward, was only two years old in 1921. And as he was fond of reminding people, his three eldest boys were among the county's first to volunteer to fight the Germans in the World War. Gus Williams was a bona fide war hero and returned home to practice medicine in nearby McDonough, Georgia.

Born in Meriwether County in 1866, one year after the end of the Civil War, John S. Williams had grown up in the harsh times of Reconstruction. The extreme animosity toward free blacks immediately after the Civil War colored young John's attitude toward the men who would someday work on his farm. Like many Southern whites of the time, Williams was raised on the certainty that blacks were always the first suspect in any crime and, no matter how personable they may seem, were to be watched closely. Ultimately, Williams learned that blacks were useful but troublesome, and dealing with them required a certain suspension of morality that apparently came naturally to him.


John S. Williams's way of life was simple by many standards, but it put him far above that of almost any black man.

While most rural Georgians in the early twentieth century led difficult lives, even after the Civil War, poor blacks were subjected to hardships we can hardly imagine. Indeed, even many Georgians of the time had trouble believing that such conditions persisted just beyond their sophisticated city doorsteps and were key to the agricultural industry that fueled the Southern economy.

Iron John, a black laborer whose true name is not known, had a typical, tragic experience with the form of slavery practiced on the Williams plantation. Also known as Iron Jaw and Long John, he was a poor, illiterate black man who ran afoul of the law in some minor way and was unable to pay the fine of a few dollars. Consequently he was locked up in the Atlanta stockade. One day John S. Williams arrived at the stockade looking for men to work on his farm. He would pay the fine to get Iron John out of the stockade, and in return Iron John would agree to work off the fine on the Williams plantation.

The deal might have seemed fair enough, especially to a man who saw no other hope of getting out of the stockade any time soon. The work offered was exactly the type he may have been looking for when he was jailed—the hard physical labor familiar to both blacks and whites in rural Georgia. Besides, Iron John did not have a lot of say in the matter. Once Williams picked him out and paid the fine, he was obligated to go to work.

That is how Iron John ended up on the Williams plantation one spring day in 1920, helping other black workers build a hog and goat lot on a nearby piece of property Williams had rented. Manning was working on the job along with Iron John and several other men. Iron John's job was to roll the fence wire up a hill to where the lot would be built. Leroy Williams, one of the four adult sons of the plantation owner, was supervising the work, and he let Manning know that he did not like what he saw.

By Leroy's estimation, Iron John was not rolling the wire straight. Manning assured him he'd get on Iron John and make sure he did it right, but that did not satisfy the white man. After harshly reprimanding Iron John for shoddy work, Leroy decided that punishment was in order. The fencing was stopped, and Leroy took the work crew to his father's house, back to the work shelter where the whipping was done. The walk must have been a long one, because everyone knew what was about to happen.

When they arrived, Iron John was instructed to strip to the waist and lie across the large gasoline barrel positioned there for whippings, just as many of the other workers had been forced to do. And as usual, the victim's friends and coworkers were made to hold him down during the whipping. Manning stood nearby as Clyde Freeman and Charlie Chisolm held Iron John's arms tight, whispering words of encouragement as they anticipated the brutality to come.

The Williams men seldom dirtied their hands with the actual act of whipping. Leroy stood by to supervise, but he forced a black hand to take the buggy whip and apply it. Again and again, the whip cracked across the man's bare back, welts rising, breaking, and finally oozing with shining blood. All the while, Iron John cried out with each lash and begged for mercy.

No mercy was forthcoming. Leroy periodically reminded the hand wielding the whip that he would get the same treatment if he slackened. Iron John struggled with each searing blow, fighting against the fellow black men who held him down and exposed his back. He could not see the tears and the terror in their eyes, but Manning could.

As the pain grew more intense, and as the indignity welled up in Iron John's throat, he found the breath and the courage to make a statement to Leroy. "Don't hit me no more," he managed to say through raspy, heaving breaths, and with a subtle note of anger. "I'd rather be dead than treated this way."

Without much hesitation, Leroy stepped up and fired a pistol shot into Iron John's shoulder. The man screamed in pain, and Manning jumped back in surprise. Leroy paused a moment, then asked, "Do you want any more?"

"Yes," Iron John managed to say. "Shoot me."

Leroy put the pistol to Iron John's head. He pulled the trigger and Iron John died, lying across a gasoline barrel stained with his blood and the blood of many men and women before him. He died because he was found guilty of some petty crime, and he died because he could not pay the five-, ten-, or twenty-dollar fine.

And in the end, he died because a white man did not like the way he rolled wire up a hill.

Leroy Williams told Manning and the other black men present to take Iron John's clothes off. They then took the man's bloody corpse down near the pond on the Williams property and laid it next to some fallen logs. Clyde Freeman was sent back to the house to get some wire from several bales of hay, and the men used that wire to tie Iron John's body to a large rotting log. They then rolled the grisly construction along until they got it to the edge of the pond and could load it onto a boat.

Iron John's body was rowed out to the middle of the pond and dumped in the water.

Disposing of bodies was almost routine work on the Jasper County farm. The Williams plantation—the big farms still were referred to as plantations in 1920—lay on the banks of the recently formed Jackson Lake. John S. Williams maintained the largest piece of property and oversaw the entire plantation. Huland, his eldest son, had his own farm in Newton County, about five miles away; and Marvin and Leroy, two other grown sons, maintained their own homes on the Williams property. The family was successful at farming, though success in the early twentieth century in rural Georgia still meant a fairly simple lifestyle and a good deal of hard physical labor.

The main crop was cotton, but the family also raised corn, wheat, oats, and livestock. Without the conveniences of technology, that work required long hours and strong men. For that, the Williams family turned to the South's traditional source of hard labor.

Some of the approximately thirty laborers on the farm were employed for wages, at least technically, though there is considerable doubt as to whether they were fairly paid for their work. Manning, however, was regularly paid twenty dollars a month for overseeing the other workers. Gus Chapman, who would later report the appalling farm conditions to federal authorities, was paid a total of thirty-five cents in the year or so that he worked for Williams, who had obtained him from the Atlanta stockade by paying his five-dollar fine. There was no accounting of how long it would take the men to work off their indebtedness to John S. Williams and earn their freedom. And there is no record of Williams ever declaring a debt paid and allowing the worker to leave.

By the standards of the day, and by the standards of previous generations, the black laborers on the Williams plantation were well fed and well clothed. In light of their brutal treatment, the meals and clothing seem inconsequential to latter-day observers, but these details mattered to law enforcement officials and commentators of the day. Yes, the men were held in bondage, but they were not walking around in tattered clothing and starving for nourishment. For some, the fine line between slavery and cheap labor was defined by such details.

Though the men ate relatively nourishing meals, they were locked up at night, much like their forebears years before the Civil War. In fact, the laborers on the Williams plantation were probably more closely controlled than many slaves had been. They were housed in two similar small red wooden buildings, one near the home of Huland Williams and one just outside that of his father. Each building was divided into two sections. One side was for the indentured workers, the other for their black overseers. From the front the houses looked like decrepit versions of a modern duplex apartment. Two front doors opened onto the small porch area, and a wall ran down the middle of the building and divided it in two. The wall was not solid, but rather a rickety partition of boards with holes and gaps of several inches.

On the Huland Williams property, Claude Freeman was the black farmhand who acted as "boss" to the other workers. On the John S. Williams property, Clyde Manning, Freeman's third cousin, was the farm boss.

Manning and his wife of nine years, twenty-three-year-old Rena Manning, lived on the left side of the slave quarters, where the cooking for all the hands was done.

The farmhands—up to twenty in each house—crowded into the right side of the buildings at night and slept on bunks. The shutters could have been opened to let in air on warm Georgia nights, but they never were. All the windows but one were nailed shut, and when the hands retired for the night, Claude Freeman and Clyde Manning took responsibility for seeing that the men could not slip away in the dark. The shutters were boarded from the outside; the two front doors were secured with a chain that ran through holes in both doors and through the middle wall dividing the building, and was locked on the boss's side.

The men could not leave until the farm bosses unlocked the doors and pulled the chains out the next morning. To make sure they could control the men, Freeman and Manning were sometimes allowed to carry pistols.


Pistols and beatings usually kept the black workers in line, but occasionally one would try to leave the plantation. The Williams family was ready for that, too.

They kept a number of dogs, but these were not considered pets, or even the "yard dogs" that rural residents tolerate and feed but don't seem to care for much. The dogs were sometimes described as bloodhounds, but those more familiar with the breed said they were just dogs used for tracking. On Sundays, the Williams men would take the dogs out for practice, and a black man would be forced to run through the surrounding woods for them to chase and bring down.


When Manning dreamed of fleeing, his goal would have been to escape the daily beatings and threats of death. He surely had no dreams of finding an easy life. In rural Georgia whites and blacks alike expected life to be hard and demanding. Blacks expected their lot to be tougher than whites, and the expectations were lowest for the forced laborers on the Williams plantation.

They worked from dawn to nearly dark, though they were usually given time to rest on Sunday. Then they could attend church, but only a small one there on the plantation, well within sight of the Williams family. The women, of course, did not get even that meager time off because they were responsible for feeding the men, cooking for the Williams families, and caring for the children.

Aside from the hard labor, everyday life on the farm was cruel. The Williams men were feared, and John S. Williams was feared the most. When one of the Williams men told a laborer to do something, the man would run, not walk. Hastening off to do the white man's bidding was much more than a sign of subservience or fear—it was a sign that he understood the potential consequences of seeming to dawdle or, God forbid, challenge the white man's instructions.

These consequences included severe whippings, and in some cases, death. Manning had learned early on that a whipping would be meted out for even the most insignificant infraction, real or imagined, and death required only slightly more provocation. Almost all of the black farmhands, whether they had been obtained from jails or otherwise, were regularly whipped on the Williams plantation. Being found seated during the workday could prompt a whipping. Emma Freeman, a black woman who cooked for John S. Williams and also for the farmhands, recalled that Marvin Williams "whipped me a heap of times," and Huland Williams pistolwhipped her and beat her with a stick. Why? Because one of the Williams men did not like the dinner she prepared, because she did not have dinner ready in time for the farmhands, or "just to suit him."

In court, Manning also recalled times when the laborers were whipped en masse. Clyde Freeman had told him about an instance in which a group of workers had been left to pick cotton, and when John S. Williams returned, he was not happy with how much had been picked. All of the workers were taken to the gear house and whipped. The whipping was done with a plow line, a leather trace, a bridle, a buggy whip, or sometimes a long strip of rubber from an old automobile tire. Some farmers were known to tie a bolt or other small piece of metal to the end of the whip for an extra measure of damage. The beatings were always severe and usually brought blood.

"Sometimes they would make them do the whipping, one whip the others," Clyde Freeman recalled. "If he would tell one to whip one and he wouldn't do it, then they would whip that one."

The Williams men also made the laborers hold each other down during the whipping. There was no resistance to the order because the men knew that hesitation would mean they would be whipped themselves—and if they already were in line to be whipped, they would receive a far more severe whipping. Or perhaps death.

Manning knew that, in most ways, his plight was not as bad as that of the others on the plantation. But though he and Claude Freeman held special places as farm bosses and thus were not treated quite as severely, they still felt the abuse of the Williams family. Claude Freeman told the court he was never whipped, but said that Williams "made me jump about." Manning was not whipped either, but John S. Williams once hit him so hard that he broke Manning's arm. The white man was unhappy with a trade that Manning had made with another laborer.

Any time new hands came to work on the farm, Manning made a point of teaching them an important lesson about how to get along: Remember that the Williams men have short tempers and always see killing as a reasonable response. In fact, murder was not even far down the list of options. He often told the new men the story of how sixteen-year-old Frank Dozier narrowly escaped the wrath of Huland Williams after being injured by a mule.

Dozier had been arrested in Macon "for sitting down at the depot," as he recalled. He had been looking for a job, made the mistake of sitting down for a moment, and ended up charged with vagrancy. He was fined $20.75 and, because he did not have the money, put in the Macon stockade. Huland Williams showed up at the stockade shopping for farm labor that same day and took Dozier back to his farm, promising to pay him thirty-five dollars a month. He slept on the bare floor of the slave quarters that night and received his first beating within a week. Marvin Williams hit him on the head three times, hard enough to leave lasting scars. He was whipped repeatedly, so often he lost count, and "for just most anything, mostly about just anything I would do. He whipped me once because I could not pick up a log. It was too heavy and I couldn't lift it. He whipped me then."

Dozier's most frightful lesson about living with the Williams family came when he was seriously injured while working the fields one day. Dozier was thrown by a young mule and broke his leg and, as the boy lay in the field in pain, Huland sent his young son to the house for a gun. While they were waiting, Huland calmly explained that he would kill Dozier when the son returned.

"I begged and got him not to kill me," Dozier told Manning. "He called Foots and carried me to the house and told him he ought to kill that nigger anyhow. He said he ought to kill me because I was too lazy to stay on a mule."

Manning also alerted the new men to another lesson that Dozier learned the hard way: The Williams family pitted workers against one another as a way to improve productivity. Huland scolded Dozier once for not picking enough cotton, and Dozier tried to explain that another worker had taken some of his cotton from his bag. The explanation only angered Huland more, and he whipped both Dozier and the other man. After that, Dozier understood why the man had stolen the cotton from his bag. Huland had a policy that the man picking the least cotton would be whipped at the end of the day. As the sun began to set on the men, their fear of being whipped overcame their allegiance to each other, and the strong would take the prized cotton from the weak.

Though all the black men on the Williams plantation must have dreamed of escaping, they were deterred by what they knew of past attempts. Manning himself later explained that he was discouraged by what had happened to one man who escaped and was brought back to face the consequences.

Frank Dozier, who was left with a crippled leg after the incident with the mule, was often told to drive wagons and do other jobs that required little standing, and on a fall day, he was taking Nathaniel Wade, known as Blackstrap, and Johnny Benson, known as Little Bit, to John S. Williams's house to pick cotton. As they passed through the swampy area near Jackson Lake, the two men decided to run away from the Williams plantation. There was nothing Dozier could do even if he wanted to stop them.

Dozier pulled the wagon up to the Williams house and told the truth when asked where the other two men were. The anger came quickly, but the job of retrieving the men took precedence over beating Dozier, so he escaped punishment. The Williams men took their dogs and set out to find the escapees. Benson, the younger of the two, was caught after two days and whipped upon his return.

Wade made more of a run for it. It took nearly a week for the Williams men to track him down, and even then they did not find him on their own. They had put out word that the man was missing, and eventually another farmer in South Georgia called to say that he had hired Wade to work on his own farm. Since the man rightly belonged to Williams, the farmer said, Williams was welcome to come get him.

John S. Williams retrieved Wade on a Sunday morning and brought him back to the plantation. That afternoon, the white man demonstrated how much anger he had built up in the week of Wade's absence. The frightened, exhausted black man was taken to the gear shelter near Williams's home and made to lie across the gasoline barrel where most of the whippings took place. Charlie Chisolm was told to hold Wade's head, and other black workers held his arms and hands during the punishment. Manning stood nearby.

Huland administered the whipping to Wade, and Manning knew that was a bad sign. If a whipping was merely a matter of punishment, a necessary task to keep the laborers productive and obedient, that was a job the Williams men would assign to one of the black workers, just like the manual labor. But if Huland was wielding the whip himself, that meant he was mad and would make sure the whipping was particularly severe. The defiance shown by the escapee had been taken as a personal affront, and Huland would make him pay.

The whipping was fierce and rapid. Huland was throwing the whip with all his might, but concentrating hard on making the leather fall strategically on Wade's back, aiming for the raw, bloody spots he already had opened up.

The punishment continued past the point where everyone expected Huland to be satisfied. The white man was sweating and breathing hard with exertion, but he showed no signs of stopping. Between screams, Wade begged to be released. "Please don't whip me no more, Mr. Huland. Please don't whip me no more," he cried. The pain made him weak, but the terror added an urgency and despondency to his begging. "I ain't gonna run away no more, Mr. Huland, please. Please don't whip me no more."

The begging continued as the whipping continued, neither letting up, each seeming to spur more of the other. After his back had become a bloody mess, Wade stopped begging and quietly writhed with each successive sting. He gasped, lurched, and moaned, but he begged no more. After more blows, Manning heard him speak again.

"Kill me," he said softly but clearly.

Huland Williams gave his .38 pistol to Charlie Chisolm, the black farmhand who was helping hold Wade down, and told him to shoot Wade. Chisolm obeyed, firing one shot into Wade's head.

Wade rose up on his knees for a moment and looked at Chisolm, then fell over dead.

# 3

# "The River Was Full
# of Dead Negroes"

Over the years the federal government had received several reports of peonage in Jasper County, but agents were in no hurry to investigate the Williams plantation until 1921, when Gus Chapman showed up at the downtown Atlanta office of the federal Bureau of Investigation. (The bureau would not become known as the "Federal Bureau of Investigation" and the "FBI" until 1935. In 1921, it was officially the Bureau of Investigation.) Because his story seemed to involve peonage—a federal crime—he was directed to the Atlanta agent in charge of most peonage investigations, A. J. Wismer, who recently had been assigned to Atlanta from the Birmingham, Alabama, office of the bureau, and his partner, George W. Brown.

The agents told Chapman to sit down and tell his story. He started by telling them that he had come from a farm in Jasper County where he had been held against his will, and he said many more were still being held there. Then he went back to the beginning, to tell the agents how he had been imprisoned by Mr. Johnny.

Chapman's life on the Williams plantation began like that of many of his fellow peons. Without a job or money in his pocket, Chapman was arrested in Atlanta for loitering. With no way to pay the five-dollar fine, he languished in the Atlanta stockade until Huland Williams showed up and took him away. Though Williams assured the man that working off his fine would be exactly the same as if he had just been hired as a farm worker, Chapman suspected otherwise. He wasn't eager to go with Williams, but he saw working for the Williams family as slightly better than remaining in the stockade. As soon as he arrived at the cotton plantation, he was locked up with the other men, and Williams dropped all pretense of assuaging the man's fears. Chapman began experiencing the hardships of everyday life there, and he knew he had to find a way out.

His opportunity did not arrive for many months, and then he would find out just how hard it was to walk away from the Williams family. The thirty-eight-year-old man waited for the dark of night one Friday in July 1920 and slipped out of the locked building that served as the slave quarters on the John S. Williams plantation. Chapman did not have to break out of the bunkhouse. He asked Manning to let him go.

Late that evening, Chapman was on the prisoners' side of the divided building that housed the captive workers on one side and Manning and his wife and children on the other. He went to the rickety dividing wall and looked through the inch-wide gaps in the boards, softly calling for Manning to come near. When the overseer came close to see what was the matter, Chapman made his plea.

"Clyde, you got to let me go," he said quietly, so that he would not wake the other men. "I know I can get out of here if you just let me out of this house tonight, Clyde."

Manning frowned and shook his head, entirely dismissing the idea at first. "Mr. Johnny will break my neck if I let you go, Clyde," he said. "You know I can't do nothing like that. Why are you asking me to do something like that?" But Chapman continued to plead quietly, whispering through the dividing wall, saying he needed nothing more than the simple act of unlocking the door long enough for him to slip outside. Chapman softly, gently, begged for one moment of help. His keeper said little in return except, "No, Gus, I can't do it."

It must have been a plea that Manning had heard many times from many men, but, for some reason, it was effective that night. Chapman's pleading continued for a while longer, and then, without saying anything more to Chapman, Manning got up, went to the front door of the building and quietly unlocked the padlock on the chain holding the double door shut. Moving carefully to avoid waking anyone, Chapman went to the door on his side of the building, slowly pulled the chain through, opened the door, and stepped outside. As soon as he was gone, Manning locked the doors again and went to bed.

Manning's generosity was limited, however, and outweighed by his fear of John S. Williams. When Chapman turned up missing the next morning, Manning knew that Williams would be furious at him for letting Chapman escape, even if he had done so accidentally. If the farmer realized that Manning had deliberately set Chapman free, his generosity would have most likely cost the black farm boss his life. Unknown to Chapman, Manning fabricated a story about Chapman attempting to rape his wife the previous night and escaping after a scuffle. To hear Manning the morning Chapman's escape was discovered, it sounded as if he wanted to catch Chapman as much as Williams did. Whether the farmer truly believed Manning's story is unknown, but it apparently served its purpose of getting the black farm boss off the hook for permitting the escape. And when the authorities later asked about the episode, the tale of attempted rape provided a good excuse for Williams's pursuit of Chapman.

Chapman had nothing to help him on his journey; Williams had paid him a total of twenty-five cents since bringing him to Jasper County. With no money, no belongings, and no one to rely on for help, Chapman made his way along the dirt roads of Jasper County, traveling as much as possible in the night and avoiding nearly everyone, including local black residents. His months on the Williams plantation had shown him that nearly everyone in the area feared the Williams family, so he could not risk having anyone realize that he was on the run. His plight could not have been much different if he had run away from a Georgia plantation a hundred years earlier.

He headed south in the stifling heat and humidity of a Georgia summer, with the night providing only moderate relief as the mosquitoes feasted. Chapman was hoping to make it to Macon, a comparatively large city in middle Georgia with more opportunity for the kind of work that did not involve picking cotton and praying the white man would not beat you that night. If he could get as far as Monticello, the seat of Jasper County, he might be able to follow the train tracks to Macon.

The trip from the Williams plantation to Monticello would have been a very short drive, and only a few hours more to Macon. But for Chapman—on the run, tired, dreadfully afraid of every encounter with another human being—the journey seemed endless. It did end, though—on Sunday morning, with the sound of dogs fast on his heels. The Williams men had tracked down their quarry outside of Shady Dale, Georgia, where Chapman had found some train tracks to follow south. Chapman had not made it far at all.

Once they found him cowering in a stand of pine trees, the Williams men held off the dogs and sent in Manning and June Dunning, another black worker who had been procured from the Monticello jail. "Get in there and bring me that nigger," John S. Williams told them. The two men did as they were told, heading into the trees to find the exhausted runaway. They found him leaning against a pine tree, hands resting on his knees and sweat pouring off his face.

The two men grabbed Chapman, tied him up, and walked him out to where the Williams men were shouting at the dogs to shut up. They put him in the Williams car to be taken back to work—and to his inevitable punishment. Manning never let on that he had accused Chapman of trying to rape his wife.

Upon returning to the plantation, John S. Williams and Manning took Chapman down to the wagon shelter, accompanied by John Brown, another black worker. The white man continued the tongue lashing that he had administered since first retrieving Chapman and started saying that maybe the escapee was just too much trouble to fool with. "If you won't work and won't stay on the farm, maybe it's best if I just get rid of you right now," Williams told Chapman.

After a few minutes of pleading from Chapman, Williams told him that "as I was a kind of an old son of a bitch he would let me go that time, but if I ever did it again he would sure kill me like I was a snake." In the strange world of the Williams family, this amounted to leniency. Instead of killing the man for walking off the farm, he would only be whipped within an inch of his life. Chapman was made to disrobe, and the other two black men held him down over the gasoline barrel while Williams whipped Chapman with a buggy trace, the long leather straps used to attach a horse to the buggy. Williams also beat the man with his fists, and when the Williams sons had the inclination, they dealt a few more blows for good measure.

Still bleeding from his whipping and his face a swollen mess from the beatings, Chapman was ordered to go out and cut stove wood for the rest of the day. Two hours after night had fallen, after Chapman had cut wood for most of the day in a drenching rain, the Williams family sent word that he could stop.

Despite the brutal consequences of his first escape attempt, Chapman turned out to be more determined than the Williams family had counted on.

If they could have known what Chapman would do in the next year, they almost certainly would have put a bullet in his head that Sunday night in July.

Chapman decided he had to try again. On the first Thursday after Thanksgiving 1920, scarcely five months later, Chapman repeated his escape. Again, Manning quietly released Chapman from his chains and let him leave the bunkhouse. He slipped out of the slave quarters between midnight and one A.M., but this time he headed north. He was carrying ten cents, the grand total of the pay he had received from the Williams family since his previous escape.

Chapman made his way north to Atlanta, where he found sympathetic blacks who convinced him to go to the only place in town where someone might be interested in hearing from a former Georgia peon: the Atlanta office of the federal Bureau of Investigation. Going to the federal authorities was far better than approaching local law enforcement agents with charges of peonage. The federal agents were not likely to drop everything and rush out to address a poor black man's complaints either, but there was at least the chance that the complaint would be taken seriously, and the informant would not be handed right back to the white man he was accusing.

When Chapman sat in the federal agents' office in early 1921 and told his story of being held prisoner and abused, he expressed great fear of being taken back to the Williams farm. Though they did not make the case a top priority, Brown and Wismer did see reason to investigate, for Chapman's was not the only complaint they had received. Another peon, James Strickland, had also managed to escape the Williams plantation recently and report to the federal authorities. They may not have seen much reason to get excited, but the complaints were at least reliable enough to go down and shake up the farmer who was violating the federal law just a little too flagrantly. Within two weeks of Chapman's first visit to the agents, Brown and Wismer would stop by the Williams plantation while investigating other federal matters in the area.

Chapman's story did not come as any big surprise to the agents. Peonage was the South's ugly secret—the kind of secret everyone knew and just pretended not to be familiar with. Because it involved holding blacks as virtual slaves, it was a federal offense, and that is why the bureau was involved. For the past year or so, Brown and Wismer had been the federal government's point men for peonage investigations in the Deep South,

25

so the Washington office routinely sent along copies of all peonage reports they received. Some of them were being handled by other agents closer to the area, but Brown and Wismer always got copies of the complaints and updates on whatever the agents found when and if they investigated. The regular updates from Washington, plus their own work in Georgia and Alabama, kept the two agents abreast of peonage charges all over the country. The only significant action they had pursued against peonage farmers amounted to a few large fines, partly because the federal government saw it as only somewhat more important than did local law officers. After all, the agents Washington had sent to Atlanta were not Northern outsiders trekking through the dusty back roads of middle Georgia. They were Southern boys who knew how to talk to Georgia farmers—they just happened to carry federal badges.

Though the agents were only beginning to learn about the Williams plantation, conditions on the farm were well known, at least in a general sense, to most residents of Jasper and Newton Counties. But nothing was done locally to stop or even discourage Williams. Neighbors were intimidated by the powerful Williams family, and no white wanted to be seen as the protector of black laborers. In addition, Williams was not alone in using slave labor to run his farm. Williams may have been the worst practitioner of peonage, but it is more likely that he merely became the best known thanks to the eventual intervention of Brown and Wismer. The fact that the agents would find anything interesting about reports of peonage in Jasper County, when they already had files about other farms, is testimony to the degree of depravity on the Williams plantation.

Peonage took many forms, with differing degrees of legality and illegality, and with differing degrees of hopelessness for the poor blacks caught in its web. For some, the misery of daily life still seemed to hold a tiny promise that someday the debt could be repaid and the worker would be set free. For many others, there was no hope, and they knew it.

In the abstract, peonage was a gray area between slavery and legitimate labor, but it often dissolved into outright slavery once the black man or woman set foot on the farm. It existed to some extent in the North but was far more common in the South. It was not an American invention, however. Peonage thrived in Mexico, Latin America, and the Philippines long before it flourished in the Southern United States. The term *peon*, later used casually to refer to a person of low standing, originated from the Spanish *peon*, meaning a man indebted to an employer. In all cultures in which it has been present, peonage is a transitional phase between a legal slave culture and a more capitalist society without slavery. To make peonage work, a society needs abundant laborers who are illiterate and politically helpless, a rural environment in which most beneficiaries of the practice do not have to see its brutality, and a legal system that is willing to look the other way. Filipinos used mostly children for peonage, and Indians were the victims in Mexico and Latin America.

In the United States, peonage arose after the Civil War in a series of legal manipulations aimed at helping white Southern farmers make the best of that troublesome Emancipation Proclamation. Slavery was illegal, yes, but certainly ways could be found to force free blacks to work on your farm anyway. In the decades after the Civil War, Southern states enacted Black Codes restricting the mobility of blacks and limiting their ability to choose an employer and bargain for higher wages. The codes also set up a particular dilemma for black workers. They were required to work for someone, anyone, so not having a job meant they could be arrested for vagrancy. The result was that an unemployed black was almost forced to accept the first job offered, and at any wage. Otherwise, he or she could be jailed for vagrancy and then be subjected to peonage when a farmer paid the fine.

Peonage was made illegal in the United States in 1867, when Congress passed a law providing ten years' imprisonment and a $10,000 fine. Georgia added a Constitutional provision in 1868 specifically outlawing peonage, but both laws were ignored or seen as mere technicalities. Many practitioners of peonage pleaded ignorance to the laws or claimed that what they were doing was not actually peonage but rather something legal, albeit similar.

That was almost always the response when Brown and Wismer ventured into the countryside to investigate a charge that black men were being held against their will. Most would claim that their farm workers were free to leave any time they wanted, though they still owed a legal debt to the farmer and would have to pay it off in some way. That was a crucial point to make because a peonage violation required that the debtor be held against his or her will until the sum was paid off. Allowing a debtor to freely work off the debt, by choice, was not an illegal act.

In practice, however, the differences proved meaningless. As Brown and Wismer knew, the white landowners could claim that the workers were free to leave while at the same time chasing them down with dogs. Poor whites were occasionally subjected to the same forced labor, and unwitting immigrants were even recruited from up North to work in "the land where it never snows." But almost all peons were black.

There were rare reports of blacks conspiring with whites to put other blacks in peonage. In 1905, two black men were convicted of tricking a young black woman into traveling to Valdosta, Georgia, where they falsified a debt and turned her over to a local white farming family. Upon their conviction, the judge compared them to the Africans who sold their brethren into slavery in the Americas.

An 1866 act actually encouraged farmers to take on black children as peons, ostensibly for the purpose of providing orphans with guardians. White farmers took advantage of the act by driving off black fathers and then filing papers declaring that the father was absent and the mother was unable to care for the children. The children were legally obligated to work for the guardian until the age of twenty-one, at which time the farmer could come up with some sort of fictitious debt that had to be worked off. In 1867, one third of the black children in Monroe County, Georgia, were enslaved in this way. Considering the mysterious shotgun slaying of his father when Manning was thirteen or fourteen, it is not farfetched to speculate that Williams may have killed the father to obtain the rest of the family.

Peonage was one step in a continuum of forced labor, with all the variations at one time providing the muscle needed to make the South move. Slavery built the early South, and sharecropping helped white farmers continue to work large plots of land with the help of poor blacks and whites. Sharecroppers and textile workers in mill towns often experienced the same conundrum of never quite earning enough to pay off their employers. No matter how hard they worked they could not leave, because they always owed more for advanced earnings or supplies from the company store. Peonage took that idea a step further, establishing from the outset that the worker had a debt to work off. And, as with sharecroppers and mill workers, the math never seemed to work out in their favor.

Perhaps the only fate worse than peonage in the South was leased convict labor. This legal practice was similar to peonage, but the workers were seen as even less worthy of care and concern. Prisons and local jails would lease convicts to farmers and industries in the area to use however they wanted. The prisoner had no hope of escaping the work, and the work did not in any way "square" him with the legal system the way peonage absolved the worker of a fine. By many accounts, leased convict laborers, black and white, were treated worse than any other workers until the system was abolished in 1908.

The extensive use of peons resulted from pressing labor problems that encouraged Southern farmers to find the cheapest laborers and then get as much work as possible out of them. At the turn of the century, the region was beginning to experience the greatest prosperity since 1850. Farmers devoted more and more land to King Cotton and watched the price of cotton triple between 1900 and 1916. The Southern economy had flourished through World War I, but in 1920 the prosperity came to a sudden halt. Cotton prices plummeted from thirty-five cents per pound in 1919 to seventeen cents per pound in 1920. The price of cottonseed dropped at the same time from thirty-one dollars to ten dollars per ton. Corn went from $1.07 to 66 cents per bushel.

The enormous price drops came just as Georgia was suffering from the boll weevil, a small insect of legendary proportions in the South. First seen in Georgia in 1913, it spread slowly through the state for six years. High cotton prices during the war nullified some of its devastating effect upon cotton fields, but by 1919 it was beginning to drive some farm families to destitution. Cotton yields fell 30 to 45 percent per year, causing nearly 3.5 million acres to be removed from farming and left idle by 1925. Jasper County's largest cotton crop ever was 32,000 bales in 1911, but the yield was down to 8,472 bales in 1920. The county's population decreased with the cotton yield, falling from 17,000 in 1920 to 8,600 in 1930.

The average size of Georgia farms fell to 82 acres in 1920, down from 117 acres in 1900. At 2,000 acres, the Williams plantation was one of the old-style, sprawling antebellum plantations. Like many farmers with smaller acreage, John S. Williams continued to concentrate on growing cotton even after the devastation of postwar price drops and the boll weevil. While seemingly futile, the continued dependence on cotton was the result of tradition, the farmers' uncertainty about growing any other crop, and the insistence of the merchants who offered the farmers credit. Most farmers were not at all wealthy, even in prosperous times, so they depended on the extension of credit from local merchants for everyday goods and the supplies needed to run the farm. The merchants, on the other hand, wanted to be sure they would be paid eventually, so they insisted that the farmers grow the only crop that had paid off handsomely in the past—

King Cotton. The result was overproduction of a low-price crop, deeper debt, mortgaging of the farmland, and often foreclosure.

With such a huge plantation devoted to cotton, John S. Williams faced financial difficulties on a grander scale than his neighbors with smaller farms. The postwar years were not easy for him, and Williams ended up mortgaging his farmland. He once remarked that "Niggers, boll weevil, and low price of cotton just about cleaned me up. I have no idea if it was sold today I could pay my indebtedness."

The financial burden of running a large plantation and supporting an extended family in such hard economic times could only have solidified John S. Williams's determination to use the cheapest labor possible.


Agents Brown and Wismer had seen plenty of examples of peonage, either personally, in reports from Washington, or in complaints from Georgia that they never bothered to follow up. They knew that peonage was found all across the South but mostly in the cotton belt stretching from the Carolinas through the Mississippi Delta to Texas. Most reports of peonage came from the cotton industry, but the turpentine farms of south Georgia, north Florida, Alabama, and Mississippi were also heavy users of peons. One of the most exhausting types of peon labor, the work took place in large stands of pine trees, almost always located far away from populated areas or main transportation sources. Making turpentine was year-round work, with men cutting boxes into the sides of trees in the winter to catch the sap that would run later. In the spring, some men collected the gum and ladled it into big, heavy barrels, while others cut notches in the trees so that fresh sap would bleed from the wounds. After years of being bled of their sap, the trees ceased producing and the laborers moved on, leaving behind an odd-looking forest in which every mature pine tree sported a series of downward slanting notches.

The railroads also used peons during periods of heavy development in the South. When federal authorities received word in 1906 that the Oliver Brothers Construction Company might be using forced labor in a Tennessee railroad camp and killing some of the peons, two bureau agents were sent to investigate. Sooner than they expected, they learned that the charges were true. As they approached the camp from downriver, one of the agents idly asked a local resident if the fishing was good in the river. "The man said yes, but no one around there would eat the fish now," the agent later recalled. "I asked him why and he said the river was full of dead negroes."

The bureau had at one point asked agents Brown and Wismer to estimate the extent of peonage, but they found the task difficult because it was relegated to distant rural communities and not well documented in any way. They had no doubt, however, that it was practiced extensively. They came across research from 1907 that estimated that a third of all farmers in Georgia, Alabama, and Mississippi used forced labor, and peonage was reported in every county in Alabama between 1903 and 1905. When a South Carolina farmer was acquitted of peonage charges in 1910, a local newspaper stated that the acquittal was "not at all surprising, for while everybody knows that he is guilty, it is equally well known that he is not any more guilty than scores or perhaps hundreds of other men." Convicting the man for a crime so commonly committed would not serve justice, the editorial concluded.

Though Brown and Wismer, and indeed the entire federal government, were less than eager to prosecute white farmers accused of peonage, they still represented a substantial step up from the attitude of local law officers. In most communities, local law enforcement not only knew about the existence of peonage but actively facilitated it by trumping up charges against black men and helping to keep workers on the farm. Some local law officers even had their own peons working at the family farm. In most locales, the local law enforcement authorities could be counted on to help enforce the traditions and unwritten laws of peonage, and sometimes even to help beat peons into submission.

For instance, federal agents had investigated an incident that occurred when Sam Sadler, a black man, refused to work off a debt on J. D. Matheson's farm in Hartwell County, Georgia. The sheriff arrested him and took him to the local jail. Once there, the sheriff and the police chief held pistols on Sadler as the farmer's son beat him. The beating was paused every so often so the white landowner could ask Sadler, "Now, will you promise to go back and work out what you owe us?" Sadler was warned that he would be thrown in a river if he told anyone about the beating.

With the collusion of local authorities obvious to all blacks in the area, peons and those threatened with peonage had little opportunity to fight the system. If the black victims happened to know how to read and write, they used that rare skill to warn others. They wrote to friends and relatives in distant places, and the message was always the same: Don't come here.

In 1912, a black woman trapped in slavery in Grapeland, Mississippi, wrote such a letter to her husband, who had escaped the farm earlier but had to leave her behind. Though she longed to be free of the farm and reunited with her husband, she admonished him not to help her. "I don't know when I can get there because the white peoples is watching me so," she wrote. "They is trying to keep me here and they are watching for you on to the river on the Kate Adam and they say if you came down on the boat they are going to hang you to the telephone poles and break your neck. Don't you come down here, darling."

But even the treasured ability to write could be turned against the poor blacks. In another case, Henry Holifield was lured back to a plantation in Forrest, Mississippi, by a letter from his wife who assured him that things were better and the landowner would not hurt him. When he returned, Holifield found that his wife had been forced to write the letter. The farmer met him with a gun and immediately tied Holifield up. "He tied my hands behind me and put a chain on my neck, carried the chain up to the rafters, and the chain was so tight until it liked to choke me to death," the man wrote. "I prayed to the Lord to help me and so he did."

For those trapped in peonage there truly were few options. Seeking help from local law officers was out of the question, since they were as much to be feared as the farm owners. Most of the peons had no education and thus were not familiar with other options, such as contacting federal authorities. Without the ability to write or access to telephones and transportation, they had no way to get in touch with federal agents even if they were willing to risk their lives in doing so.

The isolation of life on a peon plantation was perhaps the most devastating curb to any hope the workers had of obtaining freedom. Brown and Wismer knew from their own visits to peonage farms that the workers typically had no idea what their rights were or how they might leave the farm. The blacks who grew up on the farm or nearby were at even more of a disadvantage in this regard than the peons who, presumably, had seen other parts of the state and knew what lay beyond the farm hills. For those who grew up on the Williams plantation, like Manning, the borders of the farm truly were the borders of their world.

Claude Freeman, for instance, testified that he did not know where Polk's Store was, although it was a major landmark in the area and just a few miles from the Williams plantation. Emma Freeman explained that she had heard tales of other white people living somewhere near the Williams plantation, but she had never seen them and did not know if the tales were true. Such total isolation, not to mention the fear and everyday horror of life there, must be considered when questioning why people acted the way they did.

The isolation certainly had its effect on Manning, who recalled almost nothing but living under Williams's thumb. His fear of the world beyond the plantation was a significant impediment when he was faced with awful choices later. If he harbored any secret thoughts of breaking away from the farm one day, Gus Chapman's first failed escape attempt apparently ended those dreams.

"He had been out of the United States two or three times and he run away and they caught him, and I seen what they done to him," Manning said. "If he couldn't get away, I knowed I didn't have any chance.

"And Will Napier, he had been out of the United States two or three times and he did take the chance and when they brought him back they didn't let him live. They killed him. Mr. Huland killed him because he wanted to leave and he couldn't get him to stay, and Mr. Huland shot him because he would not stay with him."

There is no indication that either Chapman or Napier had ever left the United States, and it is doubtful that poor black men in rural Georgia would ever have occasion to leave the country "two or three times." Manning was referring to the men leaving Jasper County; but in his mind, because they had escaped, they had "been out of the United States" and far, far away from his world.

So Manning decided to stay. The federal agents in Atlanta would not wonder why. They understood Manning's dilemma as few others could.

# 4

## "You Lying Scoundrel, You"

Agents Brown and Wismer arrived at the Williams plantation on Friday, February 18, 1921. As was common on weekdays, the black hands were working the fields and doing other chores, but John S. Williams and his sons were away. The federal agents called a few workers out of the field near the Williams home and began asking them about some of the tales related by Chapman and Strickland. In addition, they took note of the general condition of the farm site and the hands working it, all with the goal of reporting back to Washington whether the charges of peonage were founded and, if so, whether the crime was serious enough to warrant the effort to press charges.

The workers were mostly afraid to talk to the white investigators, especially since it was clear that Manning could see and might report them to the Williams family. Since Manning was clearly in charge of the men, the agents decided to ask him about the alleged crimes, pressing hard enough to get more than the one-word responses that came from the others. They already knew from the statements of Chapman and Strickland that Manning was much more than just another worker. They knew that he was in charge of keeping the prisoners on the plantation, and they knew that he had been implicated hands-on in much of the brutality.

Brown and Wismer approached Manning and immediately disliked what they saw. Manning was carrying a pistol as John S. Williams often required, particularly in his absence. Of all the things they saw and heard on the farm that day, the sight of a black man openly carrying a pistol was what alarmed them the most.

Clyde Manning played well the role that Williams had taught him, but, in retrospect, it would be clear that Manning's effort to protect the plantation owner was the very catalyst that set Williams on a murderous rampage driven by fear. In denying that the reports about the farm were true, Manning thought he was doing exactly what Williams would expect if he were standing right next to him. It was a fatal mistake for eleven men working the fields as Manning spoke.

After asking a few general questions, the federal agents asked Manning directly about one of Chapman's most concrete claims.

"Do you know a nigger named Gus Chapman?" Brown asked Manning.

"Yes sir, I know him," the black man replied. "He used to work on the farm here for Mr. Johnny."

"Did he run away sometime last July?" Brown asked.

"Yes sir, he did."

"Did you and Mr. Williams chase him down and bring him back here to the farm?"

"No sir, we didn't do nothing like that. He come back on his own."

After exploring the subject a little more, the agents seemed satisfied with Manning's answer and dropped the query about Gus Chapman's first escape and retrieval. They asked Manning about how much he worked and how much he got paid. The black man responded truthfully, saying he worked "all day" and got paid twenty dollars a month. Almost as a formality, the agents mentioned that the farmer really could not require his workers to toil for more than eight hours a day and should be paying a fair wage.

Soon afterward, while they were poking around the farm, John S. Williams drove up and introduced himself. He had been to town on business, and, as he drove up to meet the agents, he looked every bit the part of the Southern gentleman farmer. With his carefully trimmed mustache and sharp, angular features, and dressed in a dark suit and tie with a starched high-collar shirt, Williams cut a dashing figure. His dark, wavy hair was longish on the top and short on the sides, with little gray to indicate his age. His eyes were penetrating.

Brown and Wismer told Williams they were federal agents and were investigating charges of peonage around the country. Williams played the perfect Southern host to the two visitors, offering each a glass of iced tea and listening politely to their explanation of what brought them so far into the Georgia heartland. All the while, he kept a close eye on Manning and the other few workers nearby. They, in turn, tried to look like they cared about nothing else but the work at hand.

"Well, if that's your business here, then I'll do anything I can to help you," Williams told the agents. "Y'all can go look around my property all you like and I'll help you out if you want me to."

The agents thanked Williams for his cooperation and explained that they only needed to look around the plantation some more and ask a few questions. They did not know that Williams had seen the agents from afar and driven out into the fields to talk to the hands before showing himself. A few stern words from Williams had ensured that the black men and women would say nothing when he obligingly drove the federal agents out to see them.

Williams then asked for an explanation of peonage and just how the law could be violated.

"If you pay a nigger's fine or go on his bond and you work him on your place, you're guilty of peonage," Brown told the farmer.

"Well, if that is the case, me and most of the people who have done anything of the sort were guilty of peonage," Williams replied with a smile and a chuckle. "I don't keep any of my niggers locked up. Of course, I do tell some of them they shouldn't leave before paying the fine they rightly owe me. That's only fair."

The farmer was worried, but he got the sense that the federal agents were not eager to find violations of the peonage law and might settle for the explanation that he had accidentally committed a technical violation but would stop once he understood the law more clearly. He was right. Later on, the agents testified that they were generally content with the conditions on the plantation, and federal authorities likely would have settled for placing Williams on probation for a short time—if they got around to prosecuting him at all.

But then the agents asked Williams one of the same questions they had asked Manning moments earlier. "By the way, have you ever worked a nigger by the name of Gus Chapman?" Brown asked him.

"I have," he replied. "I paid him fifteen dollars a month, plus board, and never locked him up."

"Did he run away from you last July?"

"He did."

"Did you take some nigger laborers and bring him back?"

"I did," replied John S. Williams, content that the agents would accept the explanation that Chapman had to be retrieved because he had assaulted Manning's wife before leaving and had agreed to return to the farm instead of being handed over to the local police.

Once Williams admitted to hunting down Gus Chapman, the agents had something to work with. Brown realized that the black man carrying the pistol had lied to him, and he instantly reacted with anger.

"You lying scoundrel, you!" Brown shouted at Manning, who was standing nearby and heard Williams admit to what Manning had denied. "You ought to have your neck broke! You've just been telling me a bunch of lies. Damn it, I believed it when you were telling it."

Manning said nothing, being far less concerned with the anger voiced by Brown than the anger not yet voiced by Williams. His eyes grew large with amazement, then fear. He could not believe that the farmer had admitted to chasing down Gus Chapman. And he realized that his own denial would cost him dearly.

The agents told Williams that they needed to investigate charges that certain black men were being held against their will, as reported by Chapman and Strickland, and the farmer replied that those men were up on the Huland Williams farm. Williams offered to drive the agents up there, saying, "Gentlemen, everything is open. I'll go and show you everything that you want to see. I may be plumb guilty of peonage, but I am not going to tell a whole bunch of lies about it."

The three men climbed into Williams's seven-passenger Chandler and drove toward the Huland Williams farm. On the way there, they encountered a group of farmhands working fields, and the agents decided to stop and talk to them. The group also visited both of the slave bunkhouses, where the agents took note of the divided buildings, shackles for locking the prisoners down at night, and the way in which the doors and windows were locked from the outside. Outside the bunkhouse near the Williams home, the agents noticed something that seemed inconsequential at the time but would later prove to be an important clue to the murders on the Williams farm. An older black man, Manning's uncle Rufus, was working with equipment used to repair shoes. Used rubber tires were stacked nearby, and the agents saw that pieces of the rubber were used to resole the shoes worn by the black laborers on the plantation.

Setting out again, they saw some workers near a barn and stopped to interview them. They took the opportunity to view the livestock and some other property in and around the barn.

And ever the good host, Williams pointed out that one of the young black hands was quite a fine dancer. He instructed the young man to dance for the visiting federal agents, and he did.


As Williams was driving the federal agents around his property, they encountered his sons Leroy and Marvin working with some black hands to burn off fields. The agents took the time to interview some of the workers, including overseer Claude Freeman, outside the earshot of Williams and his sons. The agents later reported that it was clear the black workers were afraid to talk and all of them refused to provide any substantial information. Each one stated that he was well cared for and not held against his will. The agents did not believe the men were free to speak truthfully, and they noted that further investigation might require taking the men away from the Williams plantation where they might be more willing to complain of being mistreated.

After the agents had seen all they wanted to see, Williams couldn't help but ask for an appraisal.

"Well, Mr. Williams, things are much better than what we expected," Brown told him. "Technically, you may be guilty of peonage. But we've looked at your hands and they are well dressed and well fed, and all we talked with seem to be satisfied.

"I don't think you need to have any fear of any case before the federal grand jury."

The agents then thanked the farmer for his cooperation and left the plantation. Williams was left pondering how much he could trust the last statement they made, and as the sun began to set on the land he had tended for years, he must have concluded that he could not trust it much at all. The consequences would be too great if the agents decided that Williams was guilty of more than just the technical violation of peonage that they could pin on almost any of the thousands of farmers in the South. He could lose his land; he could lose his money; he could lose his reputation as a leading farmer in the community. He could be sentenced for his crimes, and his family would be left without a provider. And, perhaps worst of all, his beloved sons could be sent to prison.

As Williams mulled over the day's events, he became more and more concerned that the agents would report suspicions of serious crime and instigate more of an investigation. Judging from his actions in the next days, it seems likely that he lay down to sleep that night thinking of federal agent Brown furiously shouting at Manning.

But despite the agent's obvious anger, the lie that Manning was caught in had far more impact on John S. Williams than on the federal agents. They were only vaguely suspicious and not especially eager to pursue the case, but Williams was concluding that they posed the ultimate threat to him and his family.

He already knew that local farmers were getting more attention for peonage lately, even if there had not yet been much punishment meted out. The Jasper County sheriff himself was scheduled for trial in April on federal charges that he had kidnapped a black man and forced him back to his nephew's farm to work. And there were rumors that the some Jasper County farmers would be charged with peonage when the federal grand jury convened in April.

If the authorities returned and started asking more questions, it would only be a matter of time before one of the workers ran off at the mouth and gave them something concrete to prosecute. And since they knew the federal authorities were interested, who knows how many of the workers would make a run for it and tell the federal agents everything about the Williams plantation? He could not let that happen. It was bad enough that he could be put in prison, but he could not let his boys be locked up.

Before falling asleep that night, Williams apparently decided what had to be done. He would set off to do it the next morning.

# 5

## "I Hate to Do It"

The farmer and his black hands awoke to a frosty, damp morning that contrasted sharply with the pleasant weather of the day before. In the middle of February, Georgia was in the deepest part of its short winter but about to burst forth into the warm days of spring. It was common to have days of beautiful, sunny weather followed by a sudden return to bone-chilling cold.

A frosty morning was appropriate for the day's work. Just as he had for practically all of his adult life, John S. Williams arose early and had a hearty breakfast with his wife and younger children.

There was nothing unusual about his demeanor, no outward display of worry, fear, or anger. Just another day's work to be done. His fifty-year-old wife, Lucy, bade him a good day as she watched him walk out the back door of the house and head toward the shanty building where Manning had watched over his charges during the night.

He found Manning outside the house talking with his uncle Rufus, who was settling in for a day of making and repairing shoes with the pile of old automobile tires. Rena Manning, Clyde's wife, was inside the house cleaning pots and dishes from the black men's breakfast, singing softly to herself as she worked.

A group of about ten black men could be seen walking down the road almost out of sight, so Williams knew that Manning had already sent some of the men off to work in the fields. He came near Clyde and Rufus Manning, and Rufus nodded to Clyde, who had his back to the white man. Manning turned to face Williams, and both the black men tipped their caps and quietly said, "Mornin', Mr. Johnny."

"Clyde, come on with me," the farmer replied, without breaking his stride or waiting to see if the black man would follow.

Manning immediately stepped to follow his boss, but Williams said nothing more until they were far away from the buildings and anyone else. At that point, Williams stopped walking and turned to face Manning, who in turn faced the farmer but kept his eyes cast to the ground. He expected that the plantation owner wanted to curse him for talking to the federal agents the day before, and he knew it wouldn't do for all the other men to hear what they were talking about. Manning stood with his arms tucked inside the bib of his overalls for warmth, bracing himself for a good cursing and just hoping it wouldn't be followed by a beating.

But what came out of Williams's mouth was a surprise.

"Clyde, it won't do for those boys to get up yonder and swear against us," the farmer said, referring to Atlanta. "They will ruin us. You have got to get rid of all the stockade niggers."

The black farm boss wasn't sure what he was supposed to say at this point, and he hesitated for a long while. He explained in court later that he was confused as to exactly what Williams meant. He couldn't mean that Manning could let all those men just go free. Manning stole a glance at the white farmer's face and quickly averted his eyes. No, surely he can't be telling me to kill them all, he thought. But the farmer did not say anything more, and it was obvious he was waiting for Manning to acknowledge the instructions. The pause must have seemed unbearable, and the black man finally spoke up. "Mr. Johnny, you telling me you want me to do away with them boys?"

"Yes, we'll have to do away with them."

Manning did not know what to say. There was no doubt as to his boss's intent, but he could not stand the thought of having to kill all those men who had just slept in the same house with him and his wife and shivered through the cold night with even fewer bedclothes than he had. Mr. Johnny had been good to him and his family through the years, Manning probably thought, but he didn't like some of the things he made him do. And this was by far the worst. Manning must have been torn between the dread and disgust he felt at being told to kill, and the fear he always felt when

The terrified man began to shuffle backward, almost losing his balance on the uneven ground and struggling to face Manning as he approached with the axe. "You don't have to do this, Mr. Johnny! I didn't tell them men nothing!" he cried out. "Please don't do this, Mr. Johnny, please don't!"

Manning continued to step toward the man, and he tried to avoid looking at his face. Johnnie Williams turned his attention to his last hope and fervently begged Manning not to kill him. "Don't do this, Clyde, please! This ain't right, Clyde. Please! Please don't!" Manning kept approaching Johnnie Williams, forcing him to circle backward as he begged for his life, but he made no attempt to swing the heavy axe when he got in reach. He did not want to kill the man, and his reluctance was becoming clear to the farmer standing nearby.

"Don't you mean to do what I said?" John S. Williams called out to the pair, who were by now many yards away from him. "If you don't, just give me the axe."

Manning knew that he could not give the axe to the farmer. If he did, Johnnie Williams still would die in the next few minutes and, most likely, so would he. Manning took a few big strides toward the terrified prey, who was holding up his arms, his hat held in one hand, waiting to fend off the coming blows from the axe.

Once Manning decided to go ahead with his job, he did it well. With one blow to the left side of Johnnie Williams's head, the work was done. The man fell in a heap. Manning and Williams dragged the body over to a gully where the red Georgia clay was exposed and easy to dig. Manning used the axe to dig a hole in the side of the gully, and they stuffed the man's body into it and covered it up.

As much as Manning hated what happened in the field that day, he knew there was more to come. He told no one on the plantation about it, and when Johnnie Williams never came home from taking the cows to pasture, Manning claimed he had no idea where he was. Maybe he ran off, was all he would say about it.

The next day, Manning found out who was next in line. Williams stopped by Manning's house early in the morning after breakfast, as had been customary for years. Normally, the farmer would instruct Manning on what work he expected to be done that day. Usually it was a matter of burning off the fields, picking cotton, or moving livestock. But since their first conversation about how the men must be killed, Manning had come to hate the

45

sight of the white farmer walking toward the workers' cabin first thing in the morning, fresh overalls on and still picking his teeth from his breakfast. Now Williams was as likely to talk about killing men as he was to talk about whether it was better to take one plow team or two down to the south corn.

This morning, Williams had killing on his mind. The day's victim was to be John Will Gaither, known as Big John. Since Big John truly was a big man, John S. Williams thought a better plan was necessary than the one used to kill Johnnie Williams. If Manning hesitated again when the time came to kill, Gaither might be enough of a troublemaker to just snatch the axe away from Manning and go after both him and the farmer with it.

"Clyde, I want you and Charlie to go up to the new house and make like you're digging a well," the farmer said. He wanted Charlie Chisolm to go along so that there would be more muscle available if Gaither put up any kind of fight. Williams knew that he could trust Chisolm to go along with what he and Manning were doing.

The plan was to have the two black men recruit Gaither to help with the job of digging a well near a house on Huland Williams's property. The house, known as the Campbell place, had never been lived in. Williams had just recently purchased it from a neighboring farmer. It had a barn nearby, but since no one had lived in the house yet, no well had been dug. Even if Gaither became suspicious, the job seemed sensible enough.

"Y'all go to digging the well, and we'll get Big John down in it and knock him in the head," the farmer explained. "I'll be around to see how you're doing with it."

Clyde Manning did as he was instructed. He got Charlie Chisolm to come along, and as they went to get Gaither, Manning told Chisolm they were going to have to kill the other man. Charlie Chisolm did not ask many questions. He understood that the order came from the Williams family, and that was all he needed to know.

The three men took a wagon to the Campbell place, and Manning decided that the best spot for the "well" was right near the back door. They had brought along shovels and pickaxes to do the digging, but Gaither noticed that they had no more than that, and he knew that digging a well was a big job. The shovels and axes would get them through the morning, but after that they would need buckets, ropes, a ladder, and maybe more men to spell each other. He asked Manning why they hadn't brought more material, but the black farm boss just ignored him and told him to start working. Gaither quickly lost his curiosity as he set to digging through the cold, hard red clay. He could see a long day's work ahead of him.

The three men took turns digging, creating a narrow hole that could hold only one man at a time. One would dig for a while and then hand the shovel over to the one who had rested the longest. It was tedious, back-breaking work for all three men, but only one of them was digging his own grave.

Just before lunchtime, Williams drove up in his car to see how the men were doing and to tell them to finish the job. He found Gaither and Manning resting nearby while Charlie Chisolm stood in the hole up to his shoulders, slowly digging deeper. All three men were covered in wet Georgia clay. The white man took a quick look at the hole and decided that it was deep enough, so he said, "Charlie, looks like you're going to work yourself to death. Why don't you take a spell and let Big John do some digging?"

Charlie Chisolm let the shovel drop and rest against the walls of the hole. He reached his hands up, and the other two men grabbed him and pulled with all their might while he used his legs to climb out. Gaither jumped down in the hole and started digging.

While Charlie Chisolm was still kicking the mud off his boots, Williams silently picked up the pickaxe and handed it to him. Gaither could not see them, so the white farmer just nodded in the victim's direction. Charlie Chisolm and Manning both knew what was meant.

No one spoke, and the only noise was the sound of Gaither driving the shovel into the wet earth and grunting with each thrust. Williams and Manning watched as Charlie Chisolm held the pickaxe in two hands and slowly walked up behind Gaither. He had to keep it low to the ground to hit Gaither, whose head and shoulders barely stuck out of the hole. Without a word, Charlie Chisolm swung the pickaxe back and struck Gaither in the side of the head.

Gaither never knew he had been struck. He immediately doubled over and fell into the hole he had helped dig. Charlie Chisolm walked up and pulled the shovel out of the hole—no need to waste a good shovel—and Williams told the two men to fill the hole back up. Without pausing even a moment to see if Gaither might still be alive, Manning and Chisolm began to shovel in the clay. In just a short time, there was no longer a hole. Just a big muddy spot near the house and one less man on the Williams plantation.

Williams had determined early on that resolving this whole mess with the stockade workers and the federal agents would be his problem alone. He did not want his sons mixed up in it any more than necessary, and if worse came to worst, he did not want them around to be arrested. He told Huland, Leroy, and Marvin to leave the farm and not come back until he said so. He would make up a lie to tell their mother, because even telling her they were running away to avoid getting in trouble would be too much for her to bear.

The three sons left Georgia days after the federal agents' visit and just as their father was beginning the killings that he thought would end all their problems. "I'll let you know when it's all done with and then you can come home," he told them. But before that time could come, there were nine more men to kill.

# 6

## "I'll Go, Mr. Johnny"

John S. Williams went about the business of killing in the same manner he had run the plantation for years: When you have a job to do, go ahead and do it and get the niggers to do all they can.

Williams apparently started to think that disposing of the remaining nine men on his own property might not be such a good idea. He already had Johnnie Williams and Gaither buried there, in addition to the several men who had been killed over the years before the federal agents visited. Burying a body here and there hadn't bothered the farmer, but he didn't like the idea of having a dozen or more men buried on the property all at once. That might look too suspicious if they were ever found. And if the investigators decided to look for the missing farm workers, all those graves would be hard to hide.

So Williams decided that it was better to take the men off the property, to make use of the nearby rivers and bridges to dispose of the bodies. After all, what does one do when the cats on the farm produce too many kittens? A short trip to the bridge with a sackful solves the problem.

He clearly put some thought into exactly how he might get the men off the plantation. It was too much trouble to find a way to kill them there, so it would be better to just take them out alive. But he also worried that throwing them in the rivers might not be enough. No one would wonder too much about finding one dead black man in the river, but since there would be several, Williams feared the bodies could be traced back to him. It would be better to make sure they were not found at all.

He probably recalled how he and his boys had disposed of John Singleton, a black worker who had run afoul of the Williams family some years before. Singleton's body had been thrown into a pond on the farm after he was killed, but it had not been properly weighted. One afternoon the problem was spotted by Marvin Williams and Claude Freeman, the other black overseer, who were working in a field pulling corn when they noticed buzzards flying overhead. Curious about what was dead and worried that perhaps some livestock had died, Marvin Williams left the corn to go for a look.

When he returned he said, "That Singleton boy's come to the top." Claude Freeman knew what he meant. Marvin Williams told Freeman and another black man working with him to keep pulling corn and he'd return shortly with some rope. When he came back he told the men to follow him.

They walked a short way through the woods, and as they approached the pond, they could smell the unique stench of a rotting human body. They could see it as they got closer, horribly bloated, decaying, and floating just off the shore. Marvin Williams stood back and told the other two to go ahead and get the body. They hesitated, but went to the pond's edge and pulled the corpse closer with the aid of a long branch. Fighting the smell, gagging as they worked, the two men used the rope to attach a few large rocks to the body. Once it was secured, they waded into the pond and carried the rocks as they pulled the rotting corpse behind them. When they got as close to the middle of the pond as they could and still keep their heads above water, they tied the rocks closer to the body and let it go. Singleton sank for a second time and was never seen again.

A lesson learned, Williams must have thought.


Williams decided to get rid of a couple more men on Friday, February 25, 1921, exactly one week after the federal agents' visit. All of the farm workers had put in a hard day on Huland's property. They were told to finish plowing before dark and then take some hogs down to John S. Williams's house. Manning left the group to go home in a wagon with Willie Preston, Lindsey Peterson, and Harry Price, while the rest of the men shepherded the hogs the five miles to the main plantation house.

Manning and his companions were unhitching the mules from the wagons and putting them away for the night when Williams came by and pulled him aside. "After y'all eat your supper, go on down to your house and I'll come down there," he told Manning. "Have Rena make you boys something to eat."

After finishing their chores, the four men were joined by Charlie Chisolm. They went to the kitchen of the Williams house where Rena Manning fixed them some supper. They ate quickly and quietly as she washed the dishes from the Williamses' meal.

As the men were about to leave, John S. Williams walked into the kitchen and again pulled Manning aside.

"I'm coming down there in a little while, Clyde," he said. "We have to do away with them boys."

Manning clutched his hat in his hand and stared at the floor as he muttered, "Yessir, Mr. Johnny."

He went on down to his house, the slave quarters where the other men would be locked up that night, and he was joined by several of the black workers for some socializing before bedtime. The men were sitting around the small wooden table in Manning's side of the building, talking, smoking, and sharing a few laughs as they waited for the rest of the men and women to finish their chores and have their suppers.

They continued their socializing until they heard a knock on the door at about nine P.M. Manning stood up and moved toward the door, and the other men let their laughter die down. "Who is it?" Manning called out.

"Open the door," came the reply.

Manning opened the door and greeted his boss, followed quickly by a low chorus of the other men saying "Evening, Mr. Johnny," almost simultaneously.

The white man stepped inside. Naturally, all eyes fell on him.

"Listen up, boys," Williams called out in a clear voice. "I've been thinking about this and I've decided that all you boys can go on home if you've a mind to. I can get y'all some clothes if you want them, and I'll get you to the train station so you can go on home or go anywhere you want to go."

The white man stopped talking. The other men were dead silent. They looked around at each other, wondering if they heard correctly and, if so, what it meant. Mr. Johnny was really going to let them go? Maybe those federal men had scared Mr. Johnny more than they thought.

"So, does anybody want to go?" the farmer asked.

There was a long silence again, as the men contemplated what they had just been offered and wondered about the risk of being the first to speak up. Williams just stood there waiting. Finally, John Brown spoke up.

"I'll go, Mr. Johnny," he said.

"All right, Red," the farmer replied, using the man's nickname.

"I'll go too, Mr. Johnny," said Johnny Benson, a slightly built young man, barely beyond his teens, called Little Bit.

With the tension broken, the other men chimed in, saying they too would be glad to go. As they got more excited and started to talk loudly about the joy of going home, the farmer raised his voice to calm them down again.

"Settle down now, boys," he said. "I can't take all of you at once, but I can take a couple of you to the train station tonight. Red and Little Bit, y'all come on tonight. Go on and get in the car. I'll take some more of you tomorrow."

The two men went ahead and started toward Williams's car, but the farmer did not immediately follow them. He motioned for Manning to step out onto the porch, where he said, "Go get Charlie and come on with me and those boys."

Manning knew that the farmer had no intention of letting any of the men go home. He had stood there silently next to Williams, listening to him lie to the men who had been laughing and relaxing in his house. But he did not say anything to the two men heading toward the car, and he did not go back in the house and say anything to the other men excitedly talking about leaving the Williams plantation.

Instead, he did just as he was told. He went and got Charlie Chisolm, and they joined the others waiting in the car.

The five men drove along the dark dirt roads with Williams driving and Manning riding alongside him up front. Charlie Chisolm rode in the backseat with John Brown and Johnny Benson. None of the men spoke much, partly because of the night wind whipping by in the open car. Brown and Benson occasionally leaned toward each other and discussed what was happening, mixing moments of skepticism with moments of almost giddy excitement about being set free. Charlie Chisolm heard much of their conversation but said nothing.

After a while, Williams stopped the car along the road, long before they were near the train station. He got out, and Manning followed him around to the back of the car. Brown and Benson watched and wondered with growing fear what was going on.

"You boys come on out here for a minute," the farmer called to the three men sitting in the backseat.

Chisolm got out first and told the other two to come on, and soon all five men were standing at the rear of the Chandler car. Williams reached down and opened the trunk of the car. In the dim light, the men could make out a pile of chains.

"Hold on to 'em," the white man said, and Manning and Chisolm grabbed Brown and Benson. The captives stiffened immediately but did not fight back, partly because they still did not know what was about to happen. Williams reached in and grabbed the heavy pile of chains. Once he found the ends of one chain, he knelt down and started wrapping the chains around Brown's ankles. Brown still did not fight but was growing increasingly frightened.

The young Benson was becoming terror-stricken. "What we doing, Mr. Johnny? What we gonna do, Clyde?" he stammered. "Ain't we going to the train station?"

Neither man answered Little Bit, and he began to pull away from Manning's grip, causing them both to stumble about as Benson began to cry and plead to be let go.

Williams saw that Manning could not hold Benson all by himself, so he stopped tying Brown with the chains and stepped over to Benson. He grabbed one of the young man's arms, and all three men walked a few feet away from where Chisolm was still holding Brown.

"Now, you hush up, boy!" Williams said, with a hard shake to Benson. "Stop all this fussing! You hear me?"

When Benson had calmed down enough to hear what the farmer was saying, he continued in a low voice and with an occasional glance toward Brown.

"We ain't going to do nothing to you, boy," the farmer said, his face only inches from Benson's. "We just came out here to scare ole' Red some. We ain't even going to do anything to him. We're just going to tie him up and put the fear of God in him, and that's all. Now just stop putting up such a fuss!"

There was no reason for Benson to believe him, but Williams's comments at least calmed him down enough that Manning could continue holding him. They went back to where Brown was waiting with the chains wrapped loosely around his ankles, and Williams continued wrapping them tight. When he was done there, he took more chains and tied Brown's hands tight in front of him. At that point, Brown finally spoke.

"Mr. Johnny, I ain't gonna say nothing to nobody," he said, doing his best to sound convincing. "You can trust Big Red on that there, Mr. Johnny."

Williams made no reply. He looked over to Benson and told Manning to let him go. "Get me that piece of iron out of there, Little Bit," the farmer said.

The frightened man took a few steps toward the car and saw a heavy piece of iron in the trunk. When he reached in and lifted it out, Manning could tell that it was a heavy piece of an iron wheel from a cotton press. Benson lifted it about waist high and carried it over to Williams.

"Here, tie that here on around his neck," the white man said, handing Benson another chain to attach the weight to Brown. He then returned to checking the chains on Brown's hands. Benson did not know what else to do, so he lifted the weight higher and pushed one end of the chain through a hole and then around Brown's neck. He tied the chain together in a bulky knot so that the heavy weight was hanging on Brown like a macabre necklace. Brown just stood there, his head and neck forced down by the weight.

When the farmer saw that Brown was securely chained, he told Chisolm he could let the man go. Benson had backed away a few steps and was standing near Manning when the farmer said, "Now bring *him* over here."

Benson stepped back and turned to run, but Manning and Chisolm both seized him and dragged him toward the chained Brown. Williams grabbed still more chains out of the car and wrapped Benson's arms and hands tight, then another chain around his ankles. When he was trussed up securely, Williams grabbed him and pulled him closer to Brown. With one more chain, the farmer tied Benson to Brown, the rusty links running through the loops and layers of chains that tied their hands together, palms together.

Benson by now was crying and begging to be let go, though his pleas could barely be understood. His captors ignored him and shoved both of the chained men into the backseat of the car, where they sat nearly on top of one another, pulling at the chains. The other men climbed into the front seat and they all drove off to Water's Bridge on the Alcovy River.

When they got halfway across the bridge, Williams stopped and stepped out of the car. Speaking to Chisolm and Manning, he said, "C'mon, let's get it done."

The men in the backseat looked around for an opportunity to escape, but there was no hope. They were in the middle of a long bridge, and, though they could not see far in the darkness, the Alcovy River at that point is a wide, slow-moving body of water more resembling a lake. Their chains made them helpless.

Chisolm and Manning dragged the two men out of the backseat, pulling them along on their knees as they struggled to stand and walk in the chains. As they were being dragged to the bridge railing, both men became panic-stricken and begged for their lives. They screamed and pleaded not to be thrown over the bridge, desperately swearing to do anything they were told and not to speak a word to anyone outside the Williams plantation. Williams just stood by the car and waited for the work to be done.

As the chained men were being pulled to their feet near the bridge railing, Brown pleaded for help from Manning, any sort of help. "Oh god, Clyde, please don't throw me over in that water!" he cried. "Clyde, please, I don't want to drown in no river like that. Please, Clyde, please don't throw me in that water," he sobbed.

Manning said nothing in return, but he was startled by what Brown said next.

"Can't you just knock me in the head before you throw me over, Clyde?" Brown said through a torrent of tears. "I don't want to drown, Clyde. Can't you knock me in the head first?"

The request caught Manning off guard. He stopped trying to push Brown toward the railing. Chisolm also hesitated, and they both turned to look at the farmer. Williams had heard the request, but he waved his hand with a sign of impatience and told the men to just hurry up and do it.

Manning and Chisolm turned back toward the crying men and shoved hard so that they were both up against the bridge railing. Both men were sobbing uncontrollably and letting out shrieks of terror every time they were pushed closer to the water. Finally, Manning and Chisolm managed to shove both the men hard across the shoulders and they fell in tandem into the darkness.

Manning heard their final screams of absolute terror as they fell to the water below, and he would hear those screams for years to come. But he never heard the splash.

When Williams, Chisolm, and Manning returned to the plantation that night, they said nothing to the remaining men about what had happened. The next day the men were expecting the farmer to drive more of them to the train station, but he said nothing until late in the evening, after the day's work was done and everyone was fed and beginning to rest.

Once more, Williams went to Manning's house late in the evening and asked who wanted to go home. Several of the men answered that they were ready to go, but the farmer knew who he wanted to take. He pointed to Lindsey Peterson, Willie Preston, and Harry Price, for no discernible reason, and told them to meet him in the car. And just as he had the night before, he promised the others that he would take more of them to the train station in the next few days. He turned to Johnny Green, who lived on Huland's part of the plantation, and said, "Johnny, you come on by the house first thing in the morning and I'll take you then."

The previous night's scenario played out again as the six men drove away from the Williams plantation and toward the bridge. At a point between Polk's Store and Water's Bridge, the farmer stopped the car and ordered Manning and Chisolm to tie the others with chains and wire. He also had brought along two bags of rocks weighing about a hundred pounds each, the equivalent of about twenty-five bricks.

When the chains and bag of rocks were attached to Harry Price, Williams found that there was not quite enough chain to tie the rocks around his neck, so he rummaged around in the car until he found an old horseshoe. By hooking the links of the chain over the horseshoe, the farmer was able to secure the rocks to the frightened man.

The men forced Peterson and Preston over one bridge, terrified and begging just like the previous night's victims, and they watched Price drop himself into the water with a prayer and a quiet, sad dignity. Williams drove Chisolm and Manning back to the farm at about eleven o'clock. Once more, the white farmer went to his house and slept soundly without telling his wife or children anything about what he had done. And once more, Manning returned to the house where he slept within feet of men he might kill soon, and said nothing.

# 7

---

# "Don't Make No Miss Lick"

The next morning was Sunday, but that was no reason for Williams to put off the work he had to do. After a good breakfast, his wife and children went into town for church, and the planter went to find Manning and Johnny Green relaxing outside the slave house. The sun had been up less than an hour. Just as he'd been instructed, Johnny Green had come by first thing in the morning so Mr. Johnny could drive him to the train station. He had a small cloth bundle sitting at his feet, his baggage for the trip.

"Johnny, I need you to get down in the pasture and fix up that fence wire before we take you to the train station. We'll still have time for you to make the train," the farmer said. "Go get us some tools and Clyde and me will go on down with you."

Green trotted off to gather the tools for fixing the fence, and Williams turned his attention to the black overseer.

"We got to do away with that boy, Clyde," he said. "That nigger scares me."

Manning stared at the ground, his hands jammed deep into the pockets of his overalls. He hesitated for a moment, then spoke without looking up.

"I know, Mr. Johnny," he said in a soft voice. "I sure hate to do it, though. I sure do."

"It's your neck or theirs, Clyde. I'm sticking by my boys. These niggers ain't going to tell everything on me and get my boys in trouble," the farmer replied. "Go get Charlie and we'll get on with it."

Charlie Chisolm had been summoned by the time Green returned with the tools, and they joined Williams and Manning in a wagon for the short trip down to the broken pasture fence. They traveled to a spot near where Johnnie Williams had been killed. Green started unloading a few of the tools and headed over to the fence, and Manning grabbed a heavy axe that was left in the wagon. "Go on and hit him," the farmer told him.

Manning walked up behind Green, holding the axe across his chest and remembering the difficulty he had in making himself kill Johnnie Williams with it. He intended to walk up to Green and hit him quickly, before the man could get scared and start running, but he faltered when he got close. He ended up standing there with the axe in his hands and his heart pounding while Green looked over at him, totally oblivious, and asked how Manning wanted him to go about fixing the fence.

Green stood there waiting for an answer, a look of puzzlement slowly coming over his face as Manning failed to respond. Manning looked over at Williams, who was still standing by the wagon.

The farmer shouted out, "Johnny, I heard you was going to go off and have my boys' necks broke. I ain't going to let you do it." And before Green could reply, he added, "Go on, Clyde."

Green was still looking toward the white man, a look of calm confusion on his face, when the blunt end of the axe head slammed into the back of his head. He immediately fell to the ground in a heap. Bright red blood started pooling around his head in the dewy grass. Manning stood over his victim, the axe still raised over his shoulder. His eyes were wide with terror and panic, and his chest was heaving. He looked over at Williams.

"Hit him again," the farmer called out. "Go on and hit him again."

Manning split Green's head wide open with a heavy axe blow. Blood and brain matter splattered on Manning's blue overalls as Green's body jerked and convulsed.

"All right, let's go," Williams said calmly.

Manning said nothing, and neither did Chisolm, who had watched the killing from a short distance away. They gathered up the tools that Green had carried over the fence and, after wiping off the blood on the grass, put them back in the wagon. The three men climbed into the wagon and drove out of the pasture, leaving the fourth lying in the cool, soft grass.

The men returned to their houses and had big Sunday dinners, just like every Sunday. After the planter had had his fill of fried chicken and biscuits, he strolled on down to Manning's house again. Manning saw him coming.

But Williams walked by Manning and went to Willie Givens, a black worker who was sitting under a tree nearby and talking to a few other men. They all tipped their caps to Mr. Johnny and commented on the beautiful Sunday afternoon they were enjoying.

"It's nice, all right," the farmer replied. "I'm thinking I might walk on down to Homer's store. You want to come with me, Willie?"

"Yes sir, boss, I sure do," Givens replied, anxious for any opportunity to get off the plantation for a short while.

Givens and the farmer walked back toward Manning, who was also invited to come along for a Sunday afternoon stroll. Manning grabbed his hat and joined them. He knew Mr. Johnny wasn't taking Willie along for the company.

"Clyde, get an axe and you can cut us a foot log to cross the creek with," the planter said.

Manning shuddered slightly as he heard this. He trotted off to get the axe out of the wagon where he had left it that morning, stopping to wipe the last of Green's blood off the axe head before rejoining the farmer and Givens, who was waiting a few yards away.

When Manning approached, Williams turned on his heels so that his back was to Givens and said, "Clyde, I'm going to walk on in front, and you walk behind Willie. When we get to the woods, you brain him with that axe."

"Yes sir, Mr. Johnny," he replied.

"Don't make no miss lick," the farmer urged. "If you do, I'll take that axe and I won't miss when I swing at *you* with it."

"Yes sir, Mr. Johnny," Manning said again.

The three men then took off for their leisurely Sunday afternoon stroll to Homer's store, with the farmer leading the way. As they walked along in the warm sunlight, Givens sang softly under his breath, humming parts of the tune contentedly.

Manning hung back as they made their way through the fields along the footpath, barely a foot wide, trampled in the grass.

When they approached the area where Johnnie Williams had been killed and buried and Johnny Green still lay in a bloody heap, Manning saw that he needed to go ahead with his job before they left the field and entered the woods. Givens was still singing softly as Manning quickened his pace and caught up with him. He quickly raised the axe and brought the blade down hard on the back of Givens's neck.

Givens was knocked forward by the blow and fell on his face, his hands loose at his side, making no attempt to break the fall. Manning stood with the axe raised, ready if another blow were needed.

Williams took a couple of extra steps before he heard Givens hit the earth. He turned around and stood for a moment, looking at Givens's still body and the wide, deep wound that had nearly decapitated the man.

Manning lowered the axe head to the ground and leaned on the handle, breathing hard.

"Better cover him up some," the farmer said. "Cover him up with some pine straw."

Williams stood and watched as Manning walked into the woods, came back with an armful of pine straw, and dumped it on top of Givens's body. He repeated the trip several times until Givens was covered well, forming a conspicuous heap of brown pine straw in the middle of a path through the new grass.

"That'll do," Williams said to Manning. The farmer walked past without saying anything more, and Manning stayed with Givens for a while, staring at the man he had just killed. Then he picked up the axe, rested it on his shoulder, and followed the path back.

The two men said nothing to each other as they returned home, Manning walking a fair distance behind the man who determined who and when he would kill. When they got back, Manning dropped the axe outside and immediately went into his house and collapsed on the bed. He lay there thinking about the men he had killed and what would come next.

Suddenly, he heard the door open and looked up to see Mr. Johnny standing there.

"Clyde, I don't want to hear anything about all this or I'll take my shotgun and do the same to you," he said. "You hear?"

"Yes sir, Mr. Johnny."


Manning lay on the bed all afternoon and into the early evening, until Williams showed up at the door again. He told Manning they had to go bury the men they'd killed earlier that day. The two of them went back down to the field where the two men lay and worked together to dig two shallow graves. They dragged in the bloody bodies and covered them up.

Then Manning gathered more pine straw from the nearby woods and scattered it over the muddy graves.

The killing stopped for almost a week. Manning went about his work on the farm, fearful every time he saw Williams and becoming more withdrawn from everyone else on the plantation. The hands had become somewhat suspicious of the murdered men's disappearance, but they were not exceptionally alarmed. It was normal for men to vanish suddenly. Once in a while, it was because they had escaped. And sometimes it was because they had been killed. It also was common for the Williams family to send men to other farms to work. In any case, the disappearance of a few men would not cause widespread alarm. And as far as the black workers knew, only a few men were missing; the rest had gone home.

Manning wondered if they were done killing people or, if not, who would be next. They had gotten rid of nine men already. Maybe that was enough.

But it was not quite enough for Williams. Two weeks and a day after the visit of the federal agents, the farmer decided that Charlie Chisolm knew too much about what happened before *and* after the visit. It was bad enough that Manning knew everything, but at least he could probably be trusted. Chisolm was another matter.

Things had calmed somewhat in the days since the last killing, so Manning was not as tense about seeing his boss. He thought maybe the killing was finished, and he discussed that possibility with Chisolm. They both said they hated what they had done, but they were glad they had survived.

When Williams approached Chisolm that Saturday evening, he was wary. Chisolm was quiet and obedient, but not stupid. When the farmer offered to take him to the train station, Chisolm knew what that offer had meant for the other men. But because he already had discussed with Manning the possibility that the killing was over, the farmer's explanation may have seemed plausible. Perhaps it was just wishful thinking, or perhaps he realized he had no choice, but in any case, Chisolm went along with the farmer's explanation.

"I'm going to take you to the train station before those government men get a case together and bring it on," Williams told him. "No use in having you around to talk to them if they bring a case. You might as well go on wherever you want."

Chisolm, Manning, and Williams drove along in the car until they approached Water's Bridge over the Alcovy River. As they got within a mile of the river, the farmer did just as Chisolm had feared. He pulled the car over in the darkness.

"I heard some of your damn talk, boy," the farmer said. "I'm going to teach you a lesson."

He stepped out and ordered the two black men out of the car. Although he was scared, Chisolm was as calm and quiet as he had been on the other nights. There was no surprise in the events so far, and he knew exactly what awaited him. And with Williams and Manning standing on either side of him, ready to grab him, Chisolm saw little opportunity to escape. Even if he ran, there was a good chance the farmer had a gun and would just shoot him down.

"I ain't said nothing to nobody, Mr. Johnny," Chisolm said in a trembling voice. "I ain't said nothing and I ain't going to, neither."

"Hush! I don't want to hear a word from you," the farmer replied. "I know what you said."

He then told Manning to get some wire from under the front of the car and two sacks that were hidden under the front seat. When Manning brought those, he was then told to go find some rocks. After gathering two large rocks from the roadside and returning, Williams took a look inside the sacks and decided they were not quite heavy enough.

"Better go get another big one," he told Manning. Chisolm stood and waited as his friend ensured that he would sink to the bottom of the muddy river. When the sacks of rocks were heavy enough to satisfy the planter, he told Manning to tie them to Chisolm. Manning tied one of the sacks of rocks to the man's neck and the other to his feet, but he would not be able to recall later which had the two rocks and which only one.

Manning then tied Chisolm's feet securely with the wire, but for some reason he was not instructed to tie Chisolm's hands. The two men helped Chisolm hobble over to the passenger side and flop into the seat, hoisting the heavy bag tied to his ankles. He sat in the seat next to Williams, holding the other bag of rocks in his hands and leaning forward from the weight.

Manning was in the backseat as they drove the last mile to the bridge. Chisolm did not make another plea, apparently understanding from his previous participation that there was nothing he could do to save himself.

Williams stopped the car in the middle of the bridge and left the engine running, its headlights shining through the darkness, but not strong enough to illuminate the end of the bridge. He and Manning got out of the car and went around to the passenger side. They opened the door and pulled on the rocks tied to Chisolm's feet, helping him swing his legs out of the car and onto the wooden planks of the bridge. Then they grabbed him by his upper arms and pulled him up, helping him stand and counter the weight around his neck. Chisolm never said a word.

Manning and Williams almost dragged Chisolm to the edge of the bridge as he tried to stumble forward with the rocks. When they got him to the railing, there was no need for words. Chisolm leaned against the railing, tears streaming down his face. The farmer reached down to lift his legs and the bag of rocks at his ankles. As he lifted them up, Manning pushed Chisolm's chest and he fell over the railing into the dark waters below.

When Chisolm was gone, Manning and Williams got back into the car and drove across the bridge to the signpost that said "Jasper County." There they turned around and drove back across the bridge as the last air was escaping Chisolm's lungs below.

As they drove home in the darkness, only one sentence was spoken. "Clyde, you'll end up the same if you tell anybody," the farmer said, looking straight ahead and never glancing at the man seated next to him.

Manning was not surprised to hear the warning, but it scared him badly. He was already wondering if Mr. Johnny wanted rid of him, too, and he was beginning to think that he was going to be killed no matter what. As far as he knew, Chisolm had not said anything to anyone. Yet he was in the river.

A few days after Chisolm was killed, Manning was supervising a group of men plowing some of Huland's fields when Williams walked up carrying a double-barreled shotgun. He told Clyde Freeman and Claude Freeman to go across the branch and pick up a load of fodder to carry to Huland's house and, when they were finished, to take the mules on home with Gladys Manning. Just before they left with the mules, the farmer had a second thought. "Leave Clyde's plow here and we'll bring 'em down later," he said.

Once the men had gone, that left the white planter, Manning, and Fletcher Smith.

"Clyde, go down to the branch and get a spade and a mattock," Williams said. "Bring up them on out here in the field where Fletcher and me'll be."

Manning headed down toward the branch to get the tools. As he was returning with the spade and mattock in hand, he saw that Williams was standing with the shotgun on the near side of a small hill, and he presumed Smith was waiting on the other side of the rise out of Manning's sight. Williams turned his head and saw Manning approach, then turned and walked over the small hilltop out of Manning's sight.

Suddenly a shotgun blast boomed across the fields. Manning stopped for a moment. He knew Smith was dead.

As he crested the hill, he could see the farmer standing about fifteen feet from Smith's body, the shotgun cradled in his arms and the smell of gunpowder still in the air. Williams barely glanced at Manning as he said, "Let's dig the hole right here."

The farmer put the shotgun on the ground and reached for the mattock Manning was carrying. He started breaking up the red Georgia clay with it, and Manning followed behind him to shovel the loose earth. They worked for a while as the sun began to set. When the hole was long and deep enough to hold Smith, they rolled his body into the grave and covered him with the loose earth, Manning shoveling and the farmer using the mattock to push dirt into the hole. Once it was filled, Williams told Manning to bring his plow mule over and instructed him to plow over the grave so that it would be indistinguishable from the hundreds of other furrows in the field. Manning draped his mule's trace lines over one shoulder, and with the expert hands and voice of someone who had been running a plow team all his life, he plowed over the fresh grave of Fletcher Smith. "Get up, get up," Manning called softly to the mule. With every guttural "haw," the mule would knowingly move to the left over the dead man, and back to the right with the next call of "gee, mule, gee." The heavy steel blade of the plow bit into the dirt deeply, penetrating far into the grave that held Smith's body just a scant foot or two below the surface. Before long, it was nearly impossible to see where it had been. If anyone ever came looking for the body, the grave would be just an unmarked spot in a huge, lush field of corn.

Manning and Williams picked up the tools and started guiding the mule team back home. As they headed back, the planter once again issued a stern warning to his assistant.

"Clyde, I don't want to hear nothing from this," he said. "There is nobody knows about this but just me and you. If I ever hear it come out, I'll know where it come from."

And as he had before, Manning assured his master that there was nothing to worry about.

"Mr. Johnny, I ain't going to say nothing about it to nobody."

# 8

---

# "I Believe Clyde Can Tell You All About It"

Upon returning to Atlanta from their visit to the Williams plantation, agents Brown and Wismer had decided there was no pressing need to pursue a complete investigation of the peonage charges. They had seen nothing on the farm that amounted to serious violations of the law and concluded that all the black hands seemed to be well cared for. They had no doubt that Williams was guilty of violating the peonage laws, but that violation alone was not seen as an especially high priority for prosecution. They suspected that there were more serious crimes to investigate on the plantation, but they had been stymied by the lack of information coming from the black workers. If conditions on the farm were as bad as the informants claimed, it was understandable that the remaining black workers would not be eager to talk to two white federal agents, especially with Williams standing nearby. So the agents were not fooled by the farmer's display of humble innocence, but neither were they encouraged enough to put the full weight of the federal government behind an investigation.

They submitted reports on their visit and preliminary investigation to their headquarters in Washington, D.C., the U.S. Attorney General, and the Atlanta District Attorney's Office. Their conclusion was that nothing had been found on their visit to warrant bringing charges against Williams, not even charges of peonage. The next step, they said, was to find blacks away from the Williams plantation who could substantiate the charges of peonage. That would require a lot of legwork. If they could get around to it, and if they found useful information, the federal government would go ahead and charge Williams with the labor violation. Though still suspicious, Brown and Wismer felt it unlikely that there would be enough evidence to charge the farmer in connection with the murders and other violent crimes that had been rumored.

But a newspaper clipping changed all that. Another agent in the Atlanta office of the federal Bureau of Investigation spotted a brief news item in the *Atlanta Constitution* about the discovery of some bodies in Jasper and Newton county rivers. Finding the bodies of three unknown black men in rural Georgia was not enough news to get anyone very excited, but the circumstances were just odd enough to spark a brief report in the Atlanta newspapers and to suggest to the agent that Brown and Wismer might be interested. The agent remembered that Brown and Wismer had returned from the area only ten days earlier.

The agent forwarded the newspaper clipping to Brown and Wismer with a casual suggestion that it might have something to do with their investigation. When they looked at the report of three black men pulled from rivers very close to the Williams plantation, they were once again suspicious of the farmer who had been so hospitable and calm during their visit.

The newspaper story suggested to the agents that Williams had fallen prey to the same problem that trips up many killers—disposing of the bodies. With several bodies to dispose of, it is almost certain that at least one will be found. And, despite the chains and weights attached to the men thrown into the Yellow, the South, and the Alcovy Rivers, the bodies were beginning to surface.

A phone call to the Newton County sheriff provided the agents with more information about the discovery of the bodies. They found out that Carl Wheeler, a young local resident, and his friend Randall Parker were crossing Allen's Bridge over the Yellow River early one morning when Wheeler looked down and saw a foot sticking out of the water. As he looked more closely, he could see a body floating just below the surface. They quickly ran to town and got word to Newton County Sheriff B. L. Johnson, and the boys returned with him to show him where the body was. Before long, the sheriff arranged for it to be fished out of the river.

The boys stood on the bridge and watched the scene below, eager not to miss the outcome of their gruesome discovery. They were surprised when the bloated body was pulled from the water and they could see that there were not one, but two men—still tied together, still weighted with a hundred-pound sack of rocks, still tied at the ankles and wrists. They had been thrown into the cold water together, had struggled against their chains and weights, and had drowned. Now they were being pulled from the muddy river as a small crowd of blacks and whites looked on. Though the authorities would not know their identities right away, the first bodies to surface were those of Willie Preston and Lindsey Peterson.

Sheriff Johnson knew that the water where the men were found was only about ten feet deep—deep enough to drown them but not to keep their bodies submerged as the process of decay set in. After a quick examination that yielded only the most obvious facts, the sheriff ordered the bodies buried in the riverbank. As they were already decomposing rapidly, there was little other choice. The sheriff had to conduct an investigation and have the county coroner look into the deaths, although he did not expect much of an investigation to follow. By burying the men by the river, he could temporarily store them until the evidence was needed.

The murder investigation would be conducted by Newton County authorities because the bodies had floated up closer to the Newton County side, and because the Newton County sheriff had retrieved them. The next day, the sheriff got the first tip-off that he might have more a serious incident on his hands than he first believed. Another report came in of a body found in a river, this time the South River, about a quarter mile downstream from Mann's Bridge. It was Price, the man who chose to throw himself in the river rather than be pushed. The third body was found only about half a mile from the other two, so the connection was obvious. Sheriff Johnson followed the same procedure, fishing the body out of the river, making the preliminary identification as an unknown black man, and burying it by the riverside. He would pass on all three death reports to the county coroner, who would then try to identify the victims and determine the cause of death.

Of course, to the sheriff and anyone else who had seen the bodies taken out of the rivers, the cause of death was clear. Someone had gotten rid of some niggers.

And the federal agents were pretty sure they knew who that someone was. Here were three black men, obviously murdered and disposed of in a way that was meant to hide the evidence. With all that had been rumored about the Williams plantation, finding three murder victims so close by and so soon after a visit by federal agents was too much of a coincidence. Brown and Wismer decided to devote more attention to Williams now that they might have the evidence that could make an investigation move forward.

The discovery of the bodies was front page news in nearby Covington. "Mystery Shrouds Identity of Drowned Negroes" was the headline on a story recounting how the "gruesome horrors" were found and how hundreds of people had been to view the bodies by the riversides. No one had any idea who the dead men were, and "Sheriff B. L. Johnson of this county reports no missing negroes, and no trouble in Newton. There has been some recent trouble in Jasper County over peonage."

The people of Newton County were bothered by the discoveries enough to push for a reward in the killings, partly because, as the paper described, "such finds are unspeakably gruesome and these atrocities a reproach upon the county."

After receiving a petition from Newton County residents, Governor Hugh Dorsey offered a reward of $1,750 for the arrest of "the unidentified men who threw two negroes into the Yellow River." The reward was $500 each for the first two killers caught, then $250 each for the next three caught. At that point, Governor Dorsey had no reason to believe the killings were anything extraordinary, and his offer was routine.

At about the same time, a black man walked into the Bureau of Investigation's Atlanta office and offered another crucial piece of the puzzle. Eberhardt Crawford had made his way from his home in Covington, Georgia, just across the rivers from the Williams plantation, to report a terrifying incident. He had heard from other blacks in the area that the federal agents had been investigating the Williams plantation, and now that his own life was in danger he sought help. He sat down in the agents' office and began to tell them how an innocuous comment had put him within reach of the long arm of John S. Williams. Crawford was calm and told his story clearly, but the agents could see that underneath he was a very frightened man.

"Mr. Johnny Williams in Jasper County is after me, and I don't know what else to do," he told the agents. "I'm hoping y'all can help me, 'cause that Johnny Williams ain't nobody I want to be on the wrong side of."

"OK, we'll see what we can do," Brown replied from behind his desk. "What dealings do you have with Williams? Do you work for him?"

"No sir, I don't work for Mr. Williams. I ain't never had nothing to do with that man and I don't want nothing to do with him."

"So how'd you get tangled up with him?" Wismer asked.

Crawford began to tell a story that helped the agents understand just how much Williams was feared in Jasper and Newton Counties. The black man had been present a few days earlier at the coroner's inquest into the deaths of the first two drowned men. The inquest was held by the river, where the bodies were briefly dug up so that the coroner could make an examination and try to identify them. A number of people had gathered to watch, along with a few black workers brought along to do the heavy work. Crawford was among them.

The two bodies were unearthed, and Dr. C. T. Hardeman examined them on the spot, declaring that they had died by drowning, based on his observations of their grotesquely swollen necks and their unnaturally pro-truding tongues and eyeballs. Hardeman did not open their bodies to exam-ine the lungs or make any other more formal autopsy attempt.

Before covering the rotting bodies with earth again, the coroner and the others present tried to determine who the victims might be. The effects of drowning, plus the days in the water before being found, made it nearly impossible to identify them just from looking at their faces, so those present tried to come up with any possible matches based on the men's stature, apparent ages, and who might be missing from the surrounding areas. The group thought out loud, tossing out names of local blacks who could fit the bill, but each time someone else said no, that one has been seen lately.

Before giving up on the identification, the coroner turned to Crawford, who had been watching from close by.

"How about you, boy? You got any idea who these boys might be?"

"No sir, I sure don't," Crawford replied. "But if they come from Jasper County, I bet some of the hands on the Williams place would know 'em."

That was the sum of Crawford's contribution to the inquest, and the comment did not seem to interest the white officials very much. They had realized the same possibility already. Crawford had merely answered the ques-tion that a white man posed to him, and what he offered was just barely beyond the obvious. Nevertheless, Crawford's suggestion did not go unnoticed.

Late that evening, Crawford had just put his young nephew to bed in his small, ramshackle wooden house when he heard a car pull up outside, then a loud knock at the door. His heart must have nearly stopped when he saw the imposing image of John S. Williams standing in the doorway.

"I hear you been talking about me and my boys," Williams said angrily. "You been telling folks we had something to do with them dead niggers in the river?"

"No sir, Mr. Williams, I ain't said nothing like that. All I said was some of your hands might know who them boys are. That's all I said."

"Don't you lie to me, nigger!" Williams shouted, taking a step forward as if he were going to strike Crawford. "I know what you been saying and I won't have it. If you know what's good for you, you'll keep your damn mouth shut."

"I, I don't . . ." Crawford stammered. Sizing up the situation quickly, Crawford looked down to the floor and muttered, "Yes sir, boss."

Williams stomped off the wooden porch and back to his car, speeding off in a cloud of dust. Crawford was left severely shaken. He knew Williams's reputation quite well and had always been glad not to be under Williams's thumb. Now, though, he was in trouble. One innocent comment made earlier in the day and suddenly he had John S. Williams angry with him and scared of him.

Once the farmer left his house, Crawford grew even more frightened. He knew what could happen to a black man who ran afoul of someone like John S. Williams, and damn it, this wasn't just someone *like* John S. Williams. Crawford worried that neither the visit nor the warning would satisfy the plantation owner. He worried that he had not been sufficiently contrite.

Crawford's mind must have been racing, reviewing all the stories of lynchings he heard about through the years. He may have recalled seeing the two men being pulled out of the river and wondering if that was what Williams intended for him. That white man would be back, he decided.

He had to get out of the house. He decided to go to a neighbor's and wait out the night, and possibly get some advice on what to do next. He considered whether to take his young nephew along, but he feared being caught out on the road by Williams if he had the boy with him. If Williams intended to drown him, he wouldn't be stopped by the presence of a child. He'd just kill the child too. So Crawford left the boy sleeping in the bed they shared and hurriedly walked to the neighbor's.

He had been there only a short while when he heard gunshots down the road. He ran out to see where the shots were coming from. Just as he had feared, they were at his own house. Crawford wanted to rush back to check on his nephew, but he stayed outside his friend's house and hid behind a tree until the shooting stopped. A few minutes later, Williams sped by in his car with the seats full of white men, all laughing and brandishing rifles and pistols. When he could see that they were gone, Crawford ran as fast as he could back to his home.

The smell of gunpowder was still thick in the air as he approached and saw the front of the house riddled with gunshots. All of the windows were gone, and the door was knocked off its hinges. Crawford rushed into the house, calling for his nephew, but there was no response. He went to the bed where the boy had been sleeping, but the blanket was empty.

Fearing the men had taken the boy in lieu of finding him home, Crawford rushed about the house and out into the yard, frantically calling the boy's name. After anguished minutes of calling, Crawford finally heard a response.

"I'm in here," he heard the boy's voice crying hysterically.

Crawford rushed over to the outhouse and found the terrified boy inside, crouched in the corner.

The federal agents sat quietly and listened to Crawford's tale with great interest. His information dovetailed nicely with what they already knew of the unidentified bodies and about Williams. The more they heard about these drowning victims, the more they thought there must be a connection to the plantation owner. And then Crawford added one more bit of detail that convinced the agents there was indeed a strong connection.

The agents asked Crawford to describe the bodies, calling on what he had seen of them at the riverside coroner's inquest. He described the general condition of the bodies, the way they were tied, and their clothing. They were both wearing overalls, and they were both wearing "rubber tire shoes."

"What's that?" Wismer asked him, suddenly more interested. "They were wearing what kind of shoes?"

"Rubber tire shoes. You know, them shoes made out of old car tires. They was both wearing 'em."

Wismer and Brown looked at each other but said nothing. That was the connection that clicked for the agents. They remembered seeing Clyde Manning's uncle Rufus repairing shoes on the Williams plantation during their visit, using a stack of discarded automobile tires to half-sole them. All the workers on the plantation wore shoes half-soled with old tire rubber, but they were not so common in the surrounding area. This was one coincidence too many. The agents decided to take immediate action. They assured Crawford that they would try to help him, but they knew that the real task at hand was to apprehend Williams.

The murders were local, so the Bureau of Investigation had no clear authority to intervene in the investigation. Knowing that the local authorities might have little motivation to pursue Williams for the killing of two unknown black men, Brown and Wismer considered their options. If they did nothing, it seemed likely that local authorities would also do nothing. They wondered just how many people Williams intended to kill.

They decided that the best approach would be to request help from the state. Persuasion from a federal level might have little impact, because the local authorities would know there was no federal jurisdiction, or it could cause resentment that federal authorities were trying to bully local Southerners. To obtain help on a state level, Brown and Wismer looked to the state's highest authority, Governor Hugh Dorsey.

Going to the governor with a case like this was unusual, but Wismer and Brown saw the whole situation as unusual. It was obvious to them that their visit to the plantation had spurred the killings. That probably did not leave them feeling guilty in any sense—after all, they were only conducting a routine investigation and they hadn't been particularly aggressive about it. But their personal connection to the deaths probably did make them feel obligated to see that the killer was charged appropriately. They had little authority to bring any meaningful federal action against the Jasper County farmer, but they also knew, perhaps better than anyone outside the plantation, that John S. Williams was guilty of murder.

Still, the agents' motivation is not clear without considering a report written by the Bureau of Investigation several years later, as a summary of the Williams and Manning investigation. In that report, the bureau clearly states what Agents Wismer and Brown must have discussed at the time:

> It is extremely doubtful that Manning would have been permitted to live had not the Special Agents of the United States Bureau of Investigation taken a prompt interest and brought all pressure to bear the moment they received the news of the discovery of the first bodies. It must be borne in mind that the United States Bureau of Investigation had no jurisdiction over the murder of these negroes; that was entirely a matter for the State of Georgia. It was recognized, however, that the State, or

at least the County in which these murders had occurred, was apparently powerless to proceed, and that the latest series of murders had been brought about through reason of the activity of the Special Agents in seeking information concerning peonage conditions. For these reasons, the United States Bureau of Investigation did not hesitate to take the initiative by bringing the conditions to the attention of the Governor of the State of Georgia, and urging action by the Governor, the Attorney General, and the appointment of special prosecutors and immediate appointment of a posse for the purpose of proceeding to the plantation and seeking further evidence of a crime.

While the bureau's summary of the agents' actions can be seen as somewhat self-serving, it does provide an explanation for why they took action in a situation in which they clearly had no jurisdiction.

Soon after Crawford spoke with the agents, news of the meeting leaked to the *Covington News*, which described the discovery of a "mystery witness" who went to the agents after a threat on his life. Few details of Crawford's story were leaked, but the newspaper reported that it was thought to involve "well-known citizens" of Jasper County.

That mystery witness, Eberhardt Crawford, provided the most direct evidence available to the agents, so they decided to take him along on their visit with the governor. The black man accompanied the agents to the state capitol, not far from their office in downtown Atlanta, where he sat and told his story all over again. The governor listened attentively to Crawford's tale and then assured him that he had nothing to fear. Governor Dorsey then told Crawford to wait outside while he discussed the situation further with the federal agents. This discussion would soon spur an investigation by local authorities.

In retrospect, Governor Dorsey's significant, positive influence on the investigation of the killings on the Williams plantation is surprising and somewhat puzzling. In his second and final term as governor of Georgia, he was becoming well known throughout the South as a bit of an iconoclast among white politicians because he actively denounced lynching and other forms of persecution against blacks. Governor Dorsey's willingness to stand up for Southern blacks, and to withstand the criticism that inevitably came from many whites, had suggested to the agents that he might be willing to intervene in the unusual problem in Jasper County.

That conclusion was not automatic, however. Despite his anti-lynching stance in 1921, definitely a progressive position for the time and the region, Governor Dorsey was far from a friend of minorities. Quite to the contrary: the governor had first gained notoriety, and had greased the rails for his gubernatorial campaigns, as chief prosecutor in a murder trial that would highlight the state's bigotry. In that case, Dorsey was the chief racist, not the progressive man of reason riding in on a white horse to do the right thing.

The case was the trial of Leo Frank, to this day considered one of the most flagrant examples of anti-Semitism, injustice, and mob rule in the history of Georgia and, indeed, the entire country. The repercussions of the case would be felt for decades to come, and in 1921 the events of 1913 were still quite fresh in everyone's mind. Governor Dorsey had been the state's chief prosecutor of Frank and, as such, carried substantial responsibility for what happened in court. And what Dorsey did in court, many would argue, led to what happened outside.

Dorsey's involvement in the Frank case colored his later involvement in the trial of John S. Williams and, curiously, may have led the governor to see the Williams case as a chance for redemption. He clearly needed it.

Frank, a twenty-nine-year-old Jewish businessman who had grown up in Brooklyn, was accused of murdering thirteen-year-old Mary Phagan, a white girl who worked in Frank's National Pencil Factory in Atlanta. The girl's slight, battered body was discovered in the factory basement at three A.M. on Sunday, April 27, 1913, Confederate Memorial Day, by the factory night watchman, a black man named Newt Lee.

The girl was heavily bruised and bloodied, her fingers torn out of joint, her clothing ripped. She was left in a heap in the dirty factory basement, covered in grime, sawdust, and wood shavings. A piece of jute rope was found around her neck, and so was a strip of her own underwear. An autopsy would later determine that she had been choked and her skull crushed.

Police immediately suspected Lee, the black watchman who found the body, but he was able to come up with a reasonable alibi. Then the police turned their attention to Frank, the businessman who was the last person to report seeing Mary Phagan alive. She had been in his office the previous day to collect her pay.

Frank was a small, bespectacled, well-dressed young man, married and considered socially prominent in Atlanta's Jewish community. The Jewish community was shocked to hear of his arrest and rallied to support him. But once Frank was arrested, the case against him began to snowball. There was considerable physical evidence proving that the girl had been with Frank shortly before her death, and there was difficulty in proving Frank's whereabouts. The initial suspicion of Frank may have been warranted to some degree, simply because he was indeed closely associated with the girl who was murdered in his own factory. But when Frank was arrested and charged with murder, the case took on a character that, sadly, would come to characterize the way white Southerners reacted to a crime in their midst.

Once Frank was charged with the murder of "little Mary Phagan," as she became known, the public quickly began to invest the case with their most deeply rooted fears and assumptions. The case was exactly the sort that most readily and thoroughly inflamed both an avenging mob and a more discreet avenging white community—the murder of a white girl, with strong hints of sexual abuse and rape. More so than any other crime or alleged crime, the rape of a white woman was seen as an outright assault on the fundamental virtue of the white race. The white community naturally assumed that a black man had to be responsible, and scores of black men had been summarily lynched over the years, often after extensive torture, based only on wild rumors or hysterical accusations. It is difficult to overstate the depth of this reaction by many white Southerners. In many cases, the lynching victim was not even accused of rape. He was accused of merely *looking* at a white woman.

Mary Phagan's death immediately stirred these deep sentiments, accented by the fact that the girl was only thirteen years old. In retrospect, it seems that the black night watchman who discovered the body was lucky to escape a murder charge and/or a lynching. The fact that he apparently had nothing to do with the crime was inconsequential; he was a black man standing over the dead body of a white girl. He may have been spared only because the public's attention was turned to another, and in some ways more interesting, suspect. Rather than the black man routinely blamed for violent crimes in the South, here was a young, successful businessman who happened to be a Jew. While not relegated to the bottom of the social ladder with blacks, Jews in Atlanta in 1913 were viewed with great suspicion and general disdain. They were not often accepted into the mainstream of white society, and those achieving any financial success were viewed with a spiteful envy that almost never applied to blacks. On the other hand, many Jews prospered in the South and were able to skirt the most insidious forms of bigotry.

Frank made a particularly appealing target for the white community's vengeance. With a white girl killed and rumors rampant that the murder had been performed to cover a sex crime, someone had to pay. A black man would do just fine, as always, but Frank appealed to a sort of class and cultural envy that the persecution of a black man could not satisfy. Beyond the stereotypes attached to Jews, Frank also represented the Northern businessman who came to the South and took advantage of poor rural whites. The issue of child labor was a difficult one in the South around 1913, as many children were sent into the city from the countryside to work in cotton mills and other factories. Rural whites often had no choice but to allow, or even force, children to work there, but they resented the low pay, and there was a general impression that the factories were a threat to the purity of young girls. Little Mary Phagan represented the innocent Southern girl, and Leo Frank represented the oppressive Yankee Jew.

Frank was at a serious disadvantage once he was charged with murder. The public wanted vengeance for the death of the girl, and the public officials charged with investigating and prosecuting the case were determined to give it to them. Hugh Dorsey, then solicitor general of Atlanta's circuit, led the charge. The forty-two-year-old Dorsey was a stern-looking man, with dark features and eyes. He clearly heard the public's call for a conviction, and he badly needed one. He had recently failed to convict the accused murderers in two important cases, and the press was suggesting that another high-profile defeat could be the end of his career as solicitor general. Success, on the other hand, could translate into major political clout.

Dorsey pursued Frank's conviction vigorously, drawing on the anti-Semitic prejudices of the white community to inflame public opinion while using blatantly anti-Semitic arguments against Frank in court. The prosecution ended with a passionate, nine-hour summation speech in which Dorsey waved Mary Phagan's bloody clothes in front of the jury and called Frank a "fiendish degenerate."

Throughout the four-week trial, there had been allusions to the sexual perversion supposedly common among Jews. There was testimony from witnesses that Frank had offered money to young girls for sex, assaulted a young girl in the woods, and tried to obtain a boarding-house room in order to have sex with a young girl. Rumors circulated that little Mary Phagan's body had been mutilated, and, at one point in the trial, Dorsey brought courtroom observers to tears with an impassioned account of how the girl had sacrificed her life to preserve her honor. Dorsey also suggested that Frank was homosexual. Many of the claims were disputed or disproved by witnesses, but Dorsey's questioning clearly implied that Frank was a sex fiend.

In the kind of wordplay seen frequently in court, Dorsey pointed out to the jury that prosecutors had never mentioned the word *Jew*. Only the defense attorneys had brought up the issue of Frank being a Jew, he said. Dorsey had spent considerable time during the trial, however, recalling for the jury the heinous crimes committed by various Jews throughout history, beginning with Judas Iscariot.

Within earshot of the jury members, the judge openly discussed the possibility of a riot with the chief of police and the colonel of the Fifth Georgia Regiment, noting that a "verdict of acquittal would cause a riot such as would shock the country and cause Atlanta's streets to run with innocent blood." The judge also expressed fear that if Frank were found not guilty, the public would immediately lynch him and his lawyers. For that reason, he instructed Frank and his defense attorneys not to return for the reading of the verdict. The jury heard all of this.

Not surprisingly, Frank was found guilty and sentenced to death. The waiting crowd outside erupted into cheers and applause and the fans at a local baseball game erupted into celebration when the verdict was chalked up on the scoreboard. When Dorsey walked out of the city hall after the verdict was read, the crowd hoisted him up on their shoulders and carried him through the celebrating crowd. Dorsey reveled in the adulation with his hat held high and tears streaming down his face.

To historians and to many contemporaries, Frank's guilt was far from certain. Though a definitive answer is hard to come by, largely due to the ineffective police investigation and distorted representation of the facts during the trial, Frank was most likely innocent of the crime and was simply the victim of a virulent anti-Semitic campaign. The more likely murderer was Jim Conley, a black employee of the pencil factory who was the chief witness against Frank.

Frank's attorneys launched a spirited effort to have his conviction overturned, eventually bringing the case before the U.S. Supreme Court. Dorsey remained close on Frank's heels, vowing to do everything in his power to keep Frank behind bars. Even before the Supreme Court reached a decision, Dorsey announced that if the court freed Frank he would attempt to have Frank indicted on two other charges related to the Mary Phagan killing—criminal assault and perversion. The aura of the "Jew pervert," as he was called in more than one publication, still clung to Frank.

Even though two justices said the evidence was "overwhelming that the jury responded to the passions of the mob," the U.S. Supreme Court rejected Frank's plea on April 9, 1915.

Frank's execution was scheduled for June 22, 1915. At two A.M. on June 21, Gov. John M. Slaton ordered Frank's sentence commuted to life imprisonment. The decision came after Slaton had personally gone over all the evidence from Frank's trial and more, and it came four days before he was to leave office. The decision was widely derided as a perversion of justice, and many whites believed fervently that Slaton had been paid off by wealthy Jews. Slaton's life was threatened, and there were random attacks against Jews in Georgia as retaliation.

Even though Governor Slaton clearly thought that Jim Conley was the murderer and that Frank had been badly mistreated by the authorities, he did not pardon him and set him free. But for a white community that saw Frank as the personification of a very special type of threat to white women, life in prison was not good enough.

Frank was stabbed and nearly killed in prison four weeks after the commutation. Four weeks after that, a mob of twenty-five men stormed the prison where Frank was housed and took him away. The mob had carefully planned its assault and deliberately excluded any unsavory characters from its midst. Instead, its makeup was restricted to only what it considered the finest representatives of Marietta, the hometown of little Mary Phagan. The group included a clergyman, two former Superior Court justices, and an ex-sheriff.

They drove Frank the 175 miles from the prison in Milledgeville back to Marietta, just outside Atlanta. They stood Frank on a table under a tree, slipped a noose around his neck, and kicked the table out from under him. The lynchers later recalled with pride that they had killed the Jew in a forthright, deliberate manner and had not been crazed. Rather, they said, they were merely carrying out the death sentence that had originally been dictated by the court.

Slaton and Dorsey wound up as political enemies, largely because of their head-to-head opposition in the Frank case. Dorsey was widely hailed as the savior of white women because he had successfully prosecuted Frank and steadfastly refused to back down when there was considerable pressure to do so. He rode that wave of popularity to a landslide victory in the gubernatorial primary in 1916 and then won the seat unopposed. Some of his strongest supporters were avowed racists and defenders of the white race. During the campaign, however, Dorsey was harshly criticized by Slaton. Dorsey struck back by claiming that Slaton was a major contributor to a slush fund aimed at preventing his election, and in a public statement before the Georgia primary election in 1915, he claimed that Slaton was part of a conspiracy orchestrated by Jews.

Opposition to his election showed that "the attitude of that race [Jews] in the Frank case and in every criminal case in which a Hebrew is a defendant has demonstrated the fact that the successful prosecution of a Hebrew is regarded by members of that race as persecution," Dorsey said.

Time has not been kind in assessing Dorsey's performance in the Frank trial. Even soon after the trial, criticism was plentiful. One of Frank's defense attorneys called his trial "the most horrible persecution of a Jew since the death of Jesus Christ," and many agreed with him. The Frank case received tremendous attention in the ensuing years and was directly responsible for the formation of the Anti-Defamation League of B'nai B'rith, the Jewish organization devoted to fighting anti-Semitism. While the years have not brought answers to all of the questions in the case, it is clear that Hugh Dorsey was largely responsible for a travesty of justice. There is ample evidence that he suppressed evidence and misrepresented crucial information before the jury. One publication of the times, the *Southern Ruralist*, held Dorsey in great contempt for his part in Frank's conviction and death.

"Prejudice is the mildest possible term for such misconduct," the magazine claimed. "Such official misrepresentation of fact is the very murder of justice itself."

Dorsey's role in the prosecution—and persecution—of Frank should not be underestimated. Governor Slaton would later say that the judge in Frank's case had confided in him that Dorsey had no case; there simply was not enough evidence to even warrant prosecuting Frank, much less convicting him. If Dorsey's predecessor in the solicitor general's office had been alive to handle the case instead of Dorsey, Frank would not have been prosecuted at all, the judge supposedly told Slaton.

Another publication of the time, *Frost's Magazine*, noted, "It is evident that he has sought self-aggrandizement in his ruthless effort to make out a case where he knew beforehand that he had no case."

Clearly, Dorsey was no liberal do-gooder.


Dorsey was reelected to a second term as governor in 1918. By 1921, when the killings on the Williams plantation were raising suspicions with the federal authorities, he was in his last year of political life and becoming known in political circles as a man willing to rock the boat. While he had pulled no punches in prosecuting Leo Frank as a perverted Jew, his later years in the governor's office were devoted to a surprisingly progressive idea of race relations. He worked hard to promote an anti-lynching agenda, having the temerity to suggest that even those blacks guilty of crimes should not be summarily punished and executed by a white mob. He advocated education for both black and white children, and he decried the culture that allowed whites to systematically imprison blacks against their will or drive them off land that they rightfully owned.

Dorsey is still recalled as "the anti-lynching governor." But the discrepancies in Dorsey's career beg the question: What happened between Leo Frank's lynching in 1913, which Dorsey unofficially encouraged, and his far more progressive attitude in 1921? Could Dorsey have felt guilt for his role in Frank's prosecution and eventual death? Could he have wanted to end his political career by taking the high road?

It seems the answer is yes to both questions, though it is unlikely that Dorsey was ever completely heartless or that he became a saint in his later years. More than anything else, he was an opportunist. Frank's prosecution clearly was an opportunity to save, even to advance, his career, and Dorsey took full advantage. But the Frank trial and lynching had created considerable negative publicity for Georgia, and Dorsey's name was firmly attached to the criticism. There were rumors that Dorsey intended to practice law in New York after his term as governor of Georgia, so he may have wanted to start building a reputation that would serve him well in that community.

It is clear that as he saw his political career coming to an end, Dorsey did the right thing. And just as he had done with the Frank trial, he did it both because he believed it was right, and because it would boost his image.


Brown and Wismer filled the governor in on what they knew of the Williams plantation, including the technical violations of the labor laws and the reports of heinous crimes from those escaping the plantation. They explained that they had personally visited the plantation and found nothing extraordinary, but they also were frank in their assessment that this Williams character was much more than just a typical redneck farmer operating on the edge of the law. The evidence was mounting that Williams was a serious criminal and had been getting away with it for quite some time. Now Brown and Wismer suspected that the three drownings were connected to their own investigation and that others on the farm might be in danger. Leaving this investigation to the whims of the local sheriff might not be a good idea, they suggested.

Two visits by the agents were necessary to persuade him, but Dorsey was receptive to their concerns. It was decidedly unusual for the Bureau of Investigation to express concern over what would otherwise seem a routine, if somewhat gruesome, killing of a couple of black men in rural Georgia. And from the evidence brought to him, it seemed apparent that there was something going on in Jasper County that went beyond disparate treatment of blacks in a white society. Dorsey was not about to suggest that John S. Williams had no right to work blacks on his farm as hard as he wanted, but the federal agents were making a good case that the farmer had stepped over the line generously established by a white society that would look the other way in almost all cases of abuse. And besides, the governor could always blame it on the feds if anyone said he was coddling local blacks.

By the time the agents concluded their second visit to the state capitol, the governor had pledged to do all he could to urge local officials to move swiftly on the case. He persuaded the Judge and Solicitor General of the Stone Mountain Circuit Court in Newton County to issue grand jury subpoenas for a number of witnesses, including John S. Williams and his sons Marvin, Leroy, and Huland; and Clyde Manning, Clyde Freeman, and a list of black workers known to be on the Williams plantation, including all those who had been interviewed by the federal agents during their visit. With the subpoenas in hand, Sheriff Johnson and the two federal agents went to the Williams plantation and arrested John S. Williams, Clyde Manning, and Clyde Freeman. Curiously, the Williams sons could not be found, and neither could any of the other black hands who had been interviewed during the agents' first visit to the farm. The three men were taken to the police headquarters in Covington, the seat of Newton County. They also brought in Frank Dozier, who had earlier escaped from the Williams plantation and was living in Covington.

The federal agents, the sheriff, and the Covington police chief proceeded to question the suspects. The federal agents would later report that there was "a vigorous examination of the negroes." Exactly what that entailed is not documented, but it is safe to assume that the vigorous examination involved more than stern words. Manning and Freeman at first refused to make any statements, but Dozier, who felt more confident because he had already escaped the farm, decided to speak.

He told the authorities of being taken to the farm after being bailed out of the Macon stockade for vagrancy, and how Williams had promised to pay him thirty-five dollars a month. He went on to tell of how the Williams family had kept him locked up at night with a number of other men in the same plight, and he described several whippings and beatings he had endured on the plantation.

After getting Dozier's story, the authorities turned their attention to Freeman, the other black overseer on the plantation, and his third cousin Clyde Manning. Freeman refused to talk for several hours, but then he agreed to tell the federal agents what had happened on the farm. "I'll tell y'all about it," he said, "but if I do and then you let me go, Mr. Johnny'll kill me right away."

The agents assured Freeman that he would be protected, and he proceeded to tell them that black workers on the farm had started disappearing soon after the agents visited two weeks earlier—Willie Preston, Lindsey Peterson, and Harry Price in the first couple of days, and then Johnny Green and Charlie Chisolm.

"He told us that all them boys done gone home, but I knew that wasn't right," Freeman said.

The agents pressed for more information and Freeman insisted that he did not know exactly what had happened to the missing men, only that they disappeared.

"Well, do you have any ideas what might have happened to them, if they didn't just go home like Williams said?"

"I got an idea, but I don't know," Freeman replied.

"What's your idea?"

"I wouldn't be surprised if they put them in the river," he said.

And when they kept pressing for more information, Freeman finally said that he wasn't the one who would know. "Who is the person who would know all this?" the agents asked.

"I believe Clyde can tell you all about it."


After Freeman related some more stories about the abuses on the Williams plantation, including the killing of Iron John, the questioning moved on to Clyde Manning. He still refused to say anything to the investigators, so they decided to take Manning and Freeman to view the first two bodies found in the rivers. If nothing else, at least they might give the authorities the identities of the victims.

The two black men were taken from the Covington jail to Allen's Bridge, where the two bodies still lay buried in the riverbank. The graves were opened again so that the two men could view them. Manning remained silent as he once again saw the faces of two men he had killed.

"That's Willie Preston. That's Lindsey Peterson," Freeman said, pointing to the two bodies.

Freeman then pointed out the shoes on both bodies and said he knew they were shoes from the Williams plantation, and he recalled that Preston and Peterson both had Rufus Manning resole their shoes shortly before they disappeared.

After the riverside identification, the group returned to the Covington police headquarters and another "vigorous examination" ensued. Freeman told the investigators all he knew about the circumstances of the men's disappearances, which amounted to observing that certain men were summoned to tasks by Williams and then never seen again.

The interrogation continued throughout the day as Manning steadfastly refused to provide any information. But by three o'clock the next morning, the questioning had worn Manning out and he began to talk. The moment was pivotal. Manning must have seen that he was no longer serving John S. Williams, the white man he had belonged to most of his life, and he was now serving the white men standing in front of him. Once that realization sunk in, he began to obey them just as he would have obeyed the plantation owner. And when the white man asks you a question, you answer.

Manning also may have welcomed the opportunity to tell the story once he was certain that the white authorities really wanted to hear it. His experience on the Williams plantation, and his experience as a black man, had taught him that there was no point in running to the local authorities and reporting the crimes. Manning must have been very skeptical about their sincerity, wondering if an accusation against a respected white man would just get him into more trouble. But if Manning was an unwilling participant in the murders, he must have wanted dearly to tell the truth about how his friends had been killed.

There was only one thing still making him hesitate.

"I can tell it, but I can't go back to Jasper County if I tell it," he said to the sheriff. "I'll be dead just like them other boys."

"We ain't going to let that happen, Clyde," the sheriff said, putting a hand on Clyde's shoulder. "If you tell us what you know, we'll make sure you don't get hurt."

Manning sat quietly and thought about the promise for a moment, and then he began to speak. Once Manning began, he told the entire story.

"The first nigger I remember being killed was Will Napier. Huland Williams killed him. The next one was Blackstrap. Charlie Chisolm killed him. Huland was whipping Blackstrap and Charlie Chisolm was holding his head."

Manning continued for quite some time, providing a chronological account of all the killings he could remember on the farm. At one point, the investigators brought in a cap, shoes, and trace chains taken from the bodies of the three men found in the rivers. Manning said the cap looked like Peterson's and the shoes looked like Price's or Preston's.

Manning's statement continued into the early hours of the morning, including admissions of his own guilt and details of precisely how he had carried out his boss's orders. After a short rest, Manning was put into a car later in the morning and accompanied by the federal agents and the Newton County sheriff and deputies. They all went back to Allen's Bridge, and the two bodies were dug up yet again. This time, the authorities wanted Manning himself to identify the men.

"That's Willie Preston on the side next to the river," he said. "That's Peterson on this side."

With that task accomplished, the party piled back into their cars and drove the short distance to Mann's Bridge, where the third body had been recovered. They began the same process again, with the deputies wielding shovels to uncover the body buried in the riverbank. Perhaps remembering the way Price had fought to retain some dignity in his last moments, Manning spoke up as the deputies began digging. "Y'all don't have to uncover that one," he called out.

"That's Foots," he volunteered to the sheriff standing nearby. "We put him off here in the river."

# 9

## "Things Were Sort of Bad on the Williams Place"

After the three bodies at the bridges had been identified, Manning and Williams were taken to the Covington courthouse and immediately brought before a grand jury. Its job was to decide, based on the evidence available so far, whether there was good reason to charge Manning or Williams with murder. Five of the black workers from the Williams plantation were also brought before the grand jury to testify about the conditions on the farm. Also present were the three Williams sons who had left the state during the killings. They had showed up again just before their father was arrested.

Manning testified to the same facts that he had told the investigators. Sitting in the witness chair in the courthouse, the dark young man in over-alls gripped his hat in his hands and explained how the Williams family would obtain men from local jails. He spoke calmly and with little emotion.

"Well, they brought the niggers to the farm and put 'em to work," Manning told the grand jury. "And they kept guards over 'em all the time so as not to let 'em get away or talk too much. I don't know whether they got any pay or not. I know Mr. Johnny paid me twenty dollars a month and board.

"Of course, mister, I'm sorry I knocked all them boys in the head and helped Mr. Johnny do away with them others, but there wasn't nothing else I could do. The boss told me if I didn't do as he said, I would be the next dead nigger around here. I admits I have always been mighty afraid of Mr. Williams.

"When he got ready to kill a nigger, he would come to me and say, 'Clyde, I'm afraid of that nigger.' Then he would tell me what he wanted done, and being as I was working for him and couldn't get away myself, I had to go ahead and do it.

"Why did I do it? Because the boss said he wanted to get rid of them niggers and if I didn't make 'em disappear, he'd kill me. And I knew he meant what he said."

Manning also noted that Charlie Chisolm had "put in a little work" by killing "one suspicious nigger by braining him with an axe. Then a little later, Mr. Williams got uneasy about Charlie and made me get him. Me and Mr. Johnny took him to the river one night and pitched him off the bridge after we weighted him down. Charlie begged hard, but Mr. Johnny said, 'Let's throw him over and have it over with.'"

The other black workers told the grand jury about life on the Williams plantation, including the many instances in which the Williams men beat them. Several of the men stood in front of the grand jury members and partially disrobed to show the scars left from whippings and other forms of abuse. The jury asked the black workers how they were mistreated on the farm, and the workers responded with several tales. One man told the jury of having broken his leg on the farm one day. He was taken into town to have a doctor apply a plaster cast to the leg, he explained, and then he was forced to work for the rest of the day.

When it came time for Williams to answer questions before the grand jury, he was asked if there had been any killings on the farm, ever. The farmer looked at the grand jury members and, with a confident voice, admitted that yes, one man had been killed. He did not kill the black man himself, he explained, but his son Huland Williams had killed a man a year earlier. The killing was done in self-defense, the farmer explained.

"Was any report made to the authorities?" he was asked.

"No, I don't believe so."

Other than that, there had been no killings on the farm, he said. He and his sons had nothing to do with those boys found in the river, and there was no reason for them to be charged with any crime.

"It's all a lie," he told the grand jury members, looking them straight in the eyes and speaking with self-righteous indignation. "This trouble all began six or seven years ago and was caused by controversies over land lines and livestock. Mrs. M. Leverett and her three sons—Dave, Tom, and Roy—own a farm adjacent to mine. They claimed I had part of their land, and since then arguments over land have occurred.

"If any niggers have been killed by Manning, it was under the orders of the Leveretts and not mine. It's all a frame-up between these boys to break my neck in the federal courts."

The farmer was asked to elaborate on any recent disagreements with the Leverett family.

"Last fall they charged my boys with having reported a still to county officials and a shooting scrape almost resulted from that. Not long ago, Dave Leverett and I had a fight, and it was after this that they threatened to break my neck in the federal courts.

"If I had killed the niggers, I wouldn't have carried them fourteen miles away to dump them in a river, but would have placed them in the river near my farm, where I know the depth.

"Manning's statement is a positive lie. I never shot one of the niggers, nor ordered him to hit four of them in the head, and neither did I haul six of them to points on the Yellow River where they were 'drowned like cats,' as he says."

The Williams sons were questioned along the same lines. The jury was curious about their absence for the past two weeks or so. The sons explained that they had gone to Texas, on their father's orders, to investigate the purchase of some land.

"And why did you come back now?"

"Our father sent us a telegram telling us to come back," Huland Williams replied.

"What did the telegram say?"

"It said, 'Business is picking up. Come home.'"


The grand jury returned bills of indictment that same afternoon. The indictments charged both John S. Williams and Clyde Manning with the murders of Lindsey Peterson, Willie Preston, and Harry Price. The men were to be tried separately, and for only one murder at a time. The death of Lindsey Peterson, described in the local press as "an insignificant negro," would be handled first. (Since the evidence in the three deaths was exactly the same, the murder victims were placed in alphabetical order.) The authorities planned to try Williams and Manning, if found not guilty of Peterson's death, for the murder of Preston, and if found not guilty again, for the death of Price.

Both defendants were quickly transported to Atlanta so that they could be locked up in the Atlanta Tower, the Fulton County jail reminiscent of a medieval lockup. It was Manning's first trip to Atlanta. The large stone building offered far more security from a mob of angry whites than did the Covington jail. Already, the authorities knew that indicting a prominent white farmer for the murder of three black men would generate controversy, especially since the only evidence against him came from a black.

The investigators could see that Manning knew everything there was to know about this case. All it took was enough prodding to make him speak. The federal agents realized that they had interviewed the three men who were later found drowned, and they realized that the others they had interviewed could not be found now. The picture was becoming clear, but they needed Manning to tell the story.

Since taking him to view the bodies by the riversides seemed to prompt Manning to speak, the federal agents decided to take Manning back to the scene of the crime—the Williams plantation. Doing so would not be easy, however. The arrest of Williams, who had so far denied guilt and said little else, was already stirring up the rural area where he was known so well. Simply putting Manning in a car and driving him to the Williams plantation could result in disaster. The Bureau of Investigation considered the area dangerous even for two agents traveling alone. Taking Manning to the farm would require unusual protective measures.

To ensure their safety, the agents again relied on Governor Dorsey. After the agents explained the situation to him, Dorsey contacted Sheriff Johnson of Newton County and ordered him to organize a posse comitatus—a quasi-official group of local men, armed and authorized to shoot, whom the sheriff presumably felt could be trusted to protect Manning and the federal agents even if their neighbors sought to tear them apart.

The use of an armed group to protect a prisoner from lynching was not new in Georgia, but it is a certainty that such a group was not used nearly as often as it should have been. At least 3,724 people were lynched in the United States between 1889 and 1930, and 80 percent of them were black. The number is most likely underestimated because some assaults were never documented. Most of the lynchings occurred in the South.

When officials sought to protect prisoners, the state militia was used more frequently than a posse comitatus, a collection of local men sworn to duty for the moment. Ten companies of the state militia had been put on alert eight years earlier to protect Leo Frank and Newt Lee after rumors circulated that a mob would attack the jail where they were being held. The militia had also been ready to intervene in the riot that everybody thought would follow an acquittal of Frank. But to protect Manning from a lynch mob, Dorsey thought it would be more expeditious and less contentious to order the formation of a posse comitatus, rather than taking the highly public and more formal move of sending in the militia.

And besides, the risk of lynching was less for Manning than it had been for many other black men for whose protection the state militia was, or should have been, employed. Manning was accused of killing other blacks, a crime that would incite little more than curiosity among white residents if not for his accusation that a prominent white farmer was the real criminal. The governor recognized that the white community would not take Manning's accusation well, but he also saw that this was not the typical situation that led to a lynching. No white woman was involved.

The governor and the federal agents surmised that Manning was most at risk from the Williams family. John S. Williams was in jail, but his sons were not. Given what had already happened, they did not want to run the risk of having Manning killed by the Williams boys or their friends somewhere along the quiet back-country roads between Atlanta and Jasper County.

The sheriff organized the posse, and Manning was taken from the Atlanta Tower the next day. After a stop in Covington to meet up with the posse, Manning was driven to the farm in Jasper County. There, Manning took the sheriff, district attorney, and other investigators on a tour of the farm. He showed them where the men had worked, slept, and died. One of the more important discoveries was the stockade where Manning kept his charges at night. Williams had denied to the grand jury that such a stockade even existed or that any blacks were locked up at any time. The investigators saw for themselves how the men were locked in, with Manning explaining that he was in control of the chained door.

Manning directed the party out to the field where Johnnie Williams, Johnny Green, and Willie Givens had been killed with an axe, and he directed them to each of the graves. He then led the group to a spot about five miles from John S. Williams's house and to the top of a high hill in the middle of a large cornfield of seventy-five acres. He was walking ahead of the rest of the group when he suddenly stopped and said, "He's right here. This is Fletcher Smith."

Corn had been planted over the grave since the killing, and young, healthy plants were already sprouting up. Members of the posse began digging where Manning indicated, and they uncovered the body of the man John S. Williams had killed with a shotgun. As the group of men stood there around the body, Manning proceeded to tell them how it had happened, speaking matter-of-factly about a topic that had every one of the men mesmerized.

"He was killed about two weeks ago. He was the last nigger killed. Mr. John Williams killed him. Shot him with a double-barreled shotgun right at dark."

Manning continued with the story, filling in all the details as only a witness could. Then Manning directed the party over to the unoccupied house where Big John had been instructed to dig a well. When they reached the site, Manning once again walked directly to the appropriate spot and stopped. All the men gathered around and listened closely.

"The one buried here is a nigger called Big John. He come from the Atlanta stockade. Charlie Chisolm killed Big John. Hit him in the head with the back of an axe. I saw him hit him. Charlie Chisolm is in the river."

After hearing more details of Big John's death, the party returned to the heart of the plantation, near John S. Williams's house. The investigators searched a tool shed there and brought out an axe, a shovel, and a mattock. The axe still had dried blood on it. They took the tools to Manning and asked if they were used in the murders, and he replied that they were used in killing and burying Big John but not for burying Fletcher Smith.

Manning, the investigators, and the posse then made their way back to Covington. They had to cross over Water's Bridge on the Alcovy River. Based on what Manning had already told them, the authorities were having the river dragged for bodies. Men in boats were systematically tossing large hooks into the water and pulling on the chains, hoping to snag any bodies that were on the bottom or floating below the surface. One body had been recovered already, and it was tied and weighted in just the manner that Manning had described in the death of Charlie Chisolm. Manning looked at Chisolm's body and confirmed that it was he.

The agents started to put Manning back in the car and continue to Covington, but Manning offered more information.

"You know, this is the bridge where we put Red and Little Bit in," he said. "They're the ones with the part of that iron wheel 'round their necks."

He went on to describe just how the men were tied together and to give a close description of the piece of iron used to weight their bodies. He then offered to show the group where the men had gone over the bridge railing, suggesting that the men in the boats start dragging the river from there.

Before long, the hooks had snagged the bodies of the two men, and they were brought out of the water. They were still bound together, exactly as Manning had described, with the distinctive piece of iron that Manning had said would be attached to their bodies.

Manning provided a full accounting of all the killings and recounted how Williams had made clear his intention to kill Manning if he disobeyed any instructions or told anyone what was going on. The agents were sure Manning would have been killed soon, just as Chisolm had been killed, to eliminate the one witness to all the murders. Manning also mentioned that he had overheard Williams talking about Eberhardt Crawford and the remark he had made at the coroner's inquest.

As he showed where to find the missing men and told the investigators the gruesome stories of how they had been killed, Manning made little effort to protect himself, other than to occasionally point out that he had no choice but to do what Williams told him. His version of the story fully implicated him in the murders, as he stated flat out that he had hit the men with an axe or pushed them off bridges, and made clear he knew beforehand that they were going to die.

Aside from his early reluctance to begin talking, the investigators declared Manning to be extremely compliant and reliable. He never once changed his story or altered his version of events, and he never gave his captors any trouble. He was, in fact, a model prisoner. Sheriff Johnson called him "one of the best I ever saw."

Sheriff Johnson returned to the Williams plantation and took a number of the black residents into custody as material witnesses. They would be held at the Atlanta Tower until their testimony was needed. Included in the group was Emma Manning, Clyde's mother. The sheriff made a point of having her subpoenaed because he had received a telegram from Governor Dorsey urging him to do so. The governor had gotten word that the elderly woman was "scared to death" of reprisals from the Williams family, and he wanted her protected.

The job of prosecuting Manning and Williams fell to Newton County Solicitor A. M. Brand, a large, soft man with little round spectacles sitting on a broad nose. Soon after the grand jury indictments, Brand publicly acknowledged the magnitude of the case before him. Even before a single witness had been called, Brand saw that this would be far more than an ordinary murder trial. Due to the "unusual circumstances surrounding the charges" against Williams, Brand requested assistance from Governor Dorsey in prosecuting the case. He asked that Assistant Attorney General Graham Wright be designated to assist in the local prosecution of the charges, and the governor agreed.

"If Williams is guilty, we intend to show the jury that he must be punished to the full extent of the law," Brand told a newspaper reporter. "If he is innocent, we have no desire to see him persecuted."

Brand's statement was subtle but powerful. Punishing Williams to the "full extent of the law" meant capital punishment, death by hanging. Brand had already decided to seek the death penalty, but he also knew that the decision could put him at odds with many white residents and leaders. Prosecuting the white farmer over the deaths of some black men was one thing, and basing the prosecution almost entirely on the testimony of a black man—and an admitted killer—was already enough to make people uneasy. But trying to hang a white man on a black man's testimony? That would be way over the line for most whites.

The indictment and the prospect of hanging did not appear to faze Williams much, or at least he was able to keep up a very stony visage. Those who saw him in the Atlanta Tower reported that he was utterly calm and did not seem especially concerned about his fate. He was annoyed at being charged, and he was worried about his farm and his family, but he gave no indication that he feared a conviction or a death sentence. This nonchalance continued throughout his trial, an indicator that the farmer never thought he was in serious jeopardy. Things surely were not going the way he had hoped, and some of his fears had indeed come to pass. But on the other hand, his greatest fears had been avoided. He was not brought up on federal charges of peonage or murder, and his sons were not charged with anything.

Indeed, the trial he was about to face in Covington was Williams's version of cutting his losses. When he had thought, incorrectly as it turned out, that he was about to face a major federal investigation and to be tried on charges that might be difficult to beat, he had eliminated the witnesses that could make that possible. Eliminating them had resulted in the charges he now faced, but these were a far sight less threatening. For a white man accused of killing a black man in the rural South, there was a huge difference between being tried in federal court and being tried by local authorities with a jury made up of the farmers, store owners, and other businessmen that Williams interacted with on a daily basis.

So what if Manning tells them the whole story? he must have told himself. There's nobody else to tell it, and a local jury isn't going to convict me on the word of a nigger.

Williams's only real worry at that point was his sons. From the beginning, he had sought to avoid their involvement in the investigation, knowing that they could be indicted for murder as easily as he had been. And the risk to the boys was compounded by a story they told their father just after his indictment. They had tried to provide a witness who would say that someone else killed Lindsey Peterson and Willie Preston, but the plan backfired and gave the government more evidence against them.

Huland and Marvin Williams had carried out the plan, though it is not clear whether they did it of their own initiative or at their father's behest. The mutual devotion of the sons and the father makes either motivation equally likely. On March 17, as the government was putting together its case against John S. Williams, his sons left a note for a black man who lived near the Williams plantation, offering to pay him for testimony that would clear their father.

Floyd Johnson had no direct affiliation with the Williams family, but he knew of the family's reputation. That is probably why he at first went along with the Williams boys' plans when he found the note between his "plow-stock and a bunch of honeysuckles," as he would later recall. The note said that the Williams family wished Johnson to declare that he had been across the river in Newton County on the night of February 23, 1921—the night that Lindsey Peterson, Willie Preston, and Harry Price died. Johnson was to state that he was coming back across Allen's Bridge late that night when he came across three Ford cars and sixteen white men. Three of the men pointed pistols at Johnson and walked him to the rear of one of the cars, where he saw three dead black men in the trunk, according to the detailed note. Johnson was to say that he then watched as the dead men were thrown into the river, after which the white mob drove off and left him standing on the bridge.

Clearly, the note was intended to provide an alternate explanation for the deaths of the three men, an explanation that had nothing to do with John S. Williams and sounded like a completely plausible way that three black men could meet their deaths in rural Georgia.

Since the note came from the Williams family, Johnson was in no position to just ignore it or immediately go to the authorities. Whether he wanted to or not, he was practically obligated to carry out the note's instructions to meet the two Williams boys at Allen's Bridge on the following Thursday night. Shortly after he walked up to the bridge, the Chandler car drove up with Huland and Marvin Williams inside.

They stepped out and asked Johnson if he had the note.

"Yes, I got the note," he replied.

"Give it here," one of the boys said. Johnson handed it over, and the Williams boys looked at it quickly to see if it was the same they had left for him. It was.

"What will you take to swear to this on this note?" one of the boys asked Johnson.

Johnson wouldn't answer, so the boys offered $500. Johnson still would not say much, but he nodded agreement to the offer. Then the Williams boys gave him the rest of the instructions. Knowing the story he was to tell about the night on Allen's Bridge, Johnson still needed a way to make his account public. Huland and Marvin Williams hatched a plan that would involve another white neighbor who was oblivious to the scheme, using *his* testimony to bolster the credibility of Johnson's story.

The plan went like this: The next night, Johnson was to go to the white neighbor nearby, J. T. Stubbs, and say that he had been frightened by some men outside his home and needed help. He was to suggest to Stubbs that there was a reason the men might be after him, and that perhaps they should go to John S. Williams for help because he was known to be an influential leader in the community. Then the two of them would go to the Williams family and, in the presence of Stubbs, Johnson would explain that he had seen the men thrown off the bridge in February and that he feared the white men were terrorizing him to keep him quiet. The Williams boys promised Johnson that, if he carried out their instructions, they would meet him back at Allen's Bridge on Sunday night and give him $250, to be followed by another $250 soon after.

Johnson carried out the plan as instructed on Friday night, going first to Stubbs and then to the Williams family. In front of Huland and Marvin Williams, along with the oblivious Stubbs, Johnson recounted his story of how he had seen the white mob throw the bodies from Allen's Bridge. The Williams family assured Johnson that they would look into the matter and do whatever they could to protect him from the mob that had killed the three black men. Johnson then went back to the Stubbs residence and stayed there that night, supposedly to avoid the white men who might harass him at his own home.

So far, the plan was working perfectly. Johnson had played along beautifully and now the Williams family had one witness who could testify that

Lindsey Peterson had been killed by a mob that did not include John S. Williams, and there was another witness who could testify that Johnson appeared to be in fear of his life and sought help from the benevolent Williams family.

But before that evidence could be used, it all fell apart. After speaking with his brother, Walter Johnson, about the matter, Floyd Johnson decided he could not go through with the plan even if it meant defying the Williams family. Instead, he and his brother went to the Newton County Superior Court six days after John S. Williams's indictment and filed a sworn statement with the clerk of court. In the statement, Floyd Johnson explained the entire ruse, naming Huland and Marvin Williams as the instigators.

That document might not be used against John S. Williams, but it surely could be used in any case against Huland and Marvin. It was becoming clear to their father that his boys were in grave danger of being prosecuted for murder, so he sent word to his sons that they should leave town again. This time, he said, don't come back until it's clear that all this is done with and we can get back to our normal life. It ought to take a few weeks to get through the trial and be acquitted, he said. And once he was found innocent of one of the killings, the solicitor would drop the other charges too, he told his sons. John S. Williams was very confident.


The early word on the street also cast doubt on whether a local jury could convict the farmer. At first blush, the case seemed almost absurd for the authorities to pursue. Surely a jury couldn't even consider conviction.

But then more details began spilling out in the *Atlanta Constitution*, the *Atlanta Journal*, the *Covington News*, and among the people meeting in stores, on the streets, and at church on Sunday. There had long been rumors that "things were sort of bad on the Williams place," as one local resident told a newspaper reporter, so some of the more recent allegations did not seem totally outrageous, even if the source was a black man. Even so, no one would step forward and say they had actually seen anything illegal or unusual on the Williams property, and many residents just did not like the idea of a black man accusing a white man of anything. Whether the accusation was true was secondary.

There would be little delay in starting Williams's trial. He would be tried before Manning. Newton County Judge John B. Hutcheson announced that, because of the importance of the case, he was extending the current court session so that Williams's trial could begin immediately. Jury selection for the trial was scheduled to begin on Tuesday, April 5, 1921. The Saturday before, the small town of Covington was busy with local farmers in town for market day. Hundreds of farmers from all over Newton County, Jasper County, and some surrounding areas were in town to trade their crops, buy supplies, meet with friends, and enjoy a day in the city. Market day was always busy and spirited, but this Saturday, all had the same topic on their minds. Williams was going on trial, and some of them could end up on the jury, deciding whether to hang him for killing a black man.

Saturday also saw the arrival of some of the first national news reporters to cover the trials. Word quickly arrived in New York of a shocking case in rural Georgia. There was the sheer scope of the crime, the way it confirmed the worst assumptions about the South, and, perhaps most surprising, the way the authorities actually seemed eager to prosecute the accused white man. For such an unusual case, both the *New York Times* and the *New York World* sent correspondents down to tiny Covington.

The trials themselves were covered heavily by the nation's press, but that was not the only exposure, good or bad, that Georgia received as a result of the "death farm" trials, as they were quickly dubbed by the reporters. As the trial preparations were underway, pundits, politicians, and community leaders all over the South struck on the case as a landmark for Georgia—much more than just another murder case and much more than just another example of a white bigot wielding power over a black man. For Southerners, the killings on the Williams plantation were not a shocking revelation about something hidden and shameful. Most residents of the South knew that peonage existed (even if they didn't know the proper term for it), and they knew that a plantation owner like Williams might do away with a troublesome black. But the "death farm" case was so thoroughly gruesome, beyond anything that might be excused as normal but unpleasant, that it prompted many Georgians to openly admit that there was a systemic problem in the way blacks were treated and forced to work in the rural economy.

Williams had done what no Yankee or black community leader ever could have done. He had clearly illustrated what could really happen to blacks in the humid, pine-tree-bordered farmland far from the state capitol and the comparatively urban community of Atlanta.

On the first day of the Williams trial, before the worst of the stories had even come out yet, an editorial in the *Atlanta Constitution* noted that "newspapers from coast to coast, throughout the North, East, and West, are daily printing news stories, editorials, and cartoons bearing upon the atrocities that have been brought to light in connection with peonage and the wholesale murders of negroes in Jasper and Newton Counties." The newspaper quoted an article in the *Greensboro (NC) Daily News* with the headline "Georgia as an Object Lesson." The North Carolina paper wrote that "Georgia threatens to become a monstrosity, threatens to derogate from her proud position as one of the American states, in the very forefront of civilization, and sink to the level of such semi-barbarous countries as Albania and Bulgaria."

The paper went on to say that Georgia had neglected education, made a mockery of justice and the court system, and allowed lynch mobs to rule. North Carolinians must be careful not to follow Georgia's path, the paper cautioned, or "we shall reproduce in North Carolina every horror that has occurred in Georgia." Of course, there was ample evidence that similar horrors were already occurring in North Carolina, but that was beside the point. The "death farm" killings were drawing all eyes to the South, and Georgia's sister states were becoming uncomfortable with the attention. They resented being stigmatized, so they claimed that the real problem lay only in Georgia.

In turn, Georgia leaders grabbed the nearest soapbox and declared that, shameful as the situation was, they would use it as a starting point for improvement. "Surely, surely it is high time for the decent sentiment of Georgia to assert itself and to insist upon a general clearing up of an ugly and disgraceful situation, the existence of which is bringing not only the state, but the whole South, into disrepute," the *Constitution* urged.

The idea that the "decent sentiment" of Georgia must act was a recurring one throughout the pretrial publicity and during the trials. Some of the calls for action can be dismissed as nothing more than politicians saying practically the only thing they could say in that situation, but other calls for justice were much more sincere. It was no coincidence that the *Atlanta Constitution*'s editorial calling for action came on the first day of jury selection for Williams's trial. The editorial slant of both the morning *Constitution* and the rival afternoon *Journal* favored Manning's story. And, more surprisingly, they both implied that Williams actually should be convicted if Manning's story were true.

The magnitude of the horrors in the Williams case seemed to be what led so many Southerners to an attitude that surprised many non-Southerners. *New York World* correspondent Rowland Thompson traveled around Georgia and the South during the trials, trying to get a handle on how the average Georgian—not politicians and newspaper columnists—felt about the plantation killings. "My unqualified answer to that question is that every decent white man and woman in Georgia, which means at least 90 per cent of the state's white population, is as deeply outraged and indignant over the recent revelations as the people of any other part of the country can be," Thompson concluded. "I came South feeling that the discussion of the prevalence of peonage here was going to be a 'ticklish' topic—likely to lead to evasions and arouse sentiment. Instead of this, I have found all the people in Atlanta have raised the question themselves and have been outspoken in both the admission of conditions and determination to have the evils removed.

"I then came to the rural districts of Newton County still expecting to find a different attitude here. But again I was disappointed. The same frankness, the same indignation, the same determination to give the Negro a square deal was found." Thompson went on to say that none of the white men he spoke to in Covington was "willing to stand for any mistreatment of the Negro, both for sentimental and practical reasons."

Thompson's thoroughly positive report suggests that perhaps he was not a very good reporter, was masterfully fooled by all he met, or was putting an exceptionally good spin on the scene he found in Georgia. Even so, this Yankee reporter admitted that he expected to find virulently bigoted Southerners milling about the Williams and Manning cases, and he was pleasantly surprised. The fact that he found *none* suggests that he did not understand that bigots are unlikely to confide in reporters fresh off the train from New York. But it also suggests that the South was not what outsiders believed it to be; it was not so blatantly racist that residents would be eager to praise the killing of eleven black men. Thompson's report suggests that even in a sometimes brutal, racist South, there were some standards of decency—a point that Southerners understood, but one that would be surprising to many others.

Those assumptions about the South were at the heart of what made the Williams case so important to Southerners. While many agreed the killings were contemptible and horrific, they also knew that the case could be used to justify every stereotype about their homeland. As the *Mobile Register* newspaper wrote, "We do not reflect upon the northern people as uncivilized when some of their number are shown to be rascals, thieves, hold-up men, burglars and murderers. The northern press, however, is altogether too quick in judgment of the South, being ready to infer from the peonage disclosures in Georgia that the southern white people, as a class, have invented a method of reducing the negroes to slavery and thus have nullified the great emancipation work of Abraham Lincoln."

But of course, Southern white people had done exactly that. The crucial point was that *some* Southern white people, not all Southern white people, had done it. This distinction was critical for people faced with overwhelming evidence that evil existed in their midst. It was the only way they could retain their pride while also condemning the evil that could not be overlooked.

The distinction was razor thin, and even many Southerners would argue that it was merely the rationalization of a guilty conscience. Given that ambivalence among natives, a New York reporter can be forgiven for not knowing just where the line was drawn in rural Georgia concerning how much brutality could be overlooked. After all, John S. Williams was a true Southerner, and he had seriously misjudged that line himself.


Even before the trial started, Williams was facing public criticism that he had not expected. There was a bad portent on Sunday, April 3, 1921, two days before jury selection was to begin. In a prominent article beneath a picture of Water's Bridge, a group of white citizens publicly proclaimed their eagerness to see justice done in the two murder trials. The article was written by a well-known minister in Jasper County, the Reverend J. M. Winburn. He sent the article to the *Constitution* and asked that it be printed.

The statements in the article would have been detrimental to Williams no matter what, but they were especially damning and hurtful because they came from Reverend Winburn, the pastor of the church that Williams and his entire family attended.

"I wish to make myself perfectly understood. I am Johnnie [John S.] Williams's pastor. I am Johnnie Williams's friend. It has been my privilege to be entertained many times in his home. I have been permitted to baptize and receive into the church four of his children.

"I have prayed and will continue to pray for him, but let me say this with emphasis, I am not engaged in his defense. If he is guilty of the atrocious crimes with which he has been charged, then let justice be done—and the heart and soul of Jasper County speaks through my pen."

Reverend Winburn went on to say that he was writing on behalf of all fifteen Baptist, eight Methodist, and two Presbyterian churches in Jasper County. After a lengthy recitation of all that was right and good about Jasper County, from the residents' eagerness to fight the Germans in the World War to the fact that Jasper County schoolteachers must be certified Christian before taking their jobs, the pastor excoriated the press and the rest of the country for its vilification of Jasper County as a home to peonage and murder. It is clear that Reverend Winburn was speaking for all the Georgians who felt that Williams's true crime was in acting so outrageously as to bring national criticism on quiet little Jasper and Newton Counties.

The pastor assured readers that Williams would be given "a fair and impartial trial by a set of twelve men of the old Anglo-Saxon strain of blood, unmixed with any foreign element whatever, and I know of no better people on earth."

In his article, Reverend Winburn also noted that there had been discussion of whether it would be necessary to bring in the state militia to ensure order in Covington during the trial. The governor and the local authorities seriously considered the idea, but local residents like Reverend Winburn hated the idea. Bringing in the state militia would be a slap in the face, an accusation that the community was so violent and out of control that armed soldiers would have to patrol the streets during a murder trial. It was actually not an unreasonable suggestion, but on the Sunday before jury selection, Newton County Judge John B. Hutcheson announced that he would not request the militia from Governor Dorsey, relying instead on an expanded group of sheriff's deputies to maintain order at the courthouse, and Dorsey accepted his decision. The community was relieved. This was a matter of pride now that the nation's eyes were on them.

Meanwhile, Governor Dorsey wrote a letter to the National Association for the Advancement of Colored People in New York, which was watching the case closely, promising to do all in his power to see that justice was accomplished in Newton County. The case also attracted the attention of President Harding, who urged the Justice Department to pursue federal charges of peonage against the Williams family and others in Jasper County. *The President of the United States* was talking about John S. Williams. It was beginning to look like he had gotten himself into far more than he had bargained for.

# 10

## "He Wanted to Look Good Because He Was Going Home"

The start of the trial of John S. Williams was marked by "perfect order," according to the *Atlanta Journal*. Throughout the trial, the media and the public were preoccupied with whether a rural Georgia community could try a prominent white man for murdering a black man, on the allegation of a black man, without an outbreak of violence. For now at least, the community was defying the common expectation.

Thousands of local people crowded into Covington for what was surely going to be the biggest trial ever to take place there, and possibly the biggest to ever take place in Georgia. Many of the visitors were farmers from Jasper County, including many who knew Williams well. Some wore their usual overalls, but many had spiffed up with nicely starched white shirts, and a few even wore ties for such an important occasion.

Covington was hard pressed to accommodate all the visitors. The two small hotels in town quickly ran out of room, so they arranged for hundreds of visitors to rent rooms in private homes. There still wasn't enough space for everyone who wanted to stay in town for the week or so that the trial was expected to last. Up and down the city streets, cars were parked wherever the drivers could find an open stretch of curb. All over town, small groups of men could be found on the streets discussing the upcoming trial and debating the propriety of what was about to happen. More than a few used the occasion to reacquaint themselves with neighbors not seen in a while, and they discussed just how their own use of black labor was similar, or different from, the practices that had got Williams into this mess.

The trial was expected to last only a few days because the attorney for Williams had hinted that he would need to call very few witnesses to refute the allegations of a black man who had admitted to mass murder. Jury selection was scheduled to begin on Tuesday, April 5, 1921, but controversy began bubbling to the surface even before then.

The involvement of outside forces, including Governor Dorsey, already was becoming an issue in the case. Greene F. Johnson, the local attorney hired to represent Williams, was positioning himself as just a simple country lawyer facing all the legal artillery the state could muster. Johnson was a rather small, thin man with a lean, flat face. Indeed, he had the look of a man who should be wearing overalls instead of a suit and tie. The day before the jury selection was to begin, Johnson confronted Judge Hutcheson over what he suspected was improper influence by Governor Dorsey. Johnson argued that the trial had been scheduled much too quickly for him to prepare an adequate defense, and he suspected the governor had urged Judge Hutcheson to put his defendant on trial immediately.

In replying to the lawyer's request for a delay in the trial schedule, Judge Hutcheson admitted that he had indeed attended a conference with Governor Dorsey and Solicitor Brand, the chief prosecutor in the case, at the governor's mansion in Atlanta. The judge confirmed that the governor had been interested in seeing the Jasper County farmer tried quickly, but Judge Hutcheson insisted that by then he already had decided on his own to schedule a speedy trial. Accordingly, the judge turned down Johnson's request for a delay. Jury selection would begin the next morning.

Manning and Williams had been at the Atlanta Tower during the pre-trial proceedings, but they were both taken to Covington for the jury selection and trial. Eight of the black witnesses from the "murder farm" were also transported to Covington. Transporting Manning and the other black witnesses again raised the specter of violence, so they traveled with a number of deputies and a small posse on the Monday afternoon train. For Williams, the arrangements were easier. There was no chance that he would be assaulted on the trip, so Sheriff B. L. Johnson of Newton County went to Atlanta

# Negro Who Confessed Slaying

left the room, but others insisted that the investigation be continued, according to information. Manning finally confessed and was later carried into the jury room, where he pleaded with the jurors to protect him, and then repeated his sensational confession. Indictment of both the negro and Williams followed, and the former was rushed by automobile to Atlanta, where he was placed in the Fulton county tower.

Williams was arrested last Friday and was also carried to Atlanta. Before leaving Covington he remarked to one of his sons, who was crying, not to worry about him, but to return to the farm and care for his mother. Manning was brought here again Saturday and accompanied authorities as they searched for the bodies of victims. He pointed out each grave and the places in the Alcovy river where three bodies had been thrown. After the successful search he was sent back to Atlanta.

### Telegram to Governor.

The following telegram received by Governor Dorsey Monday from the National Association for the Advancement of Colored People has been communicated to local authorities:

"The National Association for the Advancement of Colored People urges you to use every effort to bring to justice the murderers of eleven negroes in Jasper county, Georgia, because they threatened to reveal peonage conditions in that county. We also strongly urge that you have brought into the light this vicious system of exploitation and debt slavery, which is so prevalent in other parts of Georgia as well, and which is so great a menace to the well being of Georgia, the south and America.

"Will you not also turn over to the department of justice evidence of such other cases of peonage as you have in your possession that the department may act in conjunction with state authorities in wiping out this evil. Next to lynching there is no greater cause of unrest than this vicious system."

Signed
"JAMES WELDON JOHNSON,
"Secretary."

Clyde Manning, the negro whose sensational confession of having assisted in the killing of eleven negroes on the John S. Williams plantation in Jasper county and at the Alcovy river resulted in his indictment with Williams for murder by the Newton county grand jury.

Clyde Manning at the time of his trial. From the *Atlanta Constitution*, March 29, 1921.

PRINCIPAL, JUDGE AND SOME OF THE LAWYERS IN THE WILLIAMS "MURDER FARM"
CASE, which went on trial at Covington Tuesday. In the center is John S. Williams, owner of the
farm, who is on trial n the charge of murder. At the top, left to right, are Judge John B.
Hutcheson, of the Stone Mountain circuit, who is presiding and Solicitor General A. M. Brand. At
the bottom, left, is Attorney W. M. Howard, who, as special state's attorney, is associated
with Solicitor Brand and with Assistant Atorney General Graham Wright in the prosecution. At the
right is Attorney E. Marvin Underwood, who has been employed by W. Woods White and other prominent Atlantians, to represent Clyde Manning, the negro who has confessed to killing several negroes
at the instance of Williams. Added to this array of brilliant legal talent are Attorneys General
J. Johnson, of Monticello; W. H. Key and C. C. King, who will represent Williams.

*Atlanta Journal*, April 5, 1921.

# Tense Scene in Covington Courtroom as Clyde Manning Tells His Gruesome Story

## DEATH HULL HALL GIVES DRAMATIC TOUCH TO TRIAL

Manning's Narrative of Slaying of Eleven Negroes Withstands Cross-Examination.

*STATE IS VICTORIOUS IN FIRST LEGAL CLASH*

Courtroom Crowd Held Breathless as Witness Gives Details of Succession of Slayings.

BY MARION KENDRICK.
(Staff Correspondent The Constitution.)

Covington, Ga., April 5—For six long hours Clyde Manning, negro boss of the Jasper county "murder farm," held the stand in the Newton county courthouse today and under the withering fire of cross-examination told his graphic story of how eleven negroes were sent to their deaths at the command of John S. Williams, white farmer.

And when the almost unending ordeal was completed, the negro, closely guarded, walked from the courtroom with his narrative unshaken.

For a long stretch of moments today not even the sound of an indrawn breath was audible in the jam-packed court room, and when the testimony of Lessie May Benton and Clyde Freeman, employees on Williams farm, had ended, Judge Hutcheson recessed court until Thursday.

First photograph of the interior of the quaint old Newton county courthouse at Covington to be taken during the progress of the Williams murder trial. The picture, which taken Wednesday, shows Judge John B. Hutcheson presiding, and the negro, Clyde Manning (indicated by the arrow) telling his gruesome story to the jury. The jury is seen at the extreme right rear. Directly in front of Manning are the court reporters and newspaper men. An idea of the tenseness with which the negro's story was received is given by this p

*Atlanta Constitution*, April 6, 1921.

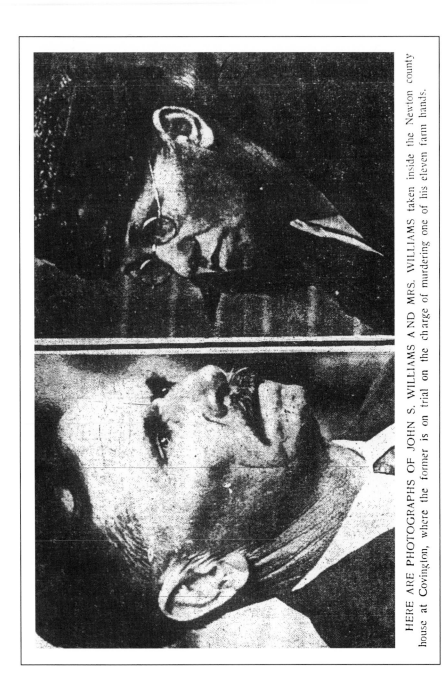

HERE ARE PHOTOGRAPHS OF JOHN S. WILLIAMS AND MRS. WILLIAMS taken inside the Newton county house at Covington, where the former is on trial on the charge of murdering one of his eleven farm hands.

John S. Williams and Mrs. Williams during his trial. From the *Atlanta Journal*, April 7, 1921.

# Leading Legal Characters in "Murder Farm" Trial

1, Greene F. Johnson, who leads defense for John S. Williams in murder trial in Covington, Ga.; 2, Judge John B. Hutcheson, who is presiding; 3, W. M. Howard, of Augusta, who is assisting the state; 4, Solicitor-General A. M. Brand, who is conducting state's case; 5, Sheriff B. L. Johnson, of Newton county; 6, Graham Wright, assistant attorney-general, who is assisting state.

## FATE OF WILLIAMS IN HANDS OF JURY

**Continued From First Page**

Johnson, who has staged a remarkable fight for his client, is expected to attract the largest crowd of the trial.

### SHERIFF TESTIFIES, COROBORATING MANNING.

The last two state's witnesses who testified were put on the stand to corroborate statement of Clyde Manning, negro farm boss. Manning told the jury yesterday Williams directed the killing of the men, three of whom were drowned in Newton county.

Rena Manning, wife of Clyde Manning, testified in corroboration of her husband's statement that the night Peterson, Willie Preston and Harry Price were last seen alive, Williams carried them and Manning and Charlie Chisbold off in his car

looked toward the jury and then to the judge.

### WILLIAMS ON STAND IN HIS OWN BEHALF.

"Your honor, the defendant will take the stand in his own behalf. I will request," he said, "you to instruct him."

With this he resumed his seat, and during the whole of the long statement of his client, he remained with his elbow propped on his knee and his chin in his hand. His eyes never left Williams. To his right, Mr. Howard, who had conducted the prosecution's examination, twirled his eyeglasses in one hand and listened attentively to Williams' every word.

Solicitor Brand smiled once or twice. Williams testified toward the table, C. C. King and W. H. Hill, associated with Mr. Johnson, glanced about the courtroom and at times made notes on parts of the statement. Mrs. Williams, sitting with them, was dressed in black and appeared nervous during the ordeal. Her eyes

those boys," he said, referring to Peterson, Price and Preston.

Williams said he asked Manning next day and the latter replied:

"They went off last night."

Williams was talking in a calm, clear voice and occasionally made a slow gesture as he addressed the jury.

He told of hearing later that the negroes' bodies had been found and of his later arrest.

"Whoever put the bodies in the river did it for a purpose," he said. "If I had done this crime, gentlemen, I would have had plenty of time to get where they could not put their hands on me," he asserted.

### DECLARES HE IS FALSELY ACCUSED.

Williams asserted he was "falsely accused," and added, "what they done to him (Manning) to make him accuse me, I don't know."

"I did not know what he was going to say till we heard him on the stand," he said.

Williams then went into details of Manning's long employment on

and in this case I say that the wife of an accomplice should not be credited.

"She made one statement alone, which should demonstrate to you that she was lying. Locked in her home, she tells you, she heard the exhaust of an automobile as far as from here to the jail. You know as well as I do that it is impossible.

Mr. King then charged that the state had trained its witnesses and that every one of them had showed their schooling when placed on the stand. He declared that the state had failed to make out its case and that when the jury considered the evidence, if there was the slightest doubt as to Williams' guilt, he should be acquitted.

### GRAHAM WRIGHT OPENS FOR STATE.

He concluded his argument at 2:15 o'clock, having spoken forty minutes. Assistant Attorney-General Graham Wright followed him.

Mr. Wright referred the court to several authorities on the extent of corroboration necessary to convict. He declared that where a series of trifling circumstances are connected

*Atlanta Constitution*, April 6, 1921.

# John Williams, As He Heard His Sentence

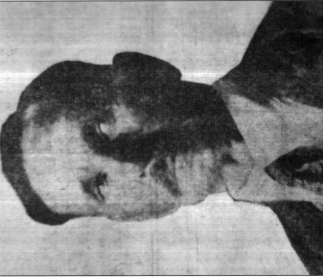

"Judge Hutcheson, Solicitor Brand and the officials and men of Newton county did splendidly what every good Georgian wanted to see done. They gave Williams the fair and impartial trial to which he was entitled. They discarded alike all prejudices and any temptation to be vengeful. In punishing him they have vindicated the law and restated the fact that every man in Georgia must stand equal at her bar of justice. I could lend only my influence to help them. I shall continue to lend it and do everything in my power to see that investigation and action wipe out every vestige of the blot which the very per county revelations put upon the state's reputation.

"If anywhere, Governor Dorsey ended, "men have been asking what Georgia thinks, means to do about such things, this superbly orderly trial, the verdict rendered this morning, the the grand jury probe which begins in Montcello next Monday are an answer. Georgia would ask to have considered.

### Pitying Silence.

From the entrance of the jury till the departure of the individual members after Williams had been sentenced, not ten minutes elapsed. Not more than a hundred persons were in the courtroom and the only demonstration was pitying silence in the face of Mrs. William's grief. And outside the result was accepted with equal quietness. It was Saturday. More automobiles than usual were parked around the courthouse square and more people were gathered in groups around the doors of the stores, but no more than there were last Saturday or any other market morning. The men in the groups talked with each other, but did not talk loudly and there was no argument. The opinion of any of them selected at random was the opinion of any other. Newton county as represented there was satisfied.

"They used horse sense," ran the narrowly between his elder son who wears a cross pinned on his breast by King George for valor on the Somme and the plump kind faced woman of fifty who is "Mother" for his twelve children. With the composure which marks her, Mrs. Williams at first sat as still as her husband. But after a moment she turned and nestled, half appealingly, half protectingly to him, and buried her wet face in his shoulder. She did not cry aloud, and there was no sound in the courtroom.

The man, his face stolcal as ever, put his strong left arm around his wife. But he seemed to feel her need of a last awkward and more expressive comfort than he was able to give her. Turning his head he whispered to his son, and "Doctor Gus" and his father quietly exchanged places.

"Gentlemen, the court thanks you for your service and excuses you from" further duty during this term," said Judge Hutcheson then, and Georgia's most dramatic and perhaps most significant murder trial had passed into her legal history. What many of her own people had been skeptical about had happened. A jury of Georgia farmers had found a Georgia farmer guilty of the murder of a negro farmhand, on the word of another negro farmhand.

### Staisrylng Verdict.

This verdict seemed to satisfy the men of whose community spirit it was an expression. And so far as can now be ascertained it satisfied Georgia at large.

"The result of the trial," said Governor Hugh M. Dorsey, "is not only what I had hoped it would be for the sake of justice and the good name of our state. It was also what I had known it would be if the wish of every good citizen could receive effective expression.

"Judge Hutcheson, Solicitor Brand and the officials and men of Newton county did splendidly what every good Georgian wanted to see

"Will you stand up, Mr. Williams,' the court asked in a voice that shook with emotion despite its modulated tones, John Williams arose, his great shoulders squared, his head thrown back, his eyes fixed on the judge with a gleam that bespoke defiance of, the words he knew would make him a striped felon for the rest of his days. There was a twitching in the muscles of his brawny throat, but otherwise his whole being seemed to shout the unspoken thought, 'There is no punishment that law can mete out that I am not man enough to bear.'

*Atlanta Constitution*, April 10, 1921.

Site of Water's Bridge on the Alcovy River, where Johnny Benson, John Brown, and Charlie Chisolm were killed. Remnants of the old bridge can still be seen next to the current bridge.

Approximate site of Allen's Bridge on the Yellow River, where Lindsey Peterson and Willie Preston were killed.

Approximate site of Mann's Bridge on the South River, where Harry Price threw himself off rather than be pushed.

with one deputy to get the defendant. The three men took the early morning train from Atlanta and arrived in Covington about 8:30 A.M. on Monday.

The train carrying Williams passed through a number of small towns on the way to Covington, and in each one a crowd gathered at the railroad in hopes of catching a glimpse of the now famous defendant. The crowds were almost entirely black. As the train passed through one small town, Williams watched the crowd of poor blacks with amusement and joked with his guards about his newfound notoriety.

"Just throw me out among them and you'll see them scatter," he joked.

Williams stayed in the Covington jail Monday night, as he would for the next several days during the trial. Manning and the other black witnesses also filled the jail.

The Williams family had already gathered in Covington to support their patriarch. In addition to his wife, the trial would be attended by his married daughter Mary (Mrs. J. A. Martin); Iva Sue, a seventeen-year-old daughter; W. T. Williams, the defendant's brother; Dr. Gus Williams, the defendant's eldest son, and his wife; and two cousins, J. L. Lane, Jr., and Tom Lane. As the trial continued, other family members, including children, were permitted to come in and watch. Sheriff Johnson announced to the media that he had given permission for the defendant to have lunch with his wife and children on each day of the trial.

Court convened in the Newton County Courthouse at nine A.M. on Tuesday, April 5, 1921. The participants filed into the red brick building with a tall clock tower on the town square of Covington, and spectators arrived early to get a seat in the courtroom. The seats filled quickly, and deputies admonished all of the spectators to resolve seating disputes immediately as they hustled latecomers back out the door. The balcony of the courtroom was reserved exclusively for blacks, who were not allowed below. It filled just as quickly as the prime seating downstairs filled with whites.

There was some surprise when the defendant drove up in front of the courthouse, escorted by three deputies. No announcement had been made about whether Williams would be present for the jury selection. A crowd of hundreds gathered around the car as the defendant tried to get out and enter the building. Four deputies cleared a path for Williams, who was dressed in a fine Sunday suit, hat, and glasses.

Though eager to be a part of the proceedings, the crowd was hushed as the defendant walked by. Williams walked confidently and showed little concern for the upcoming ordeal. He picked a few familiar faces out of the crowd and paused to speak with them, telling them, "I'll come clear. Don't you worry." He went on into the courthouse and down a hallway to the winding stairs leading to the second-floor courtroom. He went on into the courtroom with three deputies and made his way to the defense table, where he sat down and began speaking with his lawyer. The courtroom was so crowded that several minutes passed before most people realized the defendant had entered.

As the crowd waited for the day's proceedings to begin, Williams occasionally made eye contact with a familiar face in the courtroom, or smiled or paused for a short conversation and a handshake. At one point, he motioned for a deputy to come near and asked, "Is my wife here yet?" He was assured that she would be arriving soon.

The only family member to arrive this early in the day's proceedings was Dr. Gus Williams. As the courtroom door opened again, John S. Williams looked expectantly and saw his war hero son stride into the room.

Dr. Gus Williams greeted his father affectionately and then took a seat next to him at the defense table. They talked intently for some time, with hundreds of eyes watching from a distance and speculating on the content of the conversation. The defendant stroked his chin and played with his dark brown mustache as he listened to his son, his eyes staring at the ceiling or idly scanning the black faces in the balcony.

After a short wait, a deputy called for silence and announced that the judge was entering the packed courtroom. Deputies had to clear a path for Judge Hutcheson to get to the bench, and he seemed annoyed at the overflowing spectators who had convinced the deputies to allow them to fill every standing space when all the seats had been taken.

Judge Hutcheson was dressed in a dark blue suit, and his demeanor suggested he was taking the morning's proceedings very seriously. A handsome, lean man with blond hair and darker eyebrows, Judge Hutcheson always imparted an air of authority in his courtroom, but he seemed especially determined to establish order in this case from the outset.

"Everyone must be seated," he declared, and the deputies began ushering out the overflow crowd. "I will allow no one to stand. Passing in and out while witnesses are on the stand will be forbidden.

"Exclamations of approval or disapproval will not be allowed and will be handled severely."

He called the court to order and began efforts to select a jury. Clyde Manning was not present, as he was not yet needed.

Dozens of potential jurors were called and interviewed, and the court dismissed those clearly unable to serve because of age or similar reasons. Sitting among his lawyers, Williams appeared bored. He chewed gum and read a newspaper through much of it, frequently calling for a deputy to see if his wife had arrived. Before the court moved on to the selection of the actual jury, attorney Johnson once again moved for a delay in the trial. He argued that he had had very little time to meet with his client since the indictment on March 24, and he suggested that the trial was moving along so quickly only because Governor Dorsey wanted it to.

Johnson also argued that he could not properly defend Williams without having more information from the prosecution. Solicitor Brand had not even stated on what date the death of Lindsey Peterson had supposedly occurred. The indictment said March 19, but Clyde Manning had supposedly given another date. Without that information, how could he prepare an alibi showing that Williams did not commit the crime? The trial should be delayed so that Johnson could question Manning directly, he argued.

Brand pointed out that Georgia law did not require him to pinpoint the date of the murder, so the objection was irrelevant. Judge Hutcheson refused the request to delay the trial. At about that time, the defendant's wife made her entrance. Mrs. John S. Williams came into the courtroom on the arms of her two younger daughters, seventeen-year-old Iva Sue and eight-year-old Tillie. She was wearing a dark plain long dress and a modest hat. A short woman with a round nose, she wore round eyeglasses, and her graying hair was pulled back tightly and tucked neatly under her hat. Her expression was calm but solemn.

Following close behind the defendant's wife was the rest of the family. The crowd quickly saw that the family was entering, and all eyes turned to see. Mrs. Williams smiled at her husband from the back of the room and he waved back at her. As everyone in the courthouse watched, including potential jurors, Williams took a handkerchief from his pocket and dabbed at his eyes. Mrs. Williams walked quickly up to her husband, who stood and embraced her, kissing her several times on the cheek. He then turned to hug and kiss his two daughters, then to embrace and exchange hearty handshakes with the male family members following them into the courtroom.

With his request for a delay refused, Johnson moved on to another complaint. It was highly unusual for a special state-employed attorney, W. M. Howard, to assist the local prosecutor with a case, so Johnson demanded to know who was paying him for his services. He even demanded that

Howard take the stand for questioning. Judge Hutcheson granted the request, and W. M. Howard was sworn in.

"Who employed you in this case?" Johnson asked him.

"Governor Hugh M. Dorsey," Howard replied curtly. He sat in the witness chair with downturned lips and squinty eyes, the slight scowl he almost always wore.

Johnson then asked if Dorsey would pay him for his legal services in prosecuting this local murder case, and Howard explained that the governor had arranged for his fee to be paid by "a number of Atlanta men" whose names he did not know. He specifically denied being hired by the National Association for the Advancement of Colored People.

When he was finished with Howard, Johnson proceeded to question Assistant Attorney General Wright, who had been assigned by the governor to assist with the prosecution. He answered similar questions as to who was paying for his services, but he explained that he was participating in the case in an official capacity as assistant attorney general and would receive no special compensation.

Brand then rose and asked if Johnson wished to question *him* about who was paying his salary. The courtroom erupted in laughter, and Sheriff Johnson began banging on a desk to try to restore order. When the laughter died down, Judge Hutcheson sternly warned the crowd that he would clear the courtroom after any other such disturbance.

"This is not a circus or a moving picture show," the judge declared. "The court will tolerate no more of this."

Johnson then asked to question E. Marvin Underwood, the handsome young attorney from Atlanta who would represent Clyde Manning for the same killings and who was, at least in Johnson's eyes, assisting the prosecution of Williams.

Without knowing who was employing Underwood and Howard, it was possible that the jury pool would include their relatives, Johnson argued. The "secret prosecutors" would prove to be a focal point in the defense.

"I want to ascertain who our secret prosecutors are as well as who our open prosecutors are," Johnson said.

Judge Hutcheson agreed and recessed the court until 11:15 A.M. to give the state time to get the names.

As the crowd filed out of the courtroom for the recess, the defendant embraced his wife and kissed each of his children. In the first show of strong emotion since his arrest, Williams began to cry as he listened to his wife say how worried she was for him. Tears could be seen streaming down his face as his wife looked up at him and said her "heart was broken" by the trial. He hugged her again and urged her not to worry, he would be acquitted.

After the crowd had left, Williams gathered his family around him. They discussed how the plantation was faring without him, his boys, or the black workers there to take care of it. They then went to an anteroom near the courtroom, and Williams had a meal with his family for the first time since his arrest. His wife and daughters brought several baskets of lunch straight from the "death farm," and they enjoyed what the deputies later called "a picnic." Four deputies stood guard. They reported that Williams ate heartily, downing three slices of his favorite apple pie. Mrs. Williams would not eat.

The defendant asked his wife to bring more apple pie for the next day's lunch.


When the court session resumed, Howard took the stand again and said he had called Governor Dorsey, who told him that Dr. C. B. Wilmer and Dr. M. Ashby Jones were paying his fee. Underwood then took the stand and said that W. Woods White of Atlanta had hired him to represent Manning and promised that a number of socially prominent white Atlantans would pay his fee. Underwood said he did not know all of the names, but he named the same Drs. C. B. Wilmer and M. Ashby Jones, plus ten more. This information would prove important later, as the defense would argue that Williams was facing more than just a standard murder charge prosecuted by the state. With the financial support of wealthy white Atlantans, Williams was facing the state's prosecution, plus privately employed prosecutors, the defense would say.

Most of the spectators in the courtroom did not recognize the names of the Atlantans who were paying the legal fees supporting Williams's prosecution and Manning's defense, and the natural assumption was that these were just big-city liberals who saw the opportunity to do a good deed. The only one of the benefactors with any real name recognition was Dr. C. B. Wilmer, not a medical doctor but a doctor of divinity, who was well known among religious leaders in the Atlanta area because of his community activism and his regular column in the *Atlanta Journal*'s Sunday magazine. Wilmer regularly wrote on such weighty topics as the alliance of world cultures and the failure of most American cities to adequately fund their police departments, always with a biblical angle and an appeal for the community to stand up for what is right. His columns rarely touched directly on local controversies, and he never mentioned the Williams and Manning trials in his columns, even after he was revealed as one of the secret benefactors.

Nevertheless, the sentiments expressed in Wilmer's weekly columns give some indication of why he came to Manning's aid and probably encouraged the others to do the same. Wilmer may have been a big-city liberal by the standards of rural Georgians, but he was still far from revolutionary. He often took a progressive stance on racial issues, but he had a knack for couching his statements in a respectful tone of commiseration that made them fairly palatable to the average white Atlantan. In an interesting column that ran between the Williams and Manning trials, Wilmer wrote "Lessons We Can Learn from the Old South." He recounted a speech he had given to the United Daughters of the Confederacy, a group that honors the memory of Confederate veterans. After paying his respects to the aging veterans present, Wilmer discussed racial issues facing the South and suggested that it was possible to honor the past while addressing current problems in a forthright manner. "Today, we are called on in the language of the Apostle Paul in the 12th chapter of the Epistle to the Romans, to 'Provide things honest in the SIGHT of all men.' If anybody has any remedies for our racial or other ills, it is time to shout them from the house tops."

Wilmer went on to say that the Confederate veterans and their descendants were uniquely qualified to "sift Southern traditions and ideals and discriminate for the benefit of the rising generation between one sort of Southern man and a very different sort. I believe that the time has arrived when it is the duty of one set of Southern white men to say as kindly, but as firmly as possible to another set of Southern white men: You do not represent the best of the Old South and you certainly do not represent us. We deny your claim to speak for the South or the white race. We stand for justice, not injustice; for helping other people, not hindering them; for democracy and not mobocracy." Surely Wilmer must have had John S. Williams in mind.

Wilmer also told the veterans that he sometimes imagined the South as the Virgin Mary "standing hopeless by the tomb of her buried past and blinded by the tears of her inconsolable grief, unable to recognize the risen Lord of a new and better day. But as that Mary dried her tears and responded gladly when her name was called, even so the South is more and more 'forgetting the things that are behind,' laying them aside as dead weights and 'reaching forth to those that are before.'"

It is noteworthy that the reverend made such comments directly to the elderly Confederate veterans and their genteel supporters, that he was willing to enlist them in what most would consider a progressive movement that, if handled indelicately, could be considered an affront. But as Wilmer so eloquently explained, there did not have to be any contradiction between honoring the past and correcting the inadequacies of the present. That attitude must have served Wilmer well as he recruited others to fund Manning's defense. Unfortunately, the motivation of the benefactors can only be surmised because they left no public records explaining themselves; even after they were named in court, no newspaper ever interviewed them and they never appeared as part of any court proceeding.

Naming the Atlanta benefactors had slowed the proceedings, but with Johnson's complaints addressed, jury selection could resume. The first potential jurors were questioned before lunch, and the questioning resumed at 1:30 P.M. As the jury members were picked, the courtroom crowd grew increasingly excited and could not contain itself when the twelfth and final juror was chosen at 2:25 P.M. A sudden burst of conversation and shuffling erupted, and Judge Hutcheson again admonished the crowd against interruptions. The remaining men on the jury list were excused. Judge Hutcheson instructed them, and anyone else on the list of 633 potential Newton County jurors, not to attend the Williams trial because they might be needed for the trial of Clyde Manning.

Williams's jury had been chosen, and it could not have been a better representation of his peers. Of the twelve jurors, there were seven farmers, two merchants, a grocery clerk, a barber, and a druggist. Twelve of them were men. Twelve of them were local. Twelve of them were white.

The judge adjourned the proceedings until the next morning, when the prosecution would call its first witness. As the crowd began to disperse, a receiving line formed for the purpose of shaking the defendant's hand. A long queue of men, most of them farmers, waited in the hallway for Williams, offering words of encouragement and confidence as he passed by. The experience left Williams in high spirits, and he was smiling broadly as deputies led him back to the jail.

Tuesday night, on the eve of the first testimony in his father's trial for murder, Dr. Gus Williams emphatically voiced confidence that the jury would acquit him and the community would come to understand his father was just the victim of a renegade negro. The statement from Dr. Gus Williams gained considerable attention in the press because he was perhaps the most respectable, if not the most respected, member of the Williams clan. Described with great admiration in the newspapers as a "wearer of the British war cross" for heroism in the World War, the doctor seemed to have a modicum of credibility because he was not directly associated with the crimes in question. Unlike the other three Williams sons, Dr. Gus Williams lived and worked away from the Williams plantation and was not accused of direct involvement in the mistreatment of blacks.

Nevertheless, the doctor's claims were rooted more in his allegiance to his family than in the truth. Dr. Gus Williams declared that all the reports of cruelty to blacks on the plantation were greatly exaggerated and that there were no stockades used to imprison the men. He admitted that his brother Huland had killed a single black man on the plantation a year earlier in self-defense as the black man attacked him wildly with a knife. That was a justified killing, he said, and there weren't any others.

The men were even paid well, he claimed, but they gambled it all away, just as blacks are wont to do.

"I can safely say that I have not seen a single employee abused while working on our farm," the doctor told the local press. "The negroes always had plenty of food and were paid fair wages. Of course, most of them lost what they made in 'skin games,' but we couldn't help that. All the negroes had their 'skin,' and they'll be found playing on any farm in the state."

The doctor also took issue with the grand jury spectacle in which workers from the Williams plantation showed their scars inflicted by the Williams family. He contended that the scars actually were the result of mistreatment in the state's jails and prison systems, from which the Williams family had gallantly rescued the men.

"I have received letters and telephone calls from I don't know how many negroes who used to work on our place, and they always ask to be taken back," the doctor said. "I am satisfied my father will come clear. As the trial progresses, everyone will come to the same conclusion."


The Williams family returned to the plantation that night. Attorney Howard spent the evening relaxing in a rocking chair on the front porch of the Covington hotel where he was staying. Solicitor Brand could be seen on street corners, chatting with his many friends in the county. Attorney

Underwood swapped jokes with newspaper reporters in front of one of the hotels. Attorney Johnson wanted to go to a movie but took a long walk through the residential part of Covington when he found there was no movie playing that night.

The twelve members of the jury would be housed in the Flowers Hotel in Covington for the duration of the trial. After they were selected and the court was dismissed for the day, some of the jurors stayed in the courtroom and played checkers for a while, content that no one would bother them in the privacy of the courthouse. Others passed the evening playing "mumble peg" in the backyard of the hotel. Three deputies watched over them at all times, and they reported that all the jurors went to bed by ten P.M.

John S. Williams, Clyde Manning, and the black witnesses slept in the Covington jail.

The courtroom scene was duplicated the next morning, with crowds of whites fighting for every possible seat in the lower gallery and blacks crowding into the gallery above. The floor-to-ceiling windows let in the morning sun. On the wall high above the judge's bench was a banner proudly honoring "Newton County Boys Who Paid the Supreme Sacrifice" in the World War, with the names of thirteen fallen soldiers.

The day promised even more excitement than the day before, since the first witnesses were expected to testify, and the crowd in Covington was even more anxious to get into the courtroom and hear the proceedings firsthand. The deputies followed the judge's previous instructions requiring all spectators to be seated, but they allowed them to seat themselves just about anywhere an open space could be found. When he entered the courtroom at 8:45 A.M. Williams found spectators nearly shoulder to shoulder, even in the normally open spaces surrounding the judge's bench and the attorneys' tables.

The defendant chatted amiably with newspaper reporters as he entered the courtroom, and one reporter asked him why his three sons were not attending the trial. It was known that Governor Dorsey was urging the state to file murder and peonage charges against Huland, Marvin, and Leroy Williams, and their absence from their father's trial was becoming quite conspicuous.

"I cannot imagine why they were not here yesterday," Williams replied with a straight face, as if such a thing actually could be unknown to him. "But I expect they will be here today."

The defendant also told the reporters that he had slept well the night before and was "feeling good." Williams either did not notice or intentionally ignored the young black man sitting in the spectator's section behind the prosecution table. Clyde Manning had been brought to the courtroom early to minimize disruption. He now sat with several other witnesses waiting for the day's proceedings, dressed neatly in a clean pair of blue overalls and a light blue chambray shirt, freshly ironed and neatly buttoned at the neck. He held his hat in his hands, which were locked with handcuffs.

Soon after the defendant finished greeting well-wishers and took a seat, Judge Hutcheson made his way through the crowd to the bench. As he rapped his gavel to call the court to order, the clock tower on the courthouse began to strike nine.

The judge again warned the crowd that he would tolerate no disruptions, and the jury was brought in at 9:05 A.M. Just at that moment, the defendant's wife and daughters entered the courtroom and walked toward their loved one. Everyone, including the jury, watched as John S. Williams jumped to his feet with a broad smile and warmly embraced each family member. Before taking his seat again, Williams nodded pleasantly to the black maid who had brought one of Williams's grandchildren into the room.

Judge Hutcheson asked the chief prosecutor if he was ready to proceed with the case. Brand replied that the state was ready and intended to prove that the defendant ordered Lindsey Peterson killed to hide evidence of peonage on his farm.

The judge then instructed both sides to call their witnesses so that they could be confirmed present and then sequestered from the day's court proceedings. The attorneys called out the names of the witnesses they intended to call for testimony, and each one answered. When the state prosecutor got to Clyde Manning's name, all eyes turned to look at the black man. He answered "present" in a shaky voice.

The witnesses were removed from the courtroom so that they would not hear one anothers' testimony, and then the trial moved into high gear with the calling of the first witness—federal agent George W. Brown. In response to Brand's questioning, the agent explained that he and his partner, A. J. Wismer, had visited the Williams plantation on February 18, 1921, and informed the defendant that he was under investigation for peonage.

Brown testified that the agents had spoken with the defendant, his sons, Clyde Manning, and the other black workers, inquiring about the conditions on the farm and whether men were being held against their will.

Brown also testified that he and his partner had personally seen the house in which the black workers were imprisoned at night, providing details as to its size and construction.

"It was a strongly built wooden structure, with heavy shutters and wooden bars over the doors," the agent recalled, painting a picture of the building that the Williams family had said never existed. "A heavy chain ran through the two doors in front, and we were told that it was used to lock the workers in at night so they couldn't leave."

Brown went on to tell the courtroom that he had discussed with Leroy Williams, in the defendant's presence, an allegation that a worker had been killed on the farm some time earlier. Defense attorney Johnson protested vigorously, saying any information about previous killings on the farm was irrelevant to the case at hand. The jury was sent out of the room while the judge heard arguments about whether to allow the testimony.

In a stunning challenge to the defense, Brand explained that the testimony was pertinent because he intended to show that eleven men were killed on the Williams plantation and that their deaths were directly related to the defendant's motive for murder in the killing of Lindsey Peterson.

The judge met both attorneys halfway and declared that what the federal agents overheard about Leroy Williams killing a black man some time earlier would be disallowed, but the agent could continue with anything that might establish a motive for the killing of Peterson.

The jury returned, and Brown continued with his account of his visit to the farm. He told of questioning the black workers, touring the plantation, and asking Williams about how he acquired the black workers.

"I told him we had information that Clyde Manning kept some of the negroes locked up on his place," Brown said.

"What did Williams say then?" the attorney asked.

"He promised not to work any more negroes from stockades."

On cross-examination, Johnson tried to suggest that the federal agents had traveled to Jasper County to stir up trouble.

"Didn't you tell the negroes that they should only work eight hours a day?" he asked. "Didn't you tell them that they should be paid forty dollars a month?"

This was a difficult moment for Brown. The truth was that he had indeed explained to Manning that Williams had no right to work him all day for meager compensation. At the time, he thought little of making the statement to Manning because it was appropriate in the context of the investigation and there were no whites around to hear it.

But now he found himself on the stand in front of hundreds of Southern whites, in a trial being watched closely around the country. The defense attorney clearly was trying to portray Brown as a "nigger lover" just trying to stir up trouble for a farmer. In 1921 in rural Georgia, that was a serious accusation that would prompt an immediate denial in almost any white man.

Despite the good intentions he had shown before, Brown buckled under that pressure and denied the accusation.

"No, that's not what we said," Brown replied. "I think I asked him how long he had been there at Mr. Williams's farm; I asked him how many years. I did not ask him how many hours a day he was working. I did not tell him he ought to be working but eight hours a day. I did not tell him he ought to get forty dollars a month."

But the lie did not slow down the attorney. He had made his point with the jury just by asking the question.

"When you spoke the next day with Solicitor Doyle Campbell of the Ocmulgee Circuit, did you not state that you found nothing objectionable on the Williams farm?"

"I may have said there was nothing to warrant prosecution immediately," Brown replied.

"And did you not tell him that the negroes looked well fed and well cared for?"

"I only said that they looked better than the negroes on Harvey Person's place," Brown explained, referring to another Georgia farm that had been investigated.

The federal agent's testimony went on for more than an hour. As Brown testified, the accused murderer sat quietly and held a single red rose his wife had brought him. As the agent described how the black men were held prisoner on the farm, and how the federal bureau had heard of rampant physical abuse and killings, a four-year-old boy walked up to his grandfather's side. Williams greeted his grandchild warmly and hoisted the boy up onto his lap. The little boy curled up and fell asleep as his grandfather's murder trial continued, the defendant gently stroking his hair and speaking softly to him as the federal agent continued.

When the attorneys finished questioning Brown, A. J. Wismer took the stand and answered essentially the same questions with essentially the same answers. When the defense attorney asked Wismer what was the worst thing he saw on the Williams plantation, Wismer replied that the worst thing was "a negro carrying a gun."

The negro with a gun was Clyde Manning, of course.

When Judge Hutcheson asked for the next witness, Brand called out, "The state calls Clyde Manning!" The courtroom immediately erupted into a drone of excited whispering and mumbling. The courtroom doors opened and a deputy escorted Manning into the room. He walked quickly, his head held up but avoiding eye contact with anyone in the court. Williams stared at the young black man as he made his way to the stand.

Manning sat in the chair in the witness box to the judge's left, between two of the long windows and almost directly underneath a large chandelier. He looked down at his feet and held his hat in his hands as he waited for the questioning to begin.

Williams had seemed aloof and apathetic throughout the previous testimony by the federal agents but, with Manning on the stand, the defendant suddenly became alert. He began to talk frequently with the attorneys sitting at the table with him, and he leaned forward to look intently at Manning.

The judge reminded Manning that he had been sworn in earlier before being sequestered, and then Manning's attorney made a motion that the witness be reminded not to incriminate himself. Judge Hutcheson agreed and explained to Manning, "You do not have to answer questions that might incriminate you, unless you desire to do so." Manning nodded and said, "Yes sir."

The judge told the prosecution to proceed with questioning. As the courtroom became deathly silent, Howard stood up and began to address Manning in a gentle, nonthreatening tone. He began with simple questions, establishing that the witness had been employed on the Williams plantation for about thirteen years. Manning also named all the members of the Williams family and most of the black workers who had been on the farm.

The attorney asked Manning if he could drive a car, an important point because the defense intended to argue that Manning had driven some of the men to their deaths by himself and without the defendant's knowledge. Manning replied that he could not drive a car, although Mr. Johnny had let him try once.

"And what happened when you tried to drive the car?"

"I run right into Mr. Johnny's mailbox," Manning said.

Muffled laughter could be heard through the courtroom, and the defendant broke into a smile for the first time since the day's testimony began. The white farmer had been staring intently at Manning as he testified, and he now smiled and chuckled.

The prosecutors did not laugh. With the groundwork laid, Howard moved in for an important set of queries. From his position behind the prosecution's table, he leaned forward and placed both hands on the table.

He looked intently at Clyde Manning, and after a dramatic pause asked, "Do you know Lindsey Peterson?"

"I do," Manning replied.

"Where is Lindsey Peterson?"

Manning responded to the roll call of the dead with a calm, unquavering voice. The courtroom was absolutely silent as the attorney and the witness went through each name.

"He's dead."

"Now Clyde, where is Harry Price?"

"He's dead."

"And Charlie Chisolm?"

"He's dead, too."

"And Willie Givens?"

"He's dead."

"Fletcher Smith?"

"He's dead."

"The negro named Johnnie Williams?"

"Him too."

"Johnny Green?"

"He's dead."

"How about John Brown?"

"He's dead, too."

"Little Bit?"

"He's dead."

"Big John?"

"He's dead."

"And Willie Preston?"

"He's dead."

With the roll call finished, Howard paused to gather his thoughts, and many of the spectators began breathing again. The prosecutor then went back to his witness.

"Tell the jury how Lindsey Peterson died," he said.

"A weight was tied around his neck and he was thrown in Yellow River, from Allen's Bridge," Manning replied. "Willie Preston and Peterson was chained together with a trace chain, and Mr. Johnny told me and Charlie Chisolm to throw 'em in. We also weighted 'em down with a sack of rocks. They begged not to be killed, but Mr. Johnny said there wasn't a chance on earth. He made me and Charlie tie their hands together too.

"We pitched 'em over the railing of the bridge. Mr. Johnny helped us carry the sack of rocks from the automobile to the bridge. They was stubborn and a beggin' too, and me and Charlie rolled 'em over the banister of the bridge.

"We took Harry Price with us that night but Mr. Johnny decided not to drown him," Manning said, meaning that Price was not drowned at that same bridge.

The prosecutor then asked Manning why he helped throw the men in the river.

"Well, Mr. Johnny told me to."

At that point, the defense objected to the testimony involving any killings other than that of Lindsey Peterson, and the jury was sent out. Johnson cited the notorious case of Leo Frank, arguing that the U.S. Supreme Court's ruling on that case had implied that testimony in a murder case should be restricted only to information about the killing in question. Since he was referring to the court's conclusion that Frank's trial was tainted by testimony about Frank's supposed sexual perversions and wicked nature, the moment was surreal. An attorney for John S. Williams was trying to use the Supreme Court's criticism of bigotry and mob rule to protect his own client from damning testimony about how he had killed eleven men.

Howard fought back with an eloquent explanation that the trial was about much more than the one black victim named in the indictment. "This trial is about a man who plotted to kill negroes by the wholesale in order to cover up shady practices on his farm," he declared.

The defendant's wife could be heard sobbing loudly at that point, but Williams just yawned and looked up at the courtroom clock. He had spent most of the morning looking at Manning from his seat only ten feet away, his eyebrows raised and a look of bemused sarcasm on his face. The judge overruled the defense objection and then declared a dinner recess until 1:30 P.M.

When the court reconvened, more spectators had squeezed into the courtroom for what would surely be the most exciting testimony of the trial. Judge Hutcheson even made allowances. Since this was probably the one and only day that Manning would testify against Williams, the judge bent his rules and allowed spectators to stand in the rear. But he disapproved of the people who had crowded onto the windowsills for seating, and he ordered them to move. It took ten minutes for deputies to restore order.

Manning took the stand again and continued with his story.

"As soon as we threw Peterson and Preston in the Yellow River we left for South River. Mr. Johnny said we would take Harry Price there. When we got to South River, Mr. Johnny told Harry to get out of the car. We put weights on him, tied him, and threw him off the bridge.

"Price said, 'May God have mercy' as we threw him in. Price was chained around the neck and tied to a heavy sack of rocks. Mr. Johnny was right there with us when we drowned Price."

"Did he say anything?" the prosecutor asked.

"No sir, except he said to hurry up and have it over with."

Most of Manning's testimony, even the most gruesome and sorrowful portions, was presented with a steady, flat voice after his initial nervousness on the stand. He rarely became emotional or paused as if he were embarrassed to tell of his role in the killings. He answered the questions directly and quickly, with a disconcerting detachment. Spectators in the courtroom would later remark that Manning seemed to show little remorse or shame, even though he stated that he had not wanted to kill the men.

The witness went on to describe how Williams had become scared of what the black farm workers might say if he were charged with peonage.

"He said he wanted me to help get rid of them because it wouldn't do for them to testify in court, as they'd ruin him. I told him I didn't want to do it, and he said it was my neck or them other niggers'. He told me to decide which I thought the most of."

Manning then told the court about how Johnnie Williams was "knocked in the head" and buried on the farm. The defendant gave him an axe and told him to "brain Johnnie Williams," Manning testified. "He said, 'Clyde, if you don't kill that nigger, it'll be your neck.'

"I hit Johnnie one lick in the head with the flat side of the axe and he fell dead. Then I put him in one of the holes he had dug and covered him up." With the tale of Johnnie Williams's death, Manning lost his composure for the first time, choking up as he told of hitting his fellow worker with an axe. Howard paused to let Manning recover, then urged him to continue with the story.

The confessed killer went on with the story of repeated killings, explaining how he helped kill John Brown and Johnny Benson by chaining them and throwing them off a bridge. Then he moved on to the death of John Will Gaither, known as Big John.

"A nigger named Big John was next. Mr. Johnny made him dig a big hole and then made me brain him and put him in the hole. I got him with an axe and put him in the hole and covered him up.

"Johnny Green was killed with my same axe. Mr. Johnny told me to hit him.

"Willie Givens was killed the same way. Mr. Johnny watched me kill Green and Givens, and he helped me bury both of them. Charlie Chisolm was killed, too. Charlie had helped me and Mr. Johnny kill six niggers in all, but one Saturday night, Mr. Johnny told me and Charlie to come with him. We went to the Alcovy River in Mr. Johnny's car and Mr. Johnny made me tie Charlie. 'I've heard about your smart talk,' Mr. Johnny said, and we tied Chisolm and threw him in the river."

The last man killed was Fletcher Smith, Manning told the hushed court. "Mr. Johnny shot Fletcher in the head. He sent me for a spade and pick and showed me where to dig the hole to bury Fletcher."

The prosecutor paused before asking another question, and in the lull, Manning offered his own thoughts as his gaze fell to the floor. "They wasn't a bothering me," he said, referring to all the men he had killed. "Them boys wasn't doing nothing to me," he said slowly and so softly that everyone in the courtroom leaned forward to hear. "I didn't want to get 'em out of the way. But I had to."

Howard waited to see if Manning had anything else to add, but the witness had stopped talking and was just sitting there staring at the floor, lost in his own thoughts.

"Now, back to the killing in the field. Did the defendant have anything to say to you after you buried Fletcher?" the prosecutor asked.

"He told he me didn't want to hear nothing about this business," Manning replied in a soft mumble, never looking up.


The defense attorney's cross examination of Manning was short, apparently because Johnson had no interest in prompting Manning to tell the jury even more about the killings. Instead, the defense besieged the black man with questions about why he had begun to talk after first refusing to tell the authorities anything. Had he been beaten? Had he been threatened with drowning? Had he been offered a lighter sentence in return for lying about the defendant?

"I'm just telling the truth," Manning told the court. "I didn't talk at first because Mr. Johnny told me not to."

With that, Clyde Manning's testimony against Williams was finished. It had taken him six long hours to recount all of the killings.

Manning was followed on the witness stand by Lessie May Benton, a black cook on the Williams farm. She was visibly frightened and very nervous as the prosecutor questioned her in an attempt to corroborate some of Manning's testimony. She was asked when she had last seen Lindsey Peterson.

"It was one day at dinner," she stammered, referring to the South's midday meal. "I can't remember the exact time, but it was after the government officers had been there. Peterson came to the house early in the afternoon and got some shoes. I patched his overalls and he got a clean shirt, 'cause he said he was going home. He wanted to look good because he was going home. I didn't see him no more after that."

The cook's testimony ended the court proceedings for the day. As the defendant left the courtroom, John S. Williams's only comment to reporters was that Manning had been "well drilled."

That evening, Dr. Gus Williams continued to act as the family spokesman, telling reporters, "It's a lie and nobody knows it better than Manning himself." He predicted that the trial would take a major turn the next day when the defense would prove that Manning acted alone in killing all the missing black men.

"Manning knew the federal officials were after him. He knew they had the goods on him in his capture of Chapman, the negro who assaulted his wife. He brought the man back to the farm and the officers told him, according to the state's own testimony, that if my father was guilty of peonage, he was just as guilty.

"One of the agents told him that he had lied to them about the Chapman episode and Manning was afraid. They told him that they knew he was a 'boss' on the farms and he knew the negroes he had worked were the only ones who could testify against him."

Dr. Williams predicted that the next day's testimony would be even more astounding than Manning's. But that would be a hard promise to keep. Manning's testimony had gripped the courtroom observers like nothing ever seen before, and it would provide sensational reading in the next morning's newspaper.

The *Atlanta Constitution* called Wednesday "the greatest day of Georgia's greatest murder trial," declaring that Manning's testimony would be very difficult to overcome. And on the second day of the trial, the press again reported proudly that "perfect order prevailed."

# 11

# "Before God, I Am as Innocent as a Man Can Be"

The third day of John S. Williams's trial brought another packed courtroom. Having heard the black man's accusations, the crowd was eager to hear the white man's denial. After the courtroom had filled way past its capacity, the door opened and Williams entered with his wife, arm in arm.

All eyes fell upon them, and the crowd saw that on this day Mrs. Williams wore a heavy black veil. Her tired, frightened face could not be seen as the defendant gave her a hug before she took a seat with other family members. This image is essentially all that is known of Mrs. Williams; she was the ever faithful, proper wife of the respected farmer, always appearing in black to support her husband and remaining quiet, though highly visible. In accordance with the decorum of the period, she let her husband and her sons speak publicly for the family. There is no indication that she ever expressed any opinion on the matter publicly, other than her visible support for her husband, and no public record remains of her beyond these dramatic images.

Her husband then made his way to the defense table, stopping along the way to shake the hands of a few well-wishers. Williams smiled and traded quips with his supporters, but his demeanor was a bit more subdued and serious than it had been the day before. He must have been thinking ahead to what would happen in the next few hours, when he would take the stand and deny the charges against him.

Judge Hutcheson convened the court at 9:05 A.M., but before Williams could take the stand, prosecutors first had to call a couple more witnesses against him. The first witness called for the day was Rena Manning, Clyde's wife.

The twenty-three-year-old woman took the stand quickly, avoiding eye contact with anyone as she passed by. Her small frame made her look almost childlike as she sat in the big wooden chair and looked over the railing of the witness box. Howard had only a few questions for Rena, with the aim of confirming some points made the day earlier by her husband.

"Was there a night when the defendant came to your house and called out Clyde, Lindsey Peterson, Harry Price, and Willie Preston?"

"Yes sir," she replied. "He called 'em out and then I heard 'em drive away in Mr. Johnny's car."

"And when did they return?"

"Clyde come home that night about twelve o'clock," she said.

"Did Lindsey Peterson, Harry Price, or Willie Preston come back with him?"

"No sir. I never saw any of them again. They're dead now."

Howard said he was finished with the young woman, and defense attorney Johnson then took his turn. He challenged Rena Manning on her recollection of the evening, but she insisted that she did recall the events clearly. She denied that the federal agents had instructed her on what to say, and she denied the defense attorney's suggestion that she once left her husband after he beat her.

The next witness called was Sheriff B. L. Johnson of Newton County. He recalled the circumstances under which he found the first bodies, and then of Manning's original confession, trips to the rivers, and the tour of the "death farm" to identify more bodies.

"Manning identified the bodies as fast as they were discovered," the sheriff explained to the court.

"And was any attempt made by you or any other officers to force Manning to tell his story?" Howard asked.

"Absolutely not."

"Are you sure that he was not beaten, abused, or cursed in an effort to make him talk?"

"Clyde opened up and talked voluntarily."

After establishing a few more facts about how the bodies were discovered, Manning's statements about them, and the condition of the bodies when found, Howard thanked the sheriff for his time and dismissed him. With that, the prosecutor declared that the state was concluded with its evidence against John S. Williams.

He then walked back to the prosecutor's table, and asked an assistant for a drink of ice water. "I am uncomfortably dry," he said.

Soon after, the defense announced to the court that the only witness for the defense would be Williams himself. "At this time, I would like to ask Mr. Williams to take the stand," Johnson said, turning and gesturing with exaggerated politeness to the defendant. Williams stood up and quickly strode to the witness stand. He nodded politely to the judge before sitting down, but he was not sworn in because Georgia law allowed the defendant to give a statement not under oath and without any cross-examination by the prosecution. Clyde Manning watched from a seat behind the defense table but tried hard not to look Williams in the eye.

Williams settled his tall frame in the witness chair and crossed his legs. He adjusted his tie slightly and then nodded to his attorney. "I'm ready," he said. Johnson then asked the defendant, "Mr. Williams, could you please tell us your account of what happened on your farm and your involvement, if any?"

With that request, the court proceedings were in the hands of John S. Williams. He had an audience that was dying to hear whatever he had to say, anything he had to say. He paused for a moment, looking out across the courtroom at his wife and family, across the aisle at Clyde Manning, and then back to the attorney standing in front of him. Then he turned to focus on the jurors.

"Well, gentlemen. If I live to next October I will be fifty-five years old. I have a wife and twelve children, and I am a hard-working farmer. I have always taught my children to do right and have tried to do right myself. This is the first offense I have been charged with.

"I have a plantation in Jasper County, not near so large as newspaper reporters say, and what I have, it is under mortgage. Niggers, boll weevil, and low price of cotton just about cleaned me up. I have no idea if it was sold today I could pay my indebtedness. I am like most farmers I know, that at times I have bonded out and paid fines for niggers with actual agreement that they would stay there till their fines were paid, or till he was relieved from his bond, which in many instances I have rehired them after that and paid them wages just like I would any other nigger I would hire going through the country and which I thought I had a perfect right to do. I always treated all my niggers right. I could not have kept farmhands to do my work unless I dealt fairly and justly with them.

"There are two sides to every question," he continued, looking directly at the jury members sitting only a few feet away. "You have heard the other side of this case, and now I want to tell you mine. And I want to start by telling you that I am an innocent man.

"There are men in this courtroom who know me and who know I am not guilty of such charges as this. May God search my heart and bear witness that I am telling the whole truth," he said, looking from one juror to the next with an unrelenting stare. More than one juror could not withstand the farmer's penetrating eyes and glanced away.

"Clyde Manning was in charge of the niggers on the place. At times I had much trouble with Clyde. He was a hardheaded nigger. Once he tried to kill his wife and his brother, and another time he threatened his wife's life."

The defendant went on to recount his version of the visit by agents Wismer and Brown, explaining to the rapt audience that he had cooperated with the agents and showed them around the farm. Wismer and Brown watched from the second row behind the prosecutor, occasionally leaning toward each other to comment on the statement they were hearing.

"The federal officers told me they found conditions all right on my farm but one of them," pointing to agent Brown, "said I was technically guilty of peonage by bailing out niggers. I asked him what peonage was and told him I would watch myself closely in the future.

"In a few minutes after they left, Clyde Manning come up to me and says, 'Mr. Johnny, I don't think you treated me right.' He says, 'You made me out a liar right before them Revenue officers.' I says, 'How's that, Clyde?'

"He says, 'I denied everything about Gus running away and us going to catch him and bringing him back. You up and made me out a liar. Now I believe they're going to get me!' He says, 'They told me I was just as guilty of peonage as you.' That's why Clyde got so upset about that visit. Manning was a different nigger from that time on.

"Then in the morning I called all my hands—they were gathered around the wood pile up there. I says, 'Boys, all of you who want to leave, I want you to talk up.' I says, 'The federal officers have been up here and got everything stirred up. With what they say about peonage and all, if you want to stop right off you can do so. You can just go right off. You are at perfect liberty to do so.'

"Gentlemen, there is not a word of truth in Manning's statement. Goodness alive, if I had been guilty of these charges, I would have cleared out while the grand jury was investigating the finding of these bodies!"

Williams seemed at times confident of what he was saying, and at other moments stumbled as if he could not remember what he had planned to say. He gave some detailed accounts of how some of the men disappeared from his farm, with few taking him up on his generous offer to let the men go, give them a few dollars, and even drive them to the train station. He rambled on, bringing up different topics as they entered his mind. The gist of the statement was consistent, though. John S. Williams claimed to be an honest man who did his best to right any minor violation of the law, while Clyde Manning was a dangerous, angry, scheming negro.

"I know nothing about the way any of these niggers were killed. At the time Manning says I was with him and Charlie Chisolm on the way to drown Lindsey Peterson and Harry Price and Willie Preston, I was in bed in my home. I had been to Jackson that day to take a nigger home and I was mighty tired. I returned early and I wish to God my wife could take the stand and bear me out. The law don't allow her to speak, but she knows I'm an innocent man."

The defendant looked at his wife as he spoke of her confidence in him, but she could not look up at him. She looked downward and sobbed, with her hands cradling her face underneath her black veil.

"Lindsey Peterson, Willie Preston, and Harry Price came to my house one Saturday about the first of March and asked for five dollars apiece, saying they wanted to go back to their homes. I told them it was all right and gave them the money. They left my farm that night and I have never seen them since. I did not leave my home that night. I missed the niggers the next day and asked Manning where they were. He said they left for home the night before. I told him that was all right. As far as I know, Clyde was the last to see them boys, and they had fifteen dollars between 'em when I last saw 'em. I'm not going to say anything else, but fifteen dollars is a lot of money to a nigger.

"I later heard that some niggers had been found in the Yellow River. I heard a nigger named Eberhardt Crawford had said he could identify them as my niggers, so I went straight to see Crawford and he denied it. I went to see him because I was concerned, of course, and wanted to find out all I could about who those niggers were. If they were from my house I wanted to identify them and do everything I could to catch the one who did it.

"Don't you know I wouldn't have stayed around if I had been guilty? I knew nothing about it, I don't know nothing about it, and I just simply don't mean to leave and never expect to leave or anything when I am falsely accused of anything.

"Now I was subpoenaed up here on a Monday afternoon, as well as I recollect. I understand, after I was subpoenaed, that the officers went down there and arrested this nigger, Clyde Manning, and brought him to Covington. And they insisted on him telling something on me and that he positively denied knowing anything. And they took him to jail, so I was told, and threatened him, and abused him, and cussed him, and finally after the whole afternoon and most of the night. . . . Well, I don't know how they got it out of him or what they done to make him tell something on me, but I expect you could ask Mr. Hays right there, as he was the jailer.

"I was kept here till Friday and then sent to Atlanta, and I have been there in jail ever since. I have had no time to get up anything for my defense. I didn't know until this trial what that nigger was going to testify to, only what I could see from the newspaper talk. You know they have thrown hot air everywhere, nothing that they could say it looks they have failed to say. If I had been out and had time, I certainly could have got up things to contradict Clyde in these many things he has said."

Williams went on to recount how he had taken in the whole Manning family after Clyde's father was shot, only to find out that the Mannings were a wild bunch. Clyde was particularly bad, he recalled.

"He is a very cruel nigger to the niggers. The whole Manning crowd is. I done my best to help them along and I worked them and they worked several years on halves and worked on the Jack Leverett place. Clyde was so bad that Gladys asked me to move them out of Cracker Neck because the other niggers just could not put up with the way Clyde was imposing on them. And one time, Gladys went up to a little nigger church and got all shot up by a little nigger up there at the church. I paid his doctor's bill, or a part of it, and I owe a part of it yet. I have done everything in my power to help this nigger woman raise these chaps as well as I could.

"She has called me time and time again about them. They would fight each other and fight her and fight her sister here, and I have been reproving them and doing the best I could in getting them to go on and do right. I tried to get them to go on and do right but they were hardheaded, and Gladys and Clyde were much harder headed than the other named Jule.

"Clyde was a bad nigger. He run his wife off and then followed her over to where she was staying and some other niggers knocked a pistol out of his hand or he would have killed her. He was a bad nigger and they kept him from killing her. Now his wife, she's a pretty good nigger so far as niggers are concerned."

It is difficult to say whether there was any truth to Williams's claims that the whole Manning family, and Clyde in particular, were mean-spirited and difficult to get along with. Certainly it is conceivable that they were, and the fact that Manning killed eleven men with little resistance lends some shallow support to the idea. But there is no other evidence that Manning or his relatives were cruel. It is far more likely that Williams was just composing a story that he felt would best help him in the eyes of the jury. He was explaining to them that this Manning fellow was just what most whites expected from a young black man, while Williams, on the other hand, was a good citizen trying to help out the downtrodden.

"As far as the case I am on trial for now, I am absolutely innocent. I don't know anything about that at all. I didn't think anything about the niggers being gone till they found some, and I heard what Eberhardt said, and like any other man would have done, I just wanted to know if the niggers were from my place.

"Before God, I am as innocent as a man can be. That is about all I can say about this, I believe."


The testimony of John S. Williams ended the day's court proceedings for Thursday, April 8, 1921. With his confident declaration that he was as innocent as a man can be, the farmer had concluded his own short defense. His trial for the killing of eleven men came down to his word against Clyde Manning's. It was that simple. How could the jury possibly believe a black man over the word of John S. Williams?

On Friday, the closing arguments began in the morning session. The courtroom was once again packed to capacity, and on this day, local high school students were given the morning off to hear the closing arguments in this historic trial. After bringing the court to order with a rap of the gavel, Judge Hutcheson announced that he had a statement to make before proceeding with the state's closing arguments.

"I would like to take this opportunity to thank and congratulate Sheriff Johnson and his deputies for the splendid order that has been maintained during this trial," the judge said warmly, with a smile and a nod to the sheriff standing nearby. "This is a distinct compliment to you, Sheriff, and also to the entire citizenry of Newton County."

A light round of applause filled the courtroom, and Sheriff Johnson nodded in appreciation. At 9:20 A.M., the closing arguments in the murder trial of John S. Williams began with William M. Howard, the special prosecutor and former congressman.

"This is an unusual murder case," Howard said, walking slowly from the prosecutor's table toward the jury box. He continued to speak as he looked at the floor and then brought his eyes up to meet the jurors. The courtroom was completely silent and the jurors leaned forward to hear the soft-spoken attorney.

"This is a horrible case, and you are the exclusive judges of the evidence. This rapid, raving series of murders occurred within the space of two weeks, and John S. Williams, this man sitting in this courtroom right now, is the guilty party." Williams listened carefully, watching Howard as he spoke and scanning the jurors for any reaction. Williams wore a black mohair suit, silk shirt, soft collar, and blue tie. In his coat lapel was a white rose.

"These negroes caught the disease of death soon after they went from jails to the defendant's plantation. Let's approximate the date of the beginning of this diabolical scheme of self-destruction. From the testimony of federal agent G. W. Brown, the state has shown you the first murder occurred about February 24 and the last on March 8."

Howard then went on to slowly call out the names of the "victims of the scourge of death. Harry Price . . . Willie Preston . . . Lindsey Peterson . . ." After the list of eleven men, he declared that "this pestilence swept in its wake every negro who had come from stockades in cities." A summary of the testimony concerning the agents' visit to the farm followed, and then Howard addressed the defendant's own statement to the court.

The attorney held up a stenographic copy of the defendant's statement from the previous day, dangled his spectacles in the other hand, and began speaking slowly and deliberately to the jury.

"The motive for this series of horrors is plain and was borne out by the evidence," he said. "Williams told you Clyde Manning had a motive to do these things. Now if Clyde Manning had a motive, John S. Williams had an interest in it and was the primary beneficiary of that motive.

"Williams attacked Clyde Manning's statement and called it all a lie. Maybe Clyde is a liar, but even the biggest liar in the world tells the truth sometimes. A liar can say that the sun sets in the west, and it's the truth even if a liar does say it. This negro only tried to save his boss. That's all. He finally bared the awful story and his story remains unshaken. The evidence is clear that Williams was willing to kill eleven men to save himself from federal prosecution."

Even if the testimony of Clyde Manning were entirely forgotten, Howard said, the fact remained that Williams was the only person who had the motive to kill the men.

"The defense talks about lack of corroboration of Manning's statement. Well, let's see then. Do you men on the jury place any credence in the evidence given you by these government agents? By Rena Manning? By Clyde Freeman? By Sheriff Johnson and these other negroes? Has the defense impeached them? Has it even tried to impeach them? Where was Williams's evidence? What became of the witnesses his lawyers said he would introduce?

"He can't get away with it!" Howard shouted with exasperation. "It's murder, murder, MURDER!"

The crescendo having taken the breath from everyone in the courtroom, Howard paused a moment before making his final statements. He had been speaking for an hour and forty-five minutes.

"Gentlemen, the laws of this fair state have been outraged," the attorney said, once again speaking so softly that everyone was leaning forward to hear. "In the interest of justice, the state asks for a verdict of guilty without a recommendation for mercy. Make him pay with his life."

The court adjourned for lunch after Howard made his plea to execute John S. Williams. The state's closing argument had a devastating effect on the defendant's wife, who sobbed uncontrollably as the spectators filed out of the courtroom. Williams had lunch with his wife and children in the sheriff's office, and after talking for a while with each of his children, he asked them to leave. "Let me talk to Mama for a little while alone," he told them.

He shared a few moments with his wife, who still cried as her husband held her tightly. He assured her that he would be fine and that the trial was only an ordeal they must endure, an ordeal that would soon be over.

"We'll get through this, Mama. Don't you worry. It'll all be over soon."

After a long embrace, the defendant and his wife walked out of the sheriff's office and back into the courtroom. A newspaper reporter stopped them as they entered the courtroom and asked if he still expected an acquittal after the moving speech by Howard.

"Absolutely I do," he replied tersely.

"You know, even if they acquit you, the government's going to hold you for peonage," the reporter said, referring to a statement that morning by federal agent Vincent Hughes. The agent announced that federal authorities would arrest Williams "before he could leave the courthouse" if he were acquitted of the murder.

"Well, that's hard luck, ain't it?" Williams said with a grin.

He then escorted his wife back to her seat, with difficulty because the courtroom crowd had grown even larger than it was that morning. As he made his way back to his position at the defense table, he had a serious expression on his face but gave defense attorney Johnson a hearty slap on the back as he sat down next to him.

"It'll be over soon now," he said. "And I believe we whipped 'em! You've done some mighty fine work for me here."

"Thank you, John. I believe we *are* whipping 'em."

"Yes, I'm sure I'll come clear," John S. Williams said, more quietly and less assuredly. "I'll come clear."

As the court prepared to hear more of the closing arguments, the defendant's seven-year-old son Curtis got down off his mother's lap in the lower gallery and walked up to the defense table. When Williams noticed him standing at his knee, he reached down and picked him up. The little fellow was getting comfortable in the defendant's lap when Johnson stood up and said, "Your honor, it's just too hot in here!"

Indeed, the courtroom was sweltering from the heat of the hundreds of tightly packed spectators. Judge Hutcheson ordered everyone sitting in the windowsills to find other seats so that the air could circulate more freely. Once the commotion died down, Judge Hutcheson told Johnson that he could proceed with his closing argument. After taking a long drink of ice water and wiping his brow, the attorney stepped forward to the jury box and began to speak.

"I am going to make a long speech," he warned the jurors. "I want to do the defendant justice. I have nothing but the kindest feelings for Solicitor Brand. I love him. But confidentially, they haven't treated him right in this case. He worked hard for many nights and he knew this was a case in which he could make a great name for himself. But lo and behold, that Atlanta crowd took the case out of Brother Brand's hands. He hasn't had to work very hard since.

"And those private prosecutors thought so much of Clyde Manning's virtues that they employed counsels to protect him. That's a great condition of affairs: they pay their good money to prosecute Williams and shield the negro! William M. Howard is the ablest lawyer in Georgia and probably in the whole country. He has tried to stampede you into a verdict. If you allow yourselves to be stampeded, you may see the time you regret it.

"The Atlantans who guaranteed the fund to pay Howard had the right to do so, and they certainly had the right to hire another lawyer to uphold this *splendid* character, Clyde Manning. But if the fine people of Atlanta are suggesting that we in Newton County need to clean up our house, I would suggest that they need to clean up their own house first! It was 1906 when Atlanta experienced a terrible race riot that was denounced all over the country, but no one hired lawyers to punish the slayers of more than a hundred unfortunate negroes!

"The state has relied almost solely on the perjured testimony of Clyde Manning, a confessed liar and wholesale murderer. In the case on trial, which is for the murder of Lindsey Peterson, what has the state shown? Nothing."

Johnson recounted the visit to the farm by agents Wismer and Brown, arguing that they were there for more than a peonage investigation. They were there to stir up trouble by insinuating to the black workers that they weren't being treated fairly. "They put bad ideas in the heads of these negroes," he said. "They put more meanness in their minds in ten minutes than can be gotten out in ten years."

At that comment, the blacks packed into the courthouse gallery laughed in unison and Judge Hutcheson admonished them. The attorney then moved on to state bluntly the crux of the defense.

"Manning, this human butcher, told you with remarkable composure that he lied to the federal agents about everything they asked him. Gentlemen, can you doom a white man on the testimony of that kind of negro?"

Johnson looked back at his client, who was smiling. Williams gave a quick little nod of approval to the attorney.

"If that negro Manning's story were true, don't you know those other negroes on the farm would have fled from that plantation like people from a plague-stricken district? Manning's statement was an inveterate, unbelievable lie, and the state couldn't corroborate a word of it.

"Manning tells you that Williams took him and three other negroes in his car and drove up a public road early in the evening on Saturday. Then he threw these negroes off a bridge, right where he could be seen by anyone passing by," he continued, pausing and giving a look of bemused disbelief to the jury. "That's unthinkable! That's impossible, a ridiculous lie and you jurors know it. That's not a white man's conception of the way to destroy life. That's a negro's idea of how to kill somebody. Manning was the brains of the plot, and it was conceived for the purpose of committing robbery or inspired by fear over what the federal agents had told him.

"If Williams killed eleven negroes to hide peonage, he certainly would have killed the twelfth to cover up evidence of murder. He would have been the biggest idiot on earth to have let Manning live.

"According to the indictment here, Manning is an accomplice, a co-murderer. But according to his own testimony, he actually did the killings. But you can't go one step toward a conviction of Williams unless you have evidence connecting Williams with the crime and showing that he ordered the negro to take the lives of the negroes. You don't have that evidence."

The attorney then paused for a moment and walked to one end of the jury box. Looking down, he cocked his head to the side and looked at the jurors for a second before speaking. "Gentlemen, it is a well-known fact among scientists and travelers that in Africa there are peaceable tribes and there are fierce tribes, even *cannibals*, among the negroes. I am willing to venture that way back there, Clyde Manning's ancestors were cannibals. Manning's motive for this crime grew out of his natural inclination to butcher those like himself, plus the fact that these federal agents had sown the seeds of fear in his disturbed and cunning brain.

"If the killings happened at the hand of Mr. Williams, don't you know some of those negroes would have got wise and fled like rats from a sinking ship? And remember too, that none of Manning's family was touched. Remember that.

"Gentlemen, I have already pointed out the inherent improbability of this negro Manning's story," he continued, walking slowly from one end of the jury box to the other. "Let's consider it further. The state says Williams is an arch criminal. But don't you know that if Williams killed eleven negroes to hide peonage, he would have made out the dozen and got Manning too?

"It is unreasonable to believe that any man would kill eleven negroes when it had not even been established that he was guilty of peonage. No sensible man would commit such crimes. No one but a pluperfect fool would be guilty of such!

"Will you hang this white man on this negro's testimony? What will become of the negro? You know as well as I do that this negro will not be sentenced to die on the gallows. You know that he will probably be set free," Johnson said. That actually wasn't likely at all, but he was setting the scene for a tale of unequal prosecution.

"Suppose you consider this picture while you are on the subject. If you sentence Williams to hang, while his body lies moldering in the grave, Manning will be walking scot-free. What if you were to meet that negro on the road? Would you not look into his face and think what a tragic mistake you have made in hanging Williams on his evidence?"

Johnson took a few steps closer to the chief prosecutor and looked him in the eye. "And what *are* you planning to do with the black murderer, Mr. Brand? Are you planning to turn him loose to roam on Decatur Street in Atlanta? That's the kind of nigger Atlanta seems to want."

The defense attorney paused and turned back to the jury. The only sounds in the courtroom were the sobs of the defendant's wife and his youngest daughter, eight-year-old Tillie Williams, who had her head buried in her arms, leaning on the railing behind her father.

"Yes, listen to this child!" Johnson said, spinning quickly and pointing to the little girl. "Suppose you walked on and met this child whose life you had blighted. Would you not carry a burdened conscience to your grave? I ask, can you convict this man on that worthless negro's testimony? I don't believe you can. Remember, before you do anything today or tonight, remember that *you* will be called to the bar of a higher justice and *your* only plea will be that of mercy. Remember this man's children and his waiting wife."

Williams sat motionless as he listened to the final words in the plea for his life, and his eyes grew red and moist as Johnson spoke of his family. A tear rolled down his cheek, but he made no motion to wipe it away.

The charge to the jury took twenty minutes. Judge Hutcheson explained to the jurors that if they concluded that Manning acted under fear of death, there was no need for full corroboration of his testimony. If the jurors believed beyond a reasonable doubt that the defendant committed the murder with Manning, they must return a verdict of guilty. The guilty verdict could be accompanied by a recommendation of mercy. Without it, the jurors were automatically recommending the death penalty.

At four o'clock in the afternoon on Friday, April 8, 1921, the twelve jurors went to decide the fate of John S. Williams.

John S. Williams waited all evening with his family in the sheriff's office, ready to return to the courtroom and hear the jury's verdict. There was no news until midnight, when the jurors asked that the judge repeat his explanation of the charges and their obligations under the law. When the jurors once again retired to their room to continue discussing the case, a bailiff tried to convince them to retire for the night and resume deliberations the next morning. They refused, saying they felt they were close to a verdict. But at one o'clock Saturday morning, the jury finally ended deliberations and went to bed.

Early in the evening, Williams told his wife and children to go home and return the next morning. He returned to the Covington jail, where he did not sleep.

At nine the next morning, a Saturday, the court convened only for the purpose of hearing whether the jury had made any progress or needed any assistance. The jury had been brought in at eight, and, unknown to the judge, they decided to discuss the case some more and take a ballot while they waited to be called. When the jury was brought in, the courtroom was no more than half full. Williams sat with his attorney, and it was clear that neither had slept during the night. In stark contrast to each day of the trial, the defendant appeared somewhat disheveled, with an open collar and no tie. Judge Hutcheson asked who had been selected as the jury foreman and found that it was T. R. Starr, a farmer. When he rose, Judge Hutcheson asked if the jury had any questions before retiring for more deliberations.

"We don't have any questions, your honor," Starr said. "We have a verdict."

A small gasp arose from those assembled in the courtroom, and several reporters immediately dashed out of the courtroom to report the development. Williams showed no reaction to the news, but he leaned over to his attorney and asked that his family be summoned immediately.

"Well, we will hear the verdict once we have assembled all the necessary parties," Judge Hutcheson told the jurors. "Until that time, you are to take yourself to the jury room and speak to no one else. Is that understood?"

The jurors all nodded in agreement and filed out of the courtroom. The defendant remained in his seat at the defense table, and Judge Hutcheson went to his office. Over the next hour, the courtroom steadily filled to overflowing as word spread. The balcony was filled shoulder to shoulder with blacks eager to hear the outcome, but Clyde Manning was left sitting alone in his jail cell.

At 10:30 A.M. Judge Hutcheson returned and determined that all the necessary parties were present to hear the verdict. Mrs. Williams sat on the bench directly behind her husband, with her children surrounding her. As on the previous day, she wore a dark dress, a proper hat, and a black veil. She could be seen to wipe her eyes frequently under the veil and then return to holding the hands of the children on either side of her.

Williams's demeanor was markedly different as he sat waiting to hear whether his fellow farmers would sentence him to hang. He had put on a tie and added a flower to his lapel since his first appearance in court that morning, but he no longer sat with a look of complete confidence. He now sat and stared straight ahead, not acknowledging any of the well wishers who occasionally called out words of support. His eyes were vacant. The words of Judge Hutcheson suddenly caught his attention.

"Mr. Foreman, do you have a verdict?"

"Yes, Your Honor, we do."

"What is your verdict, Mr. Foreman?"

Starr looked down at the slip of paper he held in his hands, and with a slight tremble in his voice, read it aloud.

"We, the jury, find the defendant John S. Williams guilty and recommend mercy."

Mrs. Williams let out a chilling scream and began to sob openly, collapsing to her knees as her eldest children tried to support her. Little Tillie Williams also became hysterical and screamed for her father.

"My God, Daddy! I can't stand this!" she cried in a loud voice. "Daddy! Daddy!" Friends of the family moved forward to pick up Tillie and carry her outside as she screamed all the while for her father. Dr. Gus Williams managed to pick his mother up off the floor and help her to the door, making no effort to hide his own tears as he did so.

John S. Williams sat impassively, making no effort to turn toward his distraught family or even acknowledge that he heard their cries. He simply sat and stared straight ahead, seeing none of the hundreds of people staring at him. With the most vocal of the Williams family outside the courtroom and order restored, Judge Hutcheson moved on.

Taking the verdict form from the foreman, he took a moment to look it over and then read it aloud once again. "We, the jury, find the defendant John S. Williams guilty and recommend mercy." Then he added, "And the verdict is the sentence of the court." Judge Hutcheson asked Williams to rise.

"Mr. Williams, do you have anything to say to this court before I sentence you?" the judge asked. The state of Georgia looked at John S. Williams.

"I am innocent of this charge," he said, never directing his eyes to anyone. And that was all he said.

"Mr. Williams, having been found guilty of the murder of Lindsey Peterson by this court, it is my duty to sentence you to life imprisonment."

Another surge of sobbing arose from the Williams family, and a vigorous murmur arose in the rest of the courtroom. Reporters raced out, and the courtroom erupted in pandemonium, the spectators having held in their excitement as long as they could. Many shouted words of encouragement to the convicted murderer, but there were few words of anger directed to the jury, the judge, or anyone else. The black spectators in the balcony were much quieter, and more than a few decided that they should leave while the white crowd was still occupied in the courtroom. No one knew how the whites would respond to hearing a white man sentenced to prison on the word of a black man.

The sheriff quickly took the convicted murderer by the arm and escorted him out of the courtroom, down the staircase, and out to the waiting car that would take them to the Covington jail. There was a huge crowd of people to get through, but, unlike the previous days, they were not lining up to shake Williams's hand. This time, they were just watching as he passed by, fascinated by the sight of a white man going to prison for killing a black man. Once he was put in the car and driven away, the crowd dispersed and scattered to the town's lunch counters and sidewalk benches to discuss the verdict. The black spectators leaving by way of the courthouse's rear exit managed to get home without incident.

The trial of John S. Williams was over, and in many ways, so was a chapter of Georgia history.


The news of the conviction did not reach Clyde Manning for half an hour. He had heard the sheriff bringing Williams back from the courthouse, but no one had said anything to him about what had happened, so he assumed the jury was still deliberating. That Saturday was Clyde Manning's birthday, but he hadn't remembered any more than anyone else. When he saw Marvin Underwood, his attorney, approaching from down the hall, he wondered what was going on. Manning went to the bars of his cell and greeted Underwood.

"Mornin', Mr. Underwood," he said.

"Clyde, do you know what happened?"

"No sir, Mr. Underwood. Ain't nobody told me nothin'."

"He's guilty, Clyde. They sentenced him to life in prison."

"Is that right?" Clyde asked with astonishment. "They done sentenced Mr. Johnny to life in prison for killing them boys? Well, I'll be . . ."

"It was your testimony that did it, Clyde. Those jurors were convinced from the get go that Williams was guilty. You know what the jury foreman told me?"

"No sir. What'd he tell you?"

"Clyde, he said, 'All we argued about was whether to break his neck.'"

# 12

## "This Is the Spirit of Justice in Georgia"

A conviction for John S. Williams was surprising enough. But even more astounding was the fact that the jury never even came close to acquitting him. Soon after the verdict was reported, jurors told local reporters that the deliberations had resulted in a compromise between those who wanted to see the farmer swinging from a rope and those who thought he should spend the rest of his life in prison.

From the outset, the jurors agreed that they would reach a verdict no matter what. There would be no mistrial because they could not reach an agreement. The jurors understood quite clearly that the country was watching them at this moment, and it was up to them to show that the good people of Newton County could be trusted to render a verdict. But doing so was not easy. The jurors took so many ballots that they lost count, arguing each time whether to let Williams live. Each time, the results were the same: eight jurors wanted to hang Williams for his crimes and four wanted life imprisonment. Though no one on the jury argued that Williams was innocent, the four arguing for life imprisonment took a strong stance that it was just not permissible to hang a white man on the testimony of a black man. One of the four who wanted life imprisonment was described by others as "the hardest headed man in Newton County," someone known to stick with his position no matter what, so the jurors had little hope that there ever would be a unanimous decision to hang the gentleman farmer. After about eight hours of arguing and a few hours of sleep, the jurors who wanted to recommend a death sentence finally decided that they would have to give in and allow John S. Williams to live.

Though a death sentence would have been even more daring for the jury to hand down, their sentence of life imprisonment for Williams was nonetheless historic. Williams became the first Southern white man since 1877 to be convicted for the first-degree murder of a black man or woman. And he would be the last until another white man was convicted in 1966— forty-five years later.

The press did not underestimate the significance of the verdict. In most cases, the newspapers praised it as sound and necessary, but they also gave the distinct impression that Georgia was ready to move on now that this sordid affair had been dealt with. On the afternoon of the verdict, the editorial page of the *Atlanta Constitution* called the trial "one of the most remarkable criminal trials in the history of Georgia" and praised the "twelve good representative white citizens of Newton County" who served on the jury: "No more representative jury ever sat in a Georgia court than that before which this case was tried."

The paper praised the jury's determination to serve justice and said they had little choice but to reach a guilty verdict. "Every natural inclination of those twelve men would have led to an acquittal of the prisoner had there been a shadow of a doubt as to his guilt. The only conclusion to be drawn is that the evidence was so overwhelming as to justify no other verdict than that returned."

The newspaper went on to call for the elimination of "the damnable viciousness of mob law . . . grafting, official corruption, bunco steering, and all the other venal practices that have been uncovered here recently to an extent that has damned Georgia in the eyes of the world!

"Newton County has made a splendid start in that direction!"

The competing *Atlanta Journal* expressed similar sentiments, calling the verdict a message "that makes every thoughtful Georgian proud of his Commonwealth and heartened over her future, for it declares, not in words only, but by a profoundly impressive act, that the law shall be upheld, that wrongdoing shall be condemned, that righteous dealing must prevail, for even the lowliest and poorest of the land.

"This is the spirit of justice in Georgia. May it ever be lifted up."

The rest of the community responded similarly. The Atlanta Committee on Church Cooperation, a group representing all the Protestant churches in Atlanta, issued a statement saying that Christ was using the murder of eleven negroes in Jasper and Newton Counties "to wake Georgia to the need for justice to the negro, whom our fathers brought to this country, not because they desired to come, but to make the negro do our work. Slavery is gone, but the negro remains through no fault of his own. We owe justice to the negro as we owe it to no one else."

The committee went on to say that "the lawless element in certain sections of Georgia will learn, the committee believes, that the state will no longer tolerate the terrorizing of negroes in the country districts by night-riding mobs. No negro wrongdoer can escape the strong arm of the law. The mob and secret organizations are not needed to keep the negro in order."

And the Solicitor General of Jasper County told the *New York Times* that the conviction of Williams was only the beginning. "The law-abiding citizens will show to the world they believe in law enforcement. A number of citizens are involved and we have evidence sufficient to indict six or seven. We have the lynchers on the run and will clean up the county."

That was just what the readers of the *New York Times* wanted to hear about Jasper County, and it was just what Jasper County wanted them to think. Any other time, it might have sounded like an empty promise, but this wasn't just any time. John S. Williams had been convicted.

Meanwhile, the white farmer was maintaining his innocence, never deviating from his position during the trial that he had neither killed nor ordered anyone killed. Soon after the verdict, Williams told newspaper reporters at the Atlanta Tower lockup, "I am innocent and when I get my new trial I'll prove that what I say is true."

Williams and Clyde Manning had been taken back to the Atlanta prison after the end of Williams's trial. As Newton County deputies led Williams in, they came upon Clyde Manning, who had been posing in a hallway for newsreel photographers. The two men locked eyes for a moment, and then Manning rushed back to his cell. Williams chatted for a while, thanking the Newton County officers for their "many kindnesses during the trial."

Then a jailer pointed out to Williams that he had been convicted on Manning's twenty-seventh birthday.

"So they sent me up on Manning's birthday, eh?" Williams replied with a smile. And then he went on to assure everyone in attendance that his conviction was merely a momentary setback.

"They are persecuting an innocent man, but I'm not worried. I'll get a new trial and come clear next time. God will not allow this kind of injustice to be done. I will come clear when I get a new trial."

A new trial was Williams's only hope at that point, but with the overwhelming evidence presented against him at the first trial and the obvious inclination of the court and political system to see him convicted, an appeal was unlikely to succeed. Williams's attorneys dutifully pursued the appeal, but Judge Hutcheson denied it promptly on May 7, 1921. A few more futile court filings would be made in an attempt to free Williams, but it soon became clear that he was going to prison for the rest of his life.

Still, things could get worse for Williams and his family. Though Williams had been convicted of murdering Lindsey Peterson, it had become apparent that he was responsible for many more killings. A Jasper Country grand jury had been presented the evidence, including testimony by Clyde Manning, and then implored to do the right thing in issuing indictments, because "the good name of the white race rests on your actions." So only two days after he was convicted of murder in Newton County, the Jasper County grand jury issued a dozen murder indictments against John S. Williams, Manning, and the three adult Williams sons who had lived on the plantation—Huland, Marvin, and Leroy. A joint indictment charged John S. Williams and Manning with the murders of eight negroes thought to have disappeared after the visit of the federal agents, and Huland Williams was charged with murdering Blackstrap on the plantation in 1920. Leroy and Marvin Williams were indicted jointly for the killing of Iron Jaw in the summer of 1920. In addition, Marvin Williams was indicted for the murder of John Singleton, whose bones were said to be found in the pond where he had been thrown.

But before the Williams boys could be tried, they had to be found. They had been conspicuously absent during the trial of their father, and it was assumed that they had been told to leave the area to avoid arrest. The rumor around Jasper and Newton Counties was that the Williams boys were hiding out in Mexico. The governor promised to offer a reward if the fugitives did not show up soon.

News of the indictments was taken immediately to John S. Williams's wife, who was waiting in a store near the Monticello courthouse. She was standing in the modest storefront wearing a long fur coat and a black veil, with a small crowd of local residents waiting with her to hear the news. She burst into tears as her son, Dr. Gus Williams, told her that his brothers were to be tried for murder.

As soon as the Williams verdict had been returned, Governor Hugh Dorsey was up on his soapbox declaring that the state of Georgia had been vindicated by the righteous action of twelve men in Newton County. Not one to miss the momentum of the hour, Dorsey acted quickly. About a month after Williams's trial and just before the trial of Clyde Manning was to begin, Dorsey issued his landmark anti-peonage proclamation, "A Statement from Governor Hugh M. Dorsey as to the Negro in Georgia." The statement was presented to a conference of community leaders gathered to address racial problems in Georgia, and it was considered shocking for any prominent Southern politician to take such a stand in defense of blacks. It would come to be considered Dorsey's most significant, and most controversial, contribution during his two terms as governor of Georgia.

In the statement, Dorsey cited the problems of "the negro lynched, the negro held in peonage, the negro driven out by organized lawlessness." In some Georgia counties, "the negro is being driven out as though he were a wild beast. In others he is being held as a slave," Dorsey wrote.

The governor wrote an extensive admission that peonage existed in Georgia, and that there was no safe haven. He provided many examples, including instances in which men worked as slaves had run away from rural farms and sought help in Atlanta only to be arrested by Atlanta police and returned to their keepers. In another instance, a farmer offered to sell a black man to another farm for fifty-five dollars. These accounts of peonage included several incidents from the Williams plantation.

After making a remarkable confession that the white people of Georgia were guilty of systematic abuse of blacks, Dorsey went on to suggest "the remedy," which would include "publicity, namely the careful gathering and investigation by Georgians, and not by outsiders, of facts as to the treatment of the negro throughout the State and the publication of these facts to the people of Georgia." He also advocated compulsory education for both races, an organized campaign by churches to promote mutual respect, and the formation of local committees of black and white leaders to address problems. And he called for financial penalties upon any county in which a lynching occurred, prompt state investigations of lynchings, the formation of a state constabulary that could be sent into any community to quell riots, and statewide juries to hear charges against those accused of lynching.

But most significantly, Dorsey called for the repeal of Georgia Code Section 716, which addressed the "failure to perform the services so contracted for, or failure to return the money so advanced with interest thereon at the time said labor was to be performed." The wording of that law was the linchpin to a charge of "common cheat and swindler"—the charge most commonly used to return a peon to the farmer from whom he had run away. The farmer would claim that the black man had entered a contract to work off a debt, usually a fine from a previous arrest, and that the man had run away before completing the agreement; the police would then threaten to arrest the man if he did not return to the farm.

The Georgia legislature followed Dorsey's advice and repealed the law. Other portions of "the remedy" also were approved. As they had with the Williams verdict, much of the white community in Georgia publicly supported Dorsey's initiative to rid the state of peonage, even if privately they may have grumbled that the governor was moving too fast and too soon. Notable among public supporters was Dr. C. B. Wilmer, the Atlanta reverend and *Atlanta Journal Magazine* columnist who helped fund Manning's defense. He wrote a long column in support of the Dorsey's remedy, noting that "so long as employers are permitted to compel unwilling labor, we have a situation which is equivalent to imprisonment for debt, a thing that the civilized world has long ago agreed to abandon."

But others were not at all pleased with Dorsey's public confession of the state's racial sins, and sometimes that displeasure was made public.

The governor's anti-peonage statements, and the Atlanta Committee on Church Cooperation, were assaulted with fire and brimstone by the Reverend Caleb A. Ridley, pastor of Central Baptist Church in Atlanta, in a Sunday sermon in May. The pastor charged that Governor Dorsey was coddling blacks because he wanted to "open a New York office, and in order to feather his own nest up there he is willing to slander the people and the state that made him governor."

Ridley went on to proclaim that "this is a white man's country, was yesterday, is today, and will be forever, and these eloquent divines and philanthropists are doing more harm with their propaganda than all the lynchings and peonage of the years." The pastor claimed that Dorsey had given no indication of his eagerness to defend the negro during his campaign for governor—a fair assessment—so he now was betraying those who voted for him. "It is evident to sensible men everywhere that there is a nigger in the wood pile," the pastor called from his pulpit, using an aphorism that suggests trickery and deceit—a traitor among us.

Once he got warmed up, the pastor went on to decry the recent anti-peonage initiatives and the Williams conviction as a portent of very bad things to come for the white race. His comments suggest that Ridley had a clear and accurate vision of the future in Atlanta, and he didn't like what he saw.

"It is a known fact, easily established, that right in the very heart of Atlanta there is a church in which the whites and the blacks mix and mingle together, both in work and in worship. The building is a three-story affair, and up to a while ago, and I presume as yet, used in the following fashion: the first floor as a church, the second floor as a school for negroes taught by white women, and the third floor as a dance hall where the inmates go for recreation.

"These negroes are taught social equality, both by precept and example. No wonder that negro men appearing some months ago before the board of education spoke of Atlanta as sleeping over a smoldering volcano and no wonder these same negro men tell your school board that they are not asking for favors, but demanding their rights.

"So sure as the sun shines, if this race-loving committee and our beloved governor keep up their pamphlet writing, card publishing, and hobnobbing propaganda—and a few soft-brained church people keep mixing with and mollycoddling negroes—conditions will grow worse and worse until our mistakes will cost us more to repair than we want to pay.

"I count myself a most loyal friend of the negro race, but I am a white man. Almighty God set boundary lines to our cooperation that I will not and the negro must not pass."

For the pastor, Georgia was moving much too quickly to accommodate the supposed rights of negroes, and the governor's anti-peonage booklet was the best example of how big a mistake that was. But for others, the booklet was less threatening and less impressive.

Black civil rights activists in the North, for instance, derided Dorsey's anti-peonage campaign as mostly a self-serving public relations ploy. They also did not get overly excited by Williams's conviction.

"John Williams will not suffer measurably for the crimes he has committed against innocent and defenseless negroes on his peonage farm," black activists wrote in the *Messenger*, a New York publication, soon after the Williams trial. "The next governor of Georgia is not unlikely to pardon this man to clear the fair name of Georgia of the stigma of a white man's being held in prison upon the word of a mere negro. Nor are the belated statements of Governor Dorsey on the mistreatment of negroes to be taken for anything save a spectacular and sensational play to the public gallery.

"In this connection, too, it is interesting to note that he has but a few more days in office. It is also rumored that he plans to practice law in New York City. It is no amateurish piece of strategy that one employs a great public office to advertise himself favorably in a section in which he hopes to make his future abode. Besides, he gets credit for being the champion of the oppressed, although it is at the eleventh hour, when he can do the oppressed little good in relieving them of their oppression. It is highly important, today, that negroes and all other oppressed peoples 'beware of the Greeks bearing gifts, lest they receive a Trojan horse.'"

Clyde Manning's trial for the murder of Lindsey Peterson was scheduled to begin in Covington on May 30, 1921. A few days earlier, his attorney issued a statement declaring that Manning would plead not guilty, despite his detailed confession describing how he had killed Peterson and the other men. Manning would beg mercy and try to convince the jurors that he had no choice but to do what John Williams said. Everyone knew it would be a difficult argument to make. Perhaps it could be made successfully for the killing of one man, but eleven? The implied criticism was that the extent of the murders should have prompted Manning to refuse Williams's orders, but there was no public commentary suggesting exactly what he should have done. That is telling, suggesting that the public could not accept Manning's actions but still could not offer a realistic alternative.

To support his contention that Mr. Johnny's directions just could not be disobeyed, Manning would depend on corroborating testimony from other blacks on the plantation. Many of them had been detained during the Williams investigation and remained in the Atlanta Tower as they waited to testify in Manning's trial. The value of their testimony was uncertain, however, even if they backed up all of Manning's claims that Williams would kill a man for disobedience. The problem was that these were black witnesses. In the eyes of the public, that automatically diminished the value of their testimony.

A clue to the public sentiment regarding these witnesses can be found in a front page article that appeared in the *Atlanta Constitution* two weeks before the Manning trial was to begin. Headlined "Negroes Living on Fat of Land and Getting Paid," the condescending article described a scene in which lazy blacks were living a luxurious life, courtesy of the taxpayers.

The article described them as "singing 'Swing Low, Sweet Chariot' at intervals, partaking regularly of goodly portions of side meat and corn pone and other cotton field delicacies and enjoying a long, sweet rest, free from the arduous duties of 'working in the new ground,' while the United States of America pays them $1 a day each." The dollar per day was described as "sudden riches" for the blacks.

This paranoid delusion has a rich history in the South and elsewhere, a typical response from those in power who feel the need to see evil intent in the innocuous actions of those already oppressed. In this case, perhaps the accusation was a subconscious response to the first public stirrings of respect or sympathy for those whose subjugation was necessary for white superiority. By ridiculing the blacks as greedy, lazy, and ungrateful, the white community could assure themselves that their previous treatment of them was justified and should continue. If Georgians felt any sympathy or collective guilt for the way blacks had been treated on the Williams plantation, it would be reassuring to think that the witnesses were now taking advantage of the taxpayers.

Oddly enough, there was some truth to the article. Compared to what they had left on the Williams plantation, the witnesses were indeed living well while in custody. And as long as they were being held as witnesses, no white farmer could come to the jail and take them away to work.

# 13

## "There Was Fear Among the Hands"

Clyde Manning's trial began on Monday, May 30, in the same Covington courthouse where he had testified against John S. Williams. Like his former boss, Manning was on trial for the murder of Lindsey Peterson.

Manning was brought from prison under heavy guard, wearing overalls and a light blue shirt. He appeared calm and collected as he entered the courtroom and took a seat directly behind his lead defense attorney, E. Marvin Underwood. Even aside from the sensational crimes he was charged with, Manning's trial was unusual in the way he was being defended. Here was a black man who had admitted to eleven murders, yet his murder trial was to be much more than a perfunctory proceeding required before the judge could sentence him to death. He was not cajoled, tricked, or beaten in order to get a guilty plea, and it appeared that his trial would involve some reasonable attempt by his attorneys to show that there was justification to find him not guilty. For a black man in a rural Georgia courtroom, this was unheard of.

Far from being left adrift in the white man's court system, Manning had excellent legal representation. Underwood was the same young man who had been questioned in the Williams trial as one of his "secret prosecutors." That trial had made it public knowledge that Underwood had been hired by a number of wealthy Atlantans to defend Manning and that Governor Dorsey was involved with organizing that support. In addition, local Covington judge A. D. Meadows had agreed to assist Underwood in the defense.

The prosecution facing Manning was much the same team that faced Williams. Newton County Solicitor General A. M. Brand would again lead the charge to put away the killers from the "death farm," assisted by William Howard of Atlanta. The defense team that had failed to keep Williams out of prison also announced that they would attend Manning's trial, ostensibly as part of their maneuvering to appeal the white farmer's conviction. They were eager to hear how Manning, the primary witness against Williams, would defend himself against the same killing that had sent their client to prison.

Manning would be tried before the same judge who had sentenced Williams to prison, Judge John B. Hutcheson of the Stone Mountain circuit. After some preliminary tasks were taken care of that Monday morning, Judge Hutcheson proceeded with jury selection. The jury, of course, also would be very much like the one that Williams faced. It would be made up of local white men. There was no thought of taking the phrase "jury of his peers" seriously and actually including poor blacks.

During the jury selection, the defense attorneys asked the judge to require that Solicitor Brand question all the potential jurors concerning their relationship to Williams. The convicted farmer was known to have many relatives in Newton County, and the defense argued that it would be improper to allow any of his relatives to serve on a jury that would be asked to believe that Williams forced Manning to commit the murders of which he was accused. Brand resisted the requirement, arguing that there was no reason a relative of Williams could not fairly decide the fate of Manning.

The judge agreed with the defense counsel and required that Brand avoid any potential juror who was related to Williams. By 10:45 A.M. the jury was complete. It consisted of eight white farmers, a white contractor, a white manufacturer, a white bus line operator, and a white bookkeeper—not one of whom had any idea what it meant to have his life utterly controlled by someone like John S. Williams.

There had been some discussion with the judge about how long the trial might last and how that might affect practical arrangements for the jurors.

Attorneys for both sides agreed that the trial of a black man accused of murder would not last long. The jury could probably retire to consider a verdict by Tuesday afternoon, they predicted. That would be scarcely a day and a half of court proceedings, including all the preliminaries before the first witness took the stand. Even those responsible for defending Manning knew that there was not a great deal to say about the case. With most of the facts known and not contested, the trial would hinge almost entirely on Manning's explanation for *why* he had done what he admitted to doing. Once those words were spoken, it would merely be a matter of waiting to see if the jury of white men believed him—or even understood him.

Despite the strong defense team, the public perception was that Manning did not have much of a chance of escaping the hangman's noose. With support from wealthy Atlantans and an undeniably competent, determined defense, perhaps a poor black man could escape conviction and execution for a less sensational crime, for maybe one murder in which the facts were not so clearly established and to which the defendant had not confessed. But Manning faced a formidable challenge when he pleaded not guilty to the murder of Lindsey Peterson, and by assumption, the other ten murders connected to the Williams plantation. The observers who had watched the Williams trial so keenly drifted away when it came time to try Manning for the same crimes. They kept an eye on the trial but didn't bother to watch it with equal intensity. After all, the big question—could a white, prosperous farmer be convicted of murder solely on the testimony of a black man?—had been answered already. Even though it concerned the same gruesome events, this trial promised only to answer a much more mundane question—could a black man be found guilty of the eleven murders he had admitted to in great detail? Of course he could. Would he be executed? Very likely.

Accordingly, the atmosphere surrounding Manning's trial was more subdued than it had been for Williams's. There was not such a circus, with people squeezing into the courtroom and hanging on every word. Not that the trial was a nonevent. It was attended regularly by newspaper reporters and interested residents. At any other time it would have been the biggest thing to happen in Covington in years.

There were a number of empty seats available in the lower part of the courtroom when the jury selection had been completed and the trial was about to proceed. But in the gallery upstairs, where blacks were required to sit, there was standing room only. For the black residents of Newton and Jasper Counties, there was more at stake here than could be seen by the whites. Could Clyde Manning convince a room full of white people that he was forced to kill eleven times? The blacks were not uniformly convinced that Manning should be believed because, just like everyone else, they found it difficult to reconcile Manning's calm, matter-of-fact presentation and his lack of emotion with the magnitude of the killings. But they at least realized that there was something to his explanation that he was in fear for his life when Williams gave him an order. They must have been eager to hear what he had to say, to hear whether this calm, composed young man could somehow be excused for brutally killing eleven of his fellows who were trapped in a life that black Southerners could understand, one that they had all experienced themselves to some degree.

Manning had pleaded not guilty to killing Lindsey Peterson, but his attorneys had made it clear in statements to the press and others that he had no intention of denying that he had played a key role in the murder. After all, Manning had been admitting to the killings practically nonstop since the day he first opened his mouth and talked to the authorities. Instead, Manning would claim that he had been forced to kill Peterson and the other men because Williams had threatened to kill him if he did not comply. This was a legitimate legal defense. If he could convince the jury—a big if— Manning conceivably could be found not guilty for the murders that he openly and repeatedly admitted.

Since both sides agreed on many of the facts concerning the killings, there was no need to provide a blow-by-blow account. Instead, both sides merely needed to establish some basic facts and then move on to providing, and refuting, Manning's motivation for what he did. The state started things off slowly, first calling Carl Wheeler and Dr. C. T. Hardeman to explain how the bodies of Peterson and Preston had been found in the river and to describe how they were tied together and weighted down. Manning's attorneys did not cross-examine them. Sheriff B. L. Johnson of Newton County was next on the stand, testifying that Manning had identified the bodies.

"Manning said he and Charlie Chisolm helped John S. Williams throw the men off the bridge," the sheriff testified. Johnson began to elaborate on what Manning had said about killing many other men, but

Underwood objected and argued that any further confession from Manning was inadmissible.

"We are not undertaking to conceal any of the facts, and we are willing for anything material to go in, but unless the state intends to show that these murders were part of a set scheme of destruction designed by this defendant, I think evidence of other murders should be excluded," he said.

For the prosecution team, Howard replied that, yes, the state did indeed intend to prove that Manning was a willing participant in a scheme to hide the evidence of peonage, and that he had a personal interest in suppressing evidence of peonage on the Williams plantation. Judge Hutcheson ruled that the sheriff could continue with his recounting of Manning's confession.

The sheriff told the entire story of the killings as the prosecutor prompted him with pertinent questions, basing his testimony on Manning's confession. After recounting Manning's explanation for the eleven killings, the sheriff was asked by Brand about the apparent motivation.

"How did he tell you it came about? What was the reason or the occasion for it?" he asked the witness. This, after all, was the whole point of Manning's defense.

"He said Mr. Johnny would just tell him they had to destroy those niggers, they had to be done away with, and that night they would make preparations and carry them out and put them away," the sheriff said.

"Did he tell you the part he acted and the part Charlie Chisolm acted in throwing these men in the river there?"

"Yes, he said they stopped and tied them and threw them in."

After questioning the sheriff more about what Manning had said regarding his involvement in the killings, Brand asked that Manning's entire testimony from the Williams trial be entered into evidence for the jury to hear. The sheriff then would be asked to confirm that Manning's sworn testimony in the Williams trial was essentially the same as his earlier confession.

For nearly an hour, Brand read Manning's previous testimony aloud. Manning's words described the entire string of killings to the jury now deciding his fate, including the many times in which he clearly admitted having struck the axe blows that killed the men or shoving terrified men off bridges in the middle of the night with his own hands.

And with that, the courtroom once again was filled with vivid images of men dying at the hands of Clyde Manning. The defendant sat quietly and listened to the sheriff recount his participation in the killings, showing no more emotion than the observers sitting behind him.

Now that the prosecution had once again drawn all eyes to the blood on Manning's hands, it was up to the defense to start arguing that Manning was a victim, not a murderer. Attorney Underwood stood up and moved forward to cross-examine Sheriff Johnson, turning to face the jury as he spoke.

"You stated in the conversations to which you testified in the last trial that 'Manning told about the various details I have testified about. He stated Mr. John S. Williams was present at each and every occasion when the deaths occurred.'"

"Yes, sir," Johnson answered.

"You further testified that Clyde Manning stated he participated in the manner of the deaths I have described, in each one of those cases, because he said he was afraid not to do so, he was afraid Mr. Williams would kill him?"

"Yes, sir, I testified to that."

"And that is true, is it?"

"Yes, sir, that is true."

"That on each and every time he made a statement to any of this killing, he said he did it on account of fear of his life from Mr. John S. Williams?"

"Yes, sir. He always said that."

"And that was the sole reason he killed them?"

"That is what he told us."

The attorney then asked if Manning had been willing to tell the entire story, and whether Manning's statements had been consistent since he began talking to the authorities. The sheriff replied that Manning's confession had been thorough and completely consistent. After establishing that Manning had been in the sheriff's custody since his initial arrest and had not been advised by any attorney before his confession, the defense attorney repeated the question several more times: Did Manning say he killed the men because he was afraid of Williams? Each time the question was worded slightly differently, but the sheriff's answer was always yes.

"You stated then, as I believe you state now, Mr. Sheriff, that the confession was entirely voluntary?"

"It was. Yes, sir."

"And that the only inducement for it made to Clyde, any inducement whatsoever that was made, was that you would protect him?"

"Yes, sir."

"He was afraid to tell it?"

"Yes, sir."

"Afraid to tell it and be out of your protection?"

"Yes, sir. He didn't want to tell it and go back to Jasper County."

"Because he was afraid of the Williamses?"

"Yes, sir."

Sheriff Johnson ended his testimony by telling the jury that Manning had given him no trouble whatsoever and was perhaps the best prisoner he had ever had.

The next witness to be called was Agent A. J. Wismer of the Bureau of Investigation. (His former partner, George W. Brown, was no longer with the government by the time Manning went on trial.) The prosecution called Wismer to the stand, apparently in hope of establishing that Manning had been frightened by comments from the federal agents suggesting that he was as guilty of peonage as Williams was. That would help establish a motive for Manning to willingly participate in the killings, rather than doing it reluctantly because Williams had threatened to kill him.

Brand began by asking Wismer to explain how he and his partner came to investigate the Williams plantation. Wismer explained that they had received tips from two men who had worked there, and then the attorney asked him to recount what they found when they visited the farm.

"When we got there, Mr. John S. Williams was not at home. We saw Clyde Manning there, John Brown, and Johnnie Williams. We talked to Clyde Manning. We were there a half hour to three-quarters of an hour to my best judgment before Mr. Williams arrived. I asked Clyde Manning about whether he acted as guard over the hands on the place and locked them up at night and so forth, as had been reported to us, and also asked him about whether or not he had gone and helped to catch one Gus Chapman and return him to the place. He denied all about it to us. He denied all of it, and he denied helping catch Gus Chapman."

Wismer recalled that he and his partner had spoken to a number of different black workers, but he couldn't always recall exactly which ones because they had made no notes when they got no information from the witness. And that was the case in almost every conversation.

But he did recall the conversation in which Brown caught Manning in a lie. He recounted for the jury how Manning had denied any knowledge about or participation in hunting down Gus Chapman, only to have Williams admit that he and Manning had indeed recaptured Chapman after his first escape attempt.

"Mr. Brown turned around to Clyde and said, 'You just told me a lie, didn't you?' Clyde I don't believe ever answered one way or another. He never answered that remark made to him. I don't recollect that Clyde said anything to Mr. Williams then either."

Wismer described how he and his partner had encountered many black workers while Williams showed them around the plantation, but that almost every single one refused to provide any information.

"As I recollect, the only information I got while I was on the place that day that had any bearing on the entire situation by anyone, I got from Johnnie Williams. He was the only negro on the place that told anything."

That statement was a bit of a surprise to everyone. There had been nothing so far in either trial indicating that Johnnie Williams had divulged any incriminating information to the federal agents. What sort of information he passed on may never be known, because it was never documented in the agents' reports and it was never discussed in detail at either trial. The comment must have involved the death of Blackstrap, because after the agents left, Manning recalled that the farmer had angrily asked Johnnie Williams what he had said about Blackstrap. The frightened man denied saying anything, but John S. Williams did not believe him and made sure he was the first to die. Whatever he said that led to him getting hit in the head with an axe, chances are good that it was merely a superficial comment that helped to confirm some of the information provided by the escaped informants. Perhaps the information even came from Manning. Whatever the source, Williams's information was correct, according to Wismer's testimony.

When Brand was finished with the agent, Underwood stepped up to cross-examine him. He began by asking if Wismer was familiar with the confession entered by Manning. Wismer replied that he was very familiar with Manning's confessions because he had been present at each meeting in which the defendant had confessed. The agent confirmed the gist of Manning's statements, that he had killed the men because Williams made it clear that was the only way to save his own life. He quoted Manning's recollection of Williams telling him "it's your neck or theirs, whichever you think the most of."

Wismer pointed out that Manning always coupled his admissions with the statement that he feared death at Williams's hands. "I have never heard him make any statement with reference to admissions that was not coupled with that assertion," he said.

That was an extremely important point to make with the jury. They understood clearly by now that Manning had admitted to the killings and

156

would, in fact, confess to them at the drop of a hat. But now the jury also heard that those admissions were always, not sometimes and not just in front of a jury, coupled with an explanation that he had committed the murders because he feared for his own life. It also helped that the testimony came from a federal agent, making it seem reliable because the agent was more or less on the prosecution's side.

What the jury may not have considered is whether Wismer and his partner felt just a bit of remorse over the way their investigation had unwittingly caused the deaths of eleven men, and perhaps they even saw it as causing an unbelievable ordeal for Manning. If so, it seems likely that Wismer would have welcomed the chance to bolster Manning's defense that he was an unwilling accomplice. His testimony implies that he never hesitated when given the chance to confirm Manning's position that the Williams plantation was a fearful place where such horrible acts could be compelled from a man.

Wismer explained that he had talked to all of the material witnesses taken from the Williams plantation and that he had heard many stories of terror, torture, and murder occurring long before he and Brown visited. He recounted stories of whippings, shootings, beatings, and many deaths said to have occurred over the years. He described how dogs were kept to run down escaped men, and he described in great detail the two houses in which men and women were locked up at night. He described how Blackstrap, whose real name was Nathaniel Wade, was whipped severely while lying across a gasoline barrel and how Huland Williams had instructed Charlie Chisolm to kill him with a pistol.

"I found out there was fear among the hands on the other farms too," he said, referring to the Williams sons' farms on the same plantation. "One negro told me—I don't remember whether it was a negro on the farm then or not—told me that he came to the Williams plantation from the stockade and Leroy Williams told him he had killed four negroes the day before and that they talked about killing negroes there on the place. They told me about the deaths of the negroes Will Napier, Long John or Iron Jaw, and Blackstrap. Some of them that had heard about them didn't know the facts themselves of their own knowledge, but all of them knew of the report and some of them knew of the killings to their own knowledge. I found out also about the whippings and beatings. I think without exception they all admitted having been whipped."

"Clyde Manning here told us about these things too," Wismer said, gesturing toward Manning with a nod of the head. "He told us about it before he had counsel or anyone to advise him. He told us before he had the opportunity of talking with any other negroes on the place."

Satisfied with Wismer's endorsement of Manning's reliability, Underwood wanted to underscore a few more points before letting the agent leave the stand.

"Did the negroes on the place seem to be in great fear of Williams and his sons?" the defense attorney asked.

"Very much so," the agent replied.

"In your opinion, if Williams ordered one or all of them to do a thing, would they do it?"

Brand objected to the question, and Underwood countered that "the mental attitude of Manning and other negroes on the farm is very important."

Judge Hutcheson decided not to rule on the objection right away. Instead, he recessed the court for lunch until 1:45 P.M. When court resumed, the judge questioned the federal agent before bringing the jury back in, asking whether the material witnesses removed from the farm had expressed any fear of going back after testifying. They had expressed a great deal of fear, Wismer replied.

Satisfied that the workers' fear was relevant to Mannings' defense, the judge ruled in favor of the defense and told Underwood he could proceed with that line of questioning. The jury was brought back to the courtroom. Manning had taken a seat next to Underwood at the defense table, leaning forward and resting his chin on his hands as he listened to the proceedings.

"What manifestations did the blacks express?" he asked. Brand again objected to the line of questioning, but he was quickly overruled.

"They told me about negroes being whipped and killed before them on the plantations," Wismer replied. "Clyde Manning knew about the alleged killing of four negroes other than the eleven, and he told me about seeing Blackstrap shot."

"And did you ever ask the defendant why he didn't just leave the Williams plantation if things were as bad as all that?"

"Yes, I asked him that. He said that he never attempted to escape because he was in calling distance of Mr. Williams and that Mr. Williams often came to see him in the middle of the night. He also told me about the dogs that were kept on the place for running down negroes, and he said that if he was caught trying to escape, Mr. Williams would kill him."

Underwood thanked Agent Wismer for his testimony and told the judge that he had no further questions. Brand then rose from his seat and declared, "Your honor, the state rests."

The defense attorney then asked the judge to send the jury out so that he could register an objection. Once the jury was away, Underwood again objected to the state's admission of any evidence relating to the ten other murders that Manning had confessed to. Manning was charged only with the murder of a single man, Underwood argued, and therefore all evidence should be limited to that one murder.

"These murders have not been connected by the state," he argued. "The admission of this evidence will not show any scheme or motive for the crimes."

Judge Hutcheson asked the prosecution for a response, and Howard rose to deliver it.

"The killing of these negroes gives to legal history its most gruesome and horrible crimes. Yet they furnish a perfect example of the admissibility of independent crimes so connected as to show the motive of the defendant. The ruling on a similar question in the Frank case should apply to this. So long as one of these negroes lived, the defendant knew that testimony could be offered against him. This was the reason Manning acquiesced to taking part in these murders. It was the scheme and the motive of both Williams and the negro, the one a part of another."

Howard continued with a long explanation of why the other killings were important in showing Manning's motivation, recounting the long list of murders and explaining that Manning had to kill all the men who could have implicated him in the same peonage violations that threatened Williams. Howard made no effort to diminish Williams's involvement and obvious benefit from killing the men, but he stressed that Manning also benefited and that was why he went along with the orders to kill. He killed because he agreed with Williams's plan, Howard argued, not because he feared Williams.

The judge ruled in favor of the prosecution, admitting all the evidence regarding the eleven murders. The jury returned to the courtroom, and it was now the defense team's turn to put witnesses on the stand and try to save Manning's life.

# 14

# "Stand Up, Clyde"

The first witness for the defense was Clyde Freeman, Manning's third cousin. He testified that he had worked on the Williams plantation for thirteen years, and then Underwood began to ask about specific incidents. Freeman explained that he had either witnessed or heard accounts of the deaths of Will Napier, husband of Manning's sister Grace, and Nathaniel Wade (Blackstrap).

"Blackstrap had run away, him and Little Bit?" Underwood asked.

"Yes, sir," Freeman replied.

"How did they try to capture them? What did they do in order to catch them?"

"They had a dog after them."

"What did they use this dog for?"

"To run niggers when they got away."

"They kept a blood hound to run niggers?"

"Yes, sir."

Freeman went on to recount how Johnny Benson (Little Bit) had been whipped after his recapture, and how Wade was killed for escaping. He then explained how Iron John was whipped and then killed by Leroy Williams for not rolling fence wire properly. That killing took place "along sort of in the Spring of the year. We had just started planting cotton. We had just started breaking up and going to planting cotton."

Underwood asked a few more questions to establish that there had been killings on the plantation long before the eleven murders Manning confessed to, and then he addressed how the workers were treated on a daily basis.

"How were the negroes on the place treated in order to make them work, Clyde, down on the Williams plantation?" Underwood asked.

"You say how was they treated?" Freeman replied, with a slight look of puzzlement.

"Yes, what did they do?"

"What you mean?" Freeman asked. "You mean in the way they whipped them? They did whip them."

"You say they would whip them?"

"Yes, sir."

"How much whipping went on on the farm there and what were the whippings given for?"

"They whipped some of them about picking cotton and about anything they were doing. If they didn't do enough of that, they would whip them."

"Did they ever whip you?"

"Yes, sir."

"How often did they whip you?"

"I have been whipped lots of times."

"How many negroes on the place did they whip?"

"They whipped about all of them that they got out of the stockade. They would whip all of them."

"How often?"

"Sometimes they would whip one a week and sometimes they would not whip one at all in a week."

Freeman went on to testify about how the men were once whipped en masse, and then the attorney moved on to discussing the two black overseers. He asked if anybody other than the Williams men carried pistols on the plantation, and Freeman explained that Manning and Claude Freeman both sometimes carried pistols to keep the other men in line. He also explained how it was their responsibility to lock the men up at night after the work was done.

"What effect did the having of those pistols and the whippings, et cetera, have on the negroes on the plantation there?" Underwood asked.

"It kept them scared. It kept them cowered all the while."

"Were they very much afraid?"

"Yes, sir. They sure was."

Underwood then addressed whether Freeman was familiar with Peterson, Preston, and Price, the three men who had died on the same night. Freeman replied that he was, and that he remembered the day they left the farm. He also explained that he knew of Gus Chapman's first escape and the way he was whipped after being brought back.

"And you saw them force some of the negroes to whip others?"

"Yes, sir."

"When they were told to whip others, would they or not do it?"

"Yes, sir. They would do it when they knowed if they didn't they would get whipped themselves."

"Would they *always* do it?"

"Yes, the first of it there."

"Have you whipped other negroes yourself?"

"No, sir. I have not whipped any."

"What did they whip them with?"

"Sometimes they would whip them with a switch and sometimes with a strap or a bridle or trace."

"How severe were the whippings? Were they pretty hard whippings or not?"

"Yes, sir. It was pretty hard."

"Did it bring blood?"

"Sometimes it would."

Underwood continued by asking Freeman about some details of where the Williams plantation was located in relation to some other known points in the community, and then he asked about whether he and the other workers were free to leave the farm. Freeman explained that they were not free to leave when they wanted, but they sometimes were allowed to go to town with the Williams men or one of the black overseers. But he also alluded to some disaffection with Manning, saying, "We have not been to town together since Clyde started bossing."

Underwood then turned to the day when the federal agents had visited the farm.

"What did you tell them?" he asked.

"I didn't tell them nothing. I told them I didn't know nothing."

"Why didn't you tell them?"

"Mr. Johnny told us he had seen them that day. They had stopped by his house and he come up on the river, he come up there and told us not to tell them anything. He said not to tell them nothing, not to say nothing to them. Just tell them we didn't know nothing. He had seen them and beat

163

them to us and told us that." This was new information to the courtroom observers. There had been no discussion in Williams's trial of him reaching the potential witnesses before the agents did to warn them not to speak. Everyone had assumed that the workers understood the risk of speaking to the federal agents just from their previous experience on the plantation; now it was clear that Williams had made clear threats just in case they were not sufficiently intimidated.

"What was the reason you didn't tell them something? Did Mr. Johnny Williams tell you not to?"

"He told me not to tell them anything and I wouldn't tell them anything because I was scared."

"You were scared to tell them?"

"Yes."

"Scared of Mr. John S. Williams?"

"Yes, sir. I was scared of him and the boys too."

Then Underwood paused for a moment and took a look at the jury. He turned back to the witness and asked one last question.

"What would you have done if Mr. Williams had told you to kill somebody?"

"I would have tried," Freeman answered. "I would have been too scared not to."

The prosecution objected to the question, and the judge ordered it stricken from the record. But the point was made with the jury, and the defense was finished examining Freeman. The prosecution cross-examined with only a few quick questions to establish that Freeman had not personally witnessed many of the events he described.

The next witness for the defense was Claude Freeman, Clyde Manning's cousin and the other pistol-carrying overseer. After having Freeman recount some of the killings he had witnessed on the plantation, Underwood asked about his responsibilities in keeping Huland Williams's workers on the farm. Freeman explained that Huland Williams shared the living quarters with his workers when he first returned from a stint in the Navy, living on one side of the partitioned building. Huland later built a separate building for the workers, and Freeman described how he slept on one side while the other men were locked in their portion of the building. During the questioning, the defense attorney asked how Huland intended Freeman to handle "the negro darkies."

"He said if any of the hands got away or tried to get away or did anything to me, I was to kill them. And he said if I let anyone get away, I would know what was coming to me."

"What did he mean by that? What did you understand him to mean?" the defense attorney asked. The prosecution objected and argued that the witness's supposition would be inadmissible, but the judge allowed the witness to answer.

"I thought he meant I was going to be whipped. He would whip me if I let anyone get away."

Underwood then asked Claude Freeman about how the whipping was done on the farm, and he explained it in the same way that the other witnesses had. When the attorney asked why the other blacks would hold someone down to be whipped, Claude Freeman said "they were scared not to."

"How do you know they were afraid?" Underwood asked.

"I know they were scared by the way they acted. Anything he would tell them to do, they would do it," Claude Freeman answered, referring to Huland Williams. "And if he would tell them to do anything, if they didn't do anything in a hurry they would get whipped. He would tell them to hurry and they would go on a trot. He would tell them to do it and if they didn't do it just right or to suit him, they would get whipped. If he would tell them to go in a hurry and they didn't do it to suit him, he would take them down and whip them."

Claude Freeman testified that he had never been whipped, but that he had been threatened many times by the Williams family. When asked, he explained how Mr. Johnny had broken Clyde Manning's arm once when the white man "jumped on to him." He also offered an anecdote, without being asked, about how Huland and Marvin Williams had once gotten into a fight and Huland threatened to kill his brother.

The witness also testified about how dogs were used to run down escaped men. Then Underwood asked Claude Freeman if Huland Williams had ever instructed him to shoot one of the other men.

"Yes, he told me to shoot James Strickland."

"Did you shoot?"

"Yes, sir."

Strickland survived the shooting and later escaped, reporting his experience to the federal agents shortly before Gus Chapman arrived with the same information.

Underwood ended his questioning, and Brand stepped up to cross-examine. As with all the defense witnesses, he had only a few questions.

"Did Manning have any trouble with any of the hands that come from the stockade?" the prosecutor asked.

"Not as I know of."

165

"Did Manning know the negroes up on the place where you stayed or not?"

"No sir, he didn't know much about them."

"Did he have any quarrels or fights or any difficulties with them, anything like that?"

"No, sir."

"Did you know of any bad blood between them?"

"No, sir. Every time he would come up there or be with them he would be laughing and going on, just like he would with me."

So much for establishing that Manning may have been willing to kill the men because he was a "bad nigger" who was always fighting with the other workers, as John S. Williams had put it in his testimony before the court. The prosecutor had gone fishing for a little anecdotal evidence of bad blood between Manning and the men he killed, but with no luck.

At one point in the cross-examination by Brand, Underwood felt that his witness had become confused about what the prosecutor was asking. With a comment that only now seems a backhanded way to help Claude Freeman, the defense attorney stood and asked that the judge allow him to clarify a statement.

"This boy is an ignorant boy, your honor," Underwood said. "I don't think he understands these questions and I don't think the witness has just stated what he means."

The judge overruled Underwood, saying the witness was responsible for whatever he said on the stand.

Next on the witness stand was B. B. Bohannon, police chief of Covington. He testified that he knew of the conditions on the Williams plantation and did nothing to intervene. In a statement probably intended to show he had not helped the Williams family break peonage laws, he said that two of the Williams brothers had sought his help tracking down three escapees from the plantation. They told Bohannon they wanted to search Covington's "nigger town," but felt his presence was necessary to ensure their safety. When he found that the escaped men had no warrants, Bohannon declined to help. The brothers offered him a twenty-five dollar reward on each of the men, but he still declined. The boys left him and went off tracking the men with their dogs, Bohannon said.

Rather than proof of his magnanimity, Bohannon's refusal to help was more likely a sign of boredom or apathy. After Bohannon's brief testimony, Newton County Sheriff B. L. Johnson was recalled to the stand. Judge Meadows, assisting Underwood in the defense, proceeded to ask the sheriff about a curious incident that had occurred before Manning testified in front of the grand jury that indicted John S. Williams.

"Do you recollect about that time having a conversation with Williams concerning Manning, Mr. John S. Williams?" he asked the sheriff.

"Yes, sir. Before he was indicted, I did."

"What was that conversation?"

"The evening they brought Clyde here, he was here at the court awhile, Williams came to me and asked me to let him take him back with him and said if we needed him he would bring him back the next day."

Meadows paused and looked at the jury with raised eyebrows. He turned back to the sheriff with a look of surprise on his face and continued.

"Asked you to let him *take him home*?"

"He asked me to let him take him back home that night and he would bring him back the next day."

"Had Clyde then given testimony before the grand jury?"

"I don't think he had at that time. No, sir."

"State if any time later than that anybody else made the same request, and if so, who it was."

"Yes, sir. One of the boys the next day asked me to let him take him back with him and he said he would bring him back the next morning."

"Did you let him do it?"

"No sir, I did not."

The defense next called Gus Chapman to testify, asking him to recount what he had seen of the killings and abuse on the Williams plantation, including the times he was whipped and beaten.

"I never did see anybody resist when they were attempting to whip them," Chapman said. "Nobody ever did resist. I never seen anybody shot at that were not killed. I left before the killing of those eleven men began, and I have not been there since last Thanksgiving."

And then on Brand's cross-examination, Chapman let on that he could not overlook Manning's cooperation with the Williams family.

"Mr. Johnny Williams instructed him to shoot us if we attempted to get away," Chapman recalled. "He said to shoot us down and not to let us get away at all. They kept us locked up at night so we couldn't get away.

"Clyde done all the locking up. We could not get out without Clyde letting us out. Clyde had the keys and he could have got out himself and gone off. *He* didn't have to stay in there locked up like we all did."

Seventeen-year-old Frank Dozier followed on the witness stand, testifying about how he had been taken from jail and put to work on the Williams plantation, immediately falling prey to the vicious hands of the Williams men. He showed the jury scars on his head from being beaten with a stick, and he recounted how he had once seen John Brown whipped because the man's injured hand kept him from sawing wood as quickly as the Williams family wanted. Brown worked all day with his injured hand, and then when he returned to the farm in the evening, Leroy Williams appeared and ordered Brown to take down his pants. Dozier told of how, in front of the other workers, this grown man was forced to pull his pants down to his ankles and receive a whipping on his buttocks because he was unable to push lumber through a sawmill quickly with an injured hand.

Dozier also told of witnessing the whipping of Long John, and how the man begged to be killed. Once he was dead, Leroy Williams turned to Dozier and threatened him with the pistol.

"When he shot him, Cap'n Leroy asked me did I want some of it. He said he would give me some of it if I wanted some of it, that was some of the pistol, and I told him no, I didn't want none of it.

"If he told me to do anything, I would do it. Because I knowed if I didn't, he would get me. I knowed he would kill me."

Dozier went on to tell of how the Williams family were experts at terrorizing their field hands, keeping them constantly in fear of their lives.

"Mr. Johnny S. Williams and his three sons carried pistols. I seen them shoot at the hands. They shot at me in the field. They didn't just shoot to scare me, because one time they shot at me and the bullet went through my hat and knocked my hat off. He shot at me to make me hurry across the field, to make me trot. I was not going fast enough, so he hollered at me to go faster and then shot at me.

"One night we were doing some work there on a machine with a bolt cutter and cut the wrong bolt. They were going to whip some of us, and they beat Jake and then he snapped his pistol at him three times and it didn't fire because it didn't have nothing in it."

That testimony ended the first day of Clyde Manning's trial, and there was little to be done on the following day. The state had already rested its case, and the defense had no more witnesses to call. Clyde Manning would take the stand the next morning to plead for his life. It would be up to the jury to decide whether Manning could be forgiven for his crimes.

On the day on which his fate would be decided, Clyde Manning appeared to observers to be no more emotional than on any other day he had been seen in the courtroom. He appeared under heavy guard again, wearing the same blue overalls and a white shirt, with a big floppy farm hat that he took off as he entered the courthouse. The balcony of the court-house was filled with black spectators eager to hear Manning defend himself in his own words, but there were still plenty of open seats downstairs. The *Atlanta Journal* reported that afternoon that "on the Covington streets no indications of excitement or disorder were noted."

Manning was called to the stand immediately after court was brought to order at nine A.M. Just as John S. Williams had done in his own trial, Manning was to be allowed to make an unsworn statement to the jury, and the prosecution would not be allowed to cross-examine him. Williams had used the opportunity to make a long, sometimes rambling, argument that he had had nothing to do with the killing of the eleven men. He had speculated about why Manning may have had motivation for the murders. Since Manning admitted his involvement, his statement would be a plea for his life, a plea for understanding that he had killed the men because he had no choice.

Manning walked to the stand quickly and listened to Judge Hutcheson explain his rights to address the jury without cross-examination. When he was told to proceed, Manning turned slightly in his chair to look at the jury. While not making direct eye contact with any of the white men, he began to speak to them in a conversational tone that many in the court-room found amazing coming from a black man who was asking a group of white men not to hang him. The *Atlanta Journal* reported that he spoke as if he were addressing "a group of his neighbors met casually around the stove of a country general store. His language was simple and his manner at no time forceful or particularly earnest. Neither seeing him nor hearing him gave one the instant realization that he was pleading for his life." Many found Manning's calm composure admirable, but his lack of emotion troubled many observers who could not understand how he could speak so matter-of-factly about how he had killed eleven men. For some, that lack of emotion spoke poorly for his explanation that he hated carrying out the orders of John S. Williams but did it out of fear.

Manning sat back in the chair with his hands folded and began to speak to the jury.

"Gentlemen of the jury, and Judge, Your Honor, I am not guilty of murder. The crime what I have done, I done it to save my own life. When these crimes was started, one day when they first started, that week him and his three boys had been to Monticello. He was fixing to send them off. He knowed that the men had been down there talking to the men on the farm and he was fixing to send them off. He come home after they come from town, and he says, 'Clyde, we are going to do away with these boys and I want you to help.'

"I knowed about them other men being killed on the place and I knowed what he was going to do. I says, 'Mr. Johnny, I don't want to do that, and I don't want to do it.' And he says, 'Well, by God, it is all right with me if you don't want to. It means your neck or theirs. If you think more of their necks than of your own it is all right. If you do, it is yours.'

"I have nobody to speak to or nobody to tell or have to help me or save me and I have to go to do it. I had to go with him that night. After these killings started, he would call me all through the night. He would call me during the night to see if the cows were in the wheat or in the oats and he would say he heard a noise with the mules and for me to see if any of them were hung, and I figured he was calling me to see if I was off the place. If I had been off the place he would have found me and he would have brought me back there and would have killed me. He would have put the dog on me and caught me.

"If I had had any chance to get away, I would have tried it. I didn't do what I done of my own free will. I had to do it, and I will tell you gentlemen before God, if I done that of my own free will I hope this minute I will drop dead. It was against my will to do it, but it was against my power not to do it and live. I had done seen enough killings of them who run away to know if I tried to run away he would kill me. If I had known I could get away and knowed I could get to somebody to tell this to I would have taken the chance to get away, but I couldn't do it. I didn't know anybody. Nobody in this courthouse would have been there would have been fortunate enough to get away and not get caught. I was afraid to take the chance. I had seen them men brought back and whipped and killed.

"I knowed if I made the chance and didn't get away I would have been killed. If I had any chance to get away I would have taken the chance and done it."

Manning went to recount how he had seen men try to escape from the plantation, only to be brought back for severe whippings and sometimes death. He told the jury of seeing Blackstrap, Johnny Benson, Gus Chapman, and Will Napier brought back to the plantation for punishment. He emphasized that he had no faith in his own ability to escape from the Williams family if those men, some of whom he admired because they previously had traveled far beyond the Georgia plantation, could not make a successful escape. Then he continued with his statement, imploring God time and time again to strike him dead if he had killed the men voluntarily.

"If I done this crime with a free will of my own, I hope this minute I will drop dead. It was against my free will to do it, and it was against my power not to do it and live.

"All them boys there knowed they had to do just what he said. Every one there would do just what he said. If I had had some white man to speak to, some I knowed, then I could have gone to him and told him and would have saved myself. But you know how it was. I didn't have nobody to say nothing to. The only white man I was with was Mr. Johnny there and I would have disappeared, been killed just like these other boys.

"Mr. Johnny would come to the place where you was at work and he would disappear. He would go off and might be back before you knowed, but he might go out in the field and be gone and you would not know anything. You would not know where he was and the first thing you knowed he would be riding up in his car. There was no chance for me to get away. I didn't know anything about going nowhere.

"John Singleton, Mr. Marvin killed him. Of course, I didn't see Mr. Marvin when he killed him. There was nobody else out there with him but Mr. Marvin. When I knowed anything, Mr. Marvin he called Charlie Chisolm and he helped them to put him in the pond.

"Gentlemen of the jury and Judge, Your Honor, just come down to the natural facts. If I have done wrong in this thing, any man who lived on that place would have done wrong. Anybody on that place, white folks, that he said to do it, would tell them it had to be done like he did me, they would have done it. Any nigger who lived on that place would have done just as I done. If he said to whip one, they would have it to do. If one didn't do what they wanted, they would kill him.

"We had to do what he said, not just me, but any one of us. I didn't do this because I wanted to but I had to do it because I didn't want to do it. I was just worried and bothered and scared to death, and I didn't know any man I could go to for protection to get help or to tell it to, to help me.

"I had a family. I had my wife and my baby and there was my mother and sister and brothers. I couldn't run off with my whole family. If I had got off and told this, my wife and sister would all have been killed right there. I was not just like a loose man down there. Them that was loose, they caught them and killed some of them. When Gus Chapman run away and they caught him and brought him back and whipped him.

171

"If I had got off and reported this, or not wanted to have done it, my family would all have been killed. If I had not done as he told me, I would have caused all my family's death. I was not like just a loose man that didn't have anybody there.

"I studied about leaving every day. I studied about leaving and how to get away and I didn't know how. I figured out if them men ever come back there I would slip off with them. I would take a chance and tell them exactly what was going on. When they come back I didn't know they were back until they had a subpoena for me, when they came back and brought me up here and I asked them and the sheriff for protection.

"I asked them for protection if they would have me tell it. I didn't tell it until Mr. Sheriff here told me he would protect me. He said to tell it and he wouldn't let anybody hurt me, if I would tell it, and then when he told me he would give me protection, then I up and told them.

"I didn't do this of my own free will. I hope if I did this of my own free will that God will show it to you by killing me right here. I hope he will strike me dead if I ain't telling the truth, this minute.

"They are trying me for murder. That is a crime I am not guilty of and God in Heaven knows I am not guilty and you Judge and Jury, all I ask of you is to give me justice. I am not crying for mercy. Just give me justice, and if you do, God in Heaven knows I will be a free man because it was against my will.

"This is a thing that God will not hold me accountable for, because I had to do it just as he said to do."

Those words ended Clyde Manning's statement, and there was little more to be said.


Manning smiled faintly as he stood up and returned to the defense table. The *Atlanta Journal* would report that afternoon that "his impassivity and simple self-possession while he was on the stand were something no person who saw him today is likely to ever forget." When court adjourned for lunch soon after his statement, he spoke without emotion to reporters and assured them he would "come clear." Those were the same words used by John S. Williams when speaking to reporters.

Just before the lunch recess, both sides presented their closing arguments. Attorney Howard argued that "Manning's motive was identical with that of Williams, the owner of the place. Williams and Manning both had been practicing peonage, both feared federal investigation, and they plotted and acted together to get rid of the human evidence before the federal authorities should take a hand in the case."

"You must distinguish between moral responsibility and legal responsibility," he told the jury. "If a drunken man kills another he is not morally responsible but he is legally responsible."

Solicitor Brand went on to call Manning a "mean nigger" who took special delight in currying the favor of his white boss by abusing his black workers.

"Williams was a king, a monarch of all whom he surveyed, and his sons were worshipers at his throne," he said. "Clyde needed no threats to make him do anything. There was no fear of losing his life. He committed the crimes to please his boss, and he is just as guilty as Mr. Williams and should be meted out the same punishment.

"After drowning the three negroes in Newton County, why didn't he escape? He made no effort, he tells you, because bloodhounds were on the place and Mr. Williams called him at all times of the night. But I tell you that if this negro had gotten a half mile ahead of the hounds, no race horse in Georgia could have caught him. No, he wanted to stay and bask in the fiendish crimes of his master."

The defense countered that the evidence clearly showed Manning and every other black person on the farm was terrified of the Williams family. Underwood dismissed the notion that Manning was afraid of federal prosecution, and he plainly stated that his defendant could not have planned the murders. "How could a negro plan such a series of crimes?" he asked.

"I ask of you, and I believe that when you go to your room you will not let the fact that the defendant is a black man influence you in making your verdict," Underwood said.

After the lunch recess, the judge took care of some administrative details, then proceeded with charging the jury. This is an important step in any case because it allows the judge to explain in depth what is expected of the jury. For Clyde Manning's trial, Judge Hutcheson needed to address the central issue of Manning's defense—the idea that he was forced to commit what would otherwise be a crime.

"Gentlemen, the defendant has admitted he did certain things in conjunction with the co-defendant in the bill of indictment, John S. Williams, but he says he acted under threats and menaces and under coercion. In determining this question, you can look to all the facts and circumstances of the case, and if it appears to you that the defendant, Clyde Manning, was forced by coercion to take the part that he did, provided you believe that he did in fact take a part, and that the coercion was of such a nature as to excite in the mind of the defendant, Clyde Manning, a reasonable fear that his life or member was in danger, and the facts and circumstances were such as to cause you to believe that the defendant now on trial did whatever the evidence and the statement of the defendant show that he did do, and that he did those things by reason of threats or menaces, as I have heretofore charged you, then he would not be guilty of any crime, and it would be your duty to acquit him."

In other words, the jury had to decide whether they believed Clyde Manning. If so, he was a free man. If not, they could find him guilty of murder and then decide whether to recommend death or life in prison. The judge also allowed a third option. The jury could find Manning guilty of voluntary manslaughter, which carried a sentence of one to twenty years in prison. Involuntary manslaughter was not an option because it was clear that the men had been killed deliberately.

The case went to the jury at four P.M. The jurors took only two ballots and returned their verdict in forty minutes.

Manning was standing in the hallway smoking a cigarette when the jury began returning to the courtroom. He immediately tossed the cigarette away and went to the defense table to hear his fate. He sat forward on the edge of his seat, his chin propped in his hands and looking expectantly at the jurors.

"Have you gentlemen reached a verdict?" the judge asked.

The foreman nodded yes.

"Receive the verdict, please, Mr. Solicitor," the judge said.

Brand walked over to the foreman and took the jury verdict form. He walked over and handed it to the judge, who then read the verdict aloud.

"We, the jury, find the defendant Clyde Manning guilty and recommend that his sentence be life imprisonment. The verdict is the sentence of the court."

Manning's head fell forward and his whole body slumped as he heard the word *guilty*. But then he heard the word *life* and sat up straight, an expression of relief on his face. He would not be hanged. The white jury had been swift in finding him guilty, but remarkably lenient in deciding not to hang a black man who had confessed to eleven murders. The judge then called the opposing attorneys to the bench to discuss the way the jurors had written their verdict. They were supposed to state only that they found the defendent guilty and then add "with" or "without a recommendation of mercy." The jury's intention was clear, all the parties agreed, so the verdict was accepted as it was. The attorneys returned to their positions, then Judge Hutcheson addressed Manning.

"Stand up, Clyde," the judge said sternly.

Manning stood up, somewhat unsteadily, and leaned on his chair with one hand. The other hand moved nervously about his forehead, wiping away perspiration.

"Clyde, the jury has found you guilty with a recommendation for mercy, and the sentence of the court is that you spend the rest of your life in the penitentiary. Have a seat."

# Epilogue

The Williams plantation murders meandered through the legal system for years after the convictions. Both men appealed their convictions but were rejected. Federal charges of peonage were considered against Williams but never pressed because he already was in prison for life. There is no indication that the federal government ever considered peonage charges against Manning. The three Williams boys became fugitives once they were indicted for killings on the Williams plantation, and it was later learned that they had spent the whole time in Florida.

Leroy Williams turned himself in to Jasper County authorities after four years, followed by his brothers Huland and Marvin Williams two years later. All were released on bonds of $2,500 each as the state tried to prepare cases against them, with the aid of the federal Bureau of Investigation, which intended to bring peonage charges against them after the murder charges were resolved. Federal agents spent a great deal of time trying to track down witnesses from the two murder trials six years earlier, but they ultimately concluded that most of the principal witnesses could not be found. Incidentally, their investigation also revealed that there had been some intermarrying among the blacks who left the Williams plantation after the trials, most of them settling in Atlanta. Clyde Manning's wife, Rena, married his cousin Claude Freeman, the other black overseer on the plantation. His mother, Emma, married his uncle Rufus.

With few witnesses available to testify against the Williams brothers, it appeared that once again it would be up to Clyde Manning to provide all the evidence. But then it was reported that Manning had died of tuberculosis in a prison hospital on January 19, 1927. His death had gone unnoticed in the press until the Williams boys turned themselves in, but it is likely that their surrender was prompted by their discovery that the only real witness to their crimes could no longer testify. With little hope of putting on a strong case against the Williamses, Jasper County and the federal government both dropped all charges against the Williams boys.

Other peonage cases were prosecuted successfully in middle Georgia and throughout the South in the coming years, with many prosecutors seeing the conviction of John S. Williams as encouragement to go ahead and bring charges they might otherwise have deemed futile. By the mid-1920s, the peonage system in the South was on its last legs.

Governor Hugh Dorsey left office in 1921, just after the two murder trials. He went on to become a judge of the City Court of Atlanta and the Fulton Superior Court. When he died in 1948 at the age of seventy-seven, the *Atlanta Journal* made no mention of his role in either the trial of Leo Frank or the Williams trials, saying only that his two terms as governor covered "the eventful years 1917–1921." The *Atlanta Constitution* noted that he had attained national recognition as Frank's prosecutor.

But the final imagery from the Williams plantations killings is provided by the deaths of Williams and Manning. Before dying of tuberculosis on a prison farm, Manning had worked six years on a chain gang. He never left the life of a slave.

Williams spent ten years at the state prison in Milledgeville, Georgia, where he was made a trusty, an inmate trusted with a bit more freedom than most inmates and therefore able to work small jobs around the prison. He died one day when he was crushed by a truck against a wall. Supposedly the truck had been stolen by other prisoners who were trying to make an escape, and Williams, for some reason, jumped in front of the truck to try to stop them. Other accounts say his death was merely an accident, so it is possible that the escape story is just a legend that developed as a dramatic, though somewhat puzzling, denouement to the life of a farmer who had attracted so much attention.

But one thing is certain. Williams never showed one moment of remorse over the killings on his plantation. He was interviewed many times by federal and state authorities during his ten years in prison, and he never once admitted to the killings or indicated any regret for his actions.

# C o n c l u s i o n

The story of the Williams plantation murders offers a vivid illustration of the South in 1921, reminding us that slavery persisted in the United States far beyond the point at which we assumed it had ended neatly and abruptly. The tragedy helps us understand a complex and crucial, yet almost forgotten, moment in history, when the region was at once mired in the remnants of slavery and making the first efforts to move forward. The South had fulfilled some of the worst assumptions of outsiders, but the citizens of Georgia stood up and declared their limits.

Clyde Manning's South was very different from John S. Williams's South, and Williams's turned out to be very different from that of the jurors he assumed would set him free. Manning lived in the same South that had imprisoned his parents and grandparents. Williams also lived in an old South, one in which there was a tacit understanding that a white man could use blacks in any way he wanted, and it was no matter to violate the law along the way.

But the people of Georgia repudiated Williams, and, in doing so, they provided perhaps the most accurate portrait of the South in 1921. Certainly it would not be fair to judge all the white people of the South, past or present, by the likes of John S. Williams. The reaction of the people of Georgia showed that the extent of his crimes was, without a doubt, beyond the pale. While Georgians were willing to overlook the peonage and lynching that existed every day, they were genuinely appalled by the testimony from Manning, and supported Williams's conviction. The state wasted no time in bringing Williams to trial, prosecuting him with vigor and convicting him of all charges. That decisive reaction to his crimes seems to redeem the South as a community to some extent, but it must be balanced against the fact that Williams committed his crimes partly because he expected the community to look the other way. And while he misjudged the community's reaction, he may not have been far off the mark. If the same incidents had taken place ten years earlier, it is likely that Williams would have gotten away with his crimes or suffered only a slight punishment. And what if he had been on trial for peonage instead of murder? There is a much greater chance the jury would have excused his crimes as just the common response of a hard-working farmer looking for cheap labor.

It took crimes of great scope and horror to push the white people of Georgia past the point at which the suffering of blacks could just be dismissed as their lot in life. Unfortunately, that scenario continued for years after the Williams plantation murders, well into the civil rights struggle of the 1960s and beyond. Despite the abundance of daily suffering experienced by blacks in their midst, white America seems to need an occasional tragedy of extreme proportions to bring forth sympathy and meaningful action. Though it is some consolation that the white community of Georgia eventually rejected Williams and punished him, there is no pride in knowing that it took such terrible crimes to make the community do the right thing.

It is worth remembering, however, that his community could have acted in exactly the way Williams expected it to. Everyone could have continued the quiet conspiracy that allowed Williams to commit his crimes in the first place, demonstrating that unrelenting racism is the basis for Southern society. Instead, the community added a note of redemption and regret to Williams's dreadful representation of Georgia. That might seem a minor addition to a story that says so much about how blacks were routinely abused over fifty years after the Civil War, but, seen in context, it actually represents a significant advance in race relations and justice for Southern blacks. It was a small but meaningful step in the right direction, a small step taken when none was expected.

Despite their historical significance, the trial verdicts failed to fully answer a fundamental question of the Williams plantation murders. How could Clyde Manning have killed eleven men and then shown little emotion or apparent remorse? Unlike John S. Williams, Manning remains a bit of an enigma even after he admitted to the killings and explained his motivation.

With Williams, there is little doubt as to what he did and why he did it. In his twisted mind, he had to kill the black men on his plantation because each of them could have testified against him and his sons in any peonage investigation. He could not just let them go home because there was no way to ensure they would not go to the authorities. Gus Chapman escaped, and he did not just go home and forget about the Williams plantation.

Even though he never admitted to any crime other than a technical violation of peonage laws, it is obvious from the evidence that he was a casual killer who thought little of doing away with eleven black men if he would benefit from their deaths. More than likely, the number of blacks killed on the Williams plantation numbered at least fifteen and possibly as many as twenty. Oddly enough, Williams was far more willing to kill his slaves than his forebears had been. Plantation owners before the Civil War had to pay substantial sums for slaves, so even if they abused them terribly, they were less willing to just kill them and suffer the monetary loss. But since Williams obtained his peons often for only a few dollars, the cost was no deterrent when Williams wanted one to disappear.

But it also seems quite clear that Williams was not a bloodthirsty monster. Rather, he saw the killings as just another bit of work to be done on the plantation—nothing to enjoy but also nothing to lose sleep over. The black men were the equivalent of animals in Williams's eyes, so killing them for a good reason was merely a task that had to be completed. That cold detachment might be even more disturbing than the idea of someone who enjoys murder, but it was a central component of Williams and many white men who came before and after him. Williams was a man who loved his family deeply, a father so terrified that his grown sons might go to prison that he was willing to do anything to prevent it. He was a man who could cradle his young grandson in his arms, gently stroking the boy's hair as he listened to testimony about whipping and killing men on his plantation, apparently seeing no perversion in that moment. Williams was a man who in some ways embodied the entire white culture of the Old South— his proud, dignified persona maintained by a necessary detachment, a cold distancing from the pain and suffering he was inflicting on others.

But what about Manning? The evidence shows conclusively that Manning really did commit the killings against his will, because he *felt* he had no other choice. Did he *actually* have another choice?

What could we have expected of Manning? His lifelong experience with Williams and the daily terror on the plantation, plus his extreme isolation and lack of education, narrowed his options in ways that we might find difficult to understand. Perhaps Manning could have warned the workers on the farm that they were in line to be killed and allowed them to try escaping. Perhaps he could have taken an opportunity to kill Williams. Perhaps he could have participated in a mass escape and reported the murder plan to the authorities. These options amount to Manning leading a slave revolt against Williams—a lot to expect of a simple, uneducated, extremely isolated, and fearful young man. That is the sort of response that most of us like to *imagine* we could muster in such a situation, but the reality is that most of us could not.

And for a man like Manning, whose entire life was founded on fear and obedience to Williams, the challenge would have been much greater. Like the slaves of a previous generation, Manning learned early on that he was forbidden to make choices, to take responsibility for what he chose to do or not to do. John S. Williams made those decisions for Manning in nearly every way, from the mundane to the momentous. In addition, regular exposure to the whippings and other abuse on the plantation probably caused Manning to become hardened, less sensitive when yet another man was to be abused. A life of oppression, degradation, and physical abuse caused many slaves to become "indifferent to human sufferings," according to one researcher. One slave reported that a lifetime of cruelty caused him "to grow less feeling for the sufferings of others, and even indifferent to my own punishment," as John Blassingame writes in *The Slave Community: Plantation Life in the Antebellum South.* "Unremitting cruelty often subdued the slave and broke his will to resist."

That is not to say, however, that Manning was without any free will whatsoever. Despite the terrible effects of slavery on the human mind, even slaves of earlier generations sometimes managed to preserve some small degree of autonomy. "One of the primary reasons the slaves were able to survive the cruelty they faced was that their behavior was not totally dependent on their masters," Blassingame writes. "Convinced that God watched over him, the slave bore his earthly afflictions in order to earn a heavenly reward. Often he disobeyed his earthly master's rules to keep his Heavenly Master's commandments because he had greater fear for his immortal soul than for the pain which could be inflicted on his body."

So while Manning was a man robbed of much of his humanity, he may not have been completely without choice. In the final analysis, his response was probably prompted more by realistic expectations than by anything else. Any attempt to defy John S. Williams very likely would have just gotten Manning killed, and it might not have saved any lives. In that case, Manning would have been the twelfth victim, perhaps a martyr of sorts because he chose to die fighting instead of complying with orders to kill. Martyrdom may have left Manning with a legacy more easily understandable us today, but for someone in Manning's situation, it was a wholly unrealistic expectation. For a peon or a slave, there were opportunities nearly every day to sacrifice oneself for a fellow sufferer. One's own survival depended on being able to witness and endure the suffering of others.

It is only natural that some readers will wonder whether Manning's motives were *entirely* pure. That was the uncomfortable question that troubled me as I tried to understand his actions. It seemed necessary to consider the question and not automatically characterize Manning as such a kind, gentle soul that he had no selfish thoughts whatsoever during the murders. After all, he was human; he was not a cardboard "good" black man. Though I think the question is worth asking, it cannot be answered definitively, and it should not obscure the clear, overwhelming explanation for Manning's actions. There is no doubt that Manning did not want to kill the men and that he acted out of fear. Manning also could have feared prosecution for peonage since he controlled the peons on the farm, but that fear would not have been enough motivation for him to kill eleven men. If that fear was in the back of Manning's mind, however, it could have given Williams one more threat to use against Manning, one more thing to use in building even more terror.

Even after considering all the circumstances, the sheer number of the murders can make it very difficult to completely excuse Manning for his actions; some ambivalence is almost unavoidable. In a purely intellectual sense, perhaps we can say that we understand why he did what he did. But emotionally, we may have a hard time accepting a man who admitted killing eleven of his friends in gruesome ways. As I studied Manning's every known word for two years, I developed great sympathy for his plight but also for the men he killed. I want to support Manning, but I can't help feeling great frustration with him.

Equally troubling is the image of Manning telling his story with little emotion, expressing no remorse, or at least no pleas of regret that might be seen as appropriately earnest. His calm, unemotional demeanor caused me to wonder if it was reason to doubt his story, to doubt his claims that he was an unwilling participant. After all, his whole explanation hinged on being forced to commit heinous acts that would bring most people to tears even when recounting them afterward. An outpouring of remorse might have reassured even a sympathetic listener that Manning was not a common killer. But after I came to understand Manning more clearly, I saw that such a response would not have been consistent with the way he and the other slaves learned to survive on the Williams plantation. They learned to bury their emotions, to hold back the outrage and fear that most people would express when faced with the terror they experienced on a daily basis. The same circumstances that made him absolute clay in the hands of John S. Williams also made him appear emotionally numb, able to recount the killings without breaking down. Blassingame writes that most slaves maintained personal autonomy "by carefully masking their true personality traits from whites, while adopting 'sham' characteristics when interacting with them. According to [former slave] Lucy Ann Delaney, slaves lived behind an 'impenetrable mask. . . . How much of joy, of sorrow, of misery and anguish have they hidden from their tormentors!'" It is possible that Manning's stoic demeanor was only the face he put on for a white audience.

Perhaps these points were considered by Manning's jury as they listened to the testimony and deliberated his fate. They faced a dilemma that I am sure would frustrate a jury even more today than it did in 1921. Even if you believe the defendant was coerced or forced to kill, can you just open the courthouse doors and send home a man who admitted to killing eleven people by striking them with an axe or throwing them alive off bridges? The jury in 1921 apparently believed Manning's explanation but could not reconcile themselves to declaring a confessed mass murderer innocent and letting him go free. Their resolution of the quandary was to declare him guilty but spare him the death sentence that most certainly would have been his fate if he had not convinced the jury of his motivation.

Was that fair to Manning? Probably not. But Manning had become a victim of John S. Williams in a final way. Purely for his own gain, Williams had turned Manning into a man whom society could not understand, a man who left even his supporters with a vague sense of unease. This was the final punishment visited on Manning for obeying Mr. Johnny. No matter how much sympathy was generated for his plight, Manning would forever be trailed by lingering doubts, suspicions that he could have been a better person. Even if his actions should be excused, he still is known to history as a killer. That is a cruel legacy for a man who should be seen more appropriately as one of the final victims of American slavery.

# Notes

## Introduction

Page xiv: "Lay This Body Down": Allen, W. F., Ware, C. P., Garrison, L. M. *Slave Songs of the United States*. Bedford, Massachusetts: Applewood Books; 1867: 19–20.

## Chapter 1

The account in Chapter 1 is based on testimony by Clyde Manning, *The State of Georgia v. Clyde Manning*, May 31, 1921.

## Chapter 2

Page 9: "from someone lying in ambush": Testimony of Clyde Manning, *The State of Georgia v. Clyde Manning*, May 31, 1921.

Page 10: "I was in Jasper County": *New York Times*, April 7, 1921: p. 1.

Page 11: "three cars parked in three garages": *Covington News*, March 31, 1921: p. 1.

Page 11: "harsh times of Reconstruction": Newton County *Historical Society. History of Newton County*, Georgia; 1988: 90.

Page 11: "the form of slavery practiced on the Williams plantation": Manning testimony. Iron John's name may have been John Davis, but the records are unclear and contradictory.

Page 13: "Do you want any more": U.S. Bureau of Investigation. Summary of John S. Williams peonage investigation, October 27, 1932: 6.

Page 14: "for overseeing the other workers": *Atlanta Constitution*, April 3, 1921: p. 8A.

Page 14: "by paying his five-dollar fine": Testimony of Gus Chapman, *The State of Georgia v. Clyde Manning*, May 31, 1921.

Page 14: "well fed and well clothed": Testimony of George W. Brown and A. J. Wismer, *The State of Georgia v. Clyde Manning*, May 31, 1921.

Page 14: "two similar small red wooden buildings": Brown and Wismer testimony. The agents' testimony conflicts somewhat as to the exact locations and dimensions of the buildings, but there is reason to believe that they were imprecisely referring to the two buildings and not describing the same one. Brown described a building as 30–40 feet long and 35 feet wide, while Wismer described a building 16–20 feet long and 12 feet wide. Both agents acknowledged that their estimates may have been off.

Page 15: "sometimes allowed to carry pistols": Testimony of Clyde Freeman, *The State of Georgia v. Clyde Manning*, May 31, 1921.

Page 15: "dogs used for tracking": Clyde Freeman testimony. Federal agent Wismer testified during the Manning trial about using the tracking dogs for Sunday practice.

Page 15: "within sight of the Williams family": Testimony of Emma Freeman, *The State of Georgia v. Clyde Manning*, May 31, 1921. She testified that the church was half a mile from Williams's house, "where they could see all right."

Page 16: "the man would run, not walk": Clyde Freeman testimony.

Page 16: "regularly whipped on the Williams plantation": Wismer testimony. He testified that all the black laborers he spoke to said they had been whipped. Clyde Freeman also testified to the same fact.

Page 16: "just to suit him": Emma Freeman testimony.

Page 16: "usually brought blood": Clyde Freeman testimony.

Page 17: "a trade that Manning had made with another laborer": Claude Freeman testimony.

Page 17: "after being injured by a mule": Testimony of Frank Dozier, *The State of Georgia v. Clyde Manning*, May 31, 1921.

Page 18: "Williams's house to pick cotton": Clyde Freeman testimony. Little Bit's real name also has been cited elsewhere as Johnny Benford, not Johnny Benson.

Page 18: "welcome to come get him": Gus Chapman testimony.

Page 19: "then fell over dead": U.S. Bureau of Investigation. Summary of John S. Williams peonage investigation, October 27, 1932: p. 8.

## Chapter 3

Page 26: "before it flourished in the Southern United States": Daniel, P. *The Shadow of Slavery: Peonage in the South, 1901–1969.* Urbana, Illinois: University of Illinois Press; 1972: 12.

Page 27: "bargain for higher wages": Grant, D. L. *The Way It Was in the South: The Black Experience in Georgia.* New York: Carol Publishing Group; 1993: 96.

Page 27: "ten years' imprisonment and a $10,000 fine": Ibid., p. 149.

Page 28: "the land where it never snows": Daniel, p. 82.

Page 28: "sold their brethren into slavery in the Americas": Ibid., p. 36.

Page 28: "providing orphans with guardians": Grant, p. 150.

Page 29: "greatest prosperity since 1850": Coleman, K., ed. *A History of Georgia.* 2nd ed. Athens, Georgia: University of Georgia Press; 1991: 259.

Page 29: "prosperity came to a sudden halt": Ibid., p. 263.

Page 29: "8,472 bales in 1920": Jasper County Historical Foundation. *History of Jasper County*, Georgia. Roswell, Georgia: W. H. Wolfe Associates; 1984: 96.

Page 29: "sprawling antebellum plantations": Daniel, p. 110.

Page 29: "handsomely in the past—King Cotton": Coleman, p. 259.

Page 30: "could pay my indebtedness": Testimony of John S. Williams, *The State of Georgia v. John S. Williams*, April 5, 1921.

Page 30: "two bureau agents were sent to investigate": Daniel, p. 41.

Page 31: "Alabama between 1903 and 1905": Ibid., p. 22.

Page 31: "would not serve justice, the editorial concluded": Ibid., p. 23.

Page 31: "took him to the local jail": Daniel, p. 31.

Page 31: "had to leave her behind": Ibid., p. 29.

Page 32: "landowner would not hurt him": Ibid.

Page 32: "just a few miles from the Williams plantation": Testimony of Claude Freeman, *The State of Georgia v. Clyde Manning*, May 31, 1921.

Page 32: "did not know if the tales were true": Testimony of Emma Freeman, *The State of Georgia v. Clyde Manning*, May 31, 1921.

Page 33: "apparently ended those dreams": Testimony of Clyde Manning, *The State of Georgia v. Clyde Manning*, May 31, 1921.

## Chapter 4

Page 35: "arrived at the Williams plantation on Friday, February 18, 1921": Testimony of George W. Brown and A. J. Wismer, *The State of Georgia v. Clyde Manning*, May 31, 1921.

Page 36: "what alarmed them the most": *Atlanta Constitution*, April 7, 1921: p. 2A.

Page 36: "charges of peonage around the country": Testimony of John S. Williams, *The State of Georgia v. John S. Williams*, April 5, 1921.

Page 37: "on probation for a short time": *Atlanta Constitution*, April 3, 1921: p. 1A.

Page 38: "clue to the murders on the Williams farm": U.S. Bureau of Investigation. Summary of John S. Williams peonage investigation, October 27, 1932: p. 2.

Page 39: "not held against his will": Ibid.

Page 40: "when the federal grand jury convened in April": *Covington News*, March 24, 1921, p. 1.

## Chapter 5

Page 42: "got to get rid of all the stockade niggers": U.S. Bureau of Investigation. Summary of John S. Williams peonage investigation, October 27, 1932: p. 18.

Page 43: "I hate to do it": Testimony of Clyde Manning, *The State of Georgia v. Clyde Manning*, May 31, 1921. Manning recalled the exchange slightly differently when recounting the scene to federal investigators and others, but the gist of the conversation was always the same. This version uses phrases from Manning's recollection during his trial and also his explanation to the federal agents.

Page 44: "meet Johnnie down there": Testimony of Clyde Manning, *The State of Georgia v. Clyde Manning*, May 31, 1921.

Page 44: "blunt end of the axe head facing him": Ibid.

Page 45: "stuffed the man's body into it": During the trial of Williams, Manning testified that Johnnie Williams was buried in "one of the holes he had dug" (*Atlanta Journal*, April 6, 1921: p. 2A). While plausible that Williams would have instructed the man to dig holes for some false reason, planning to bury him in one, no other account of the killing of Johnnie Williams makes reference to him having dug his own grave. On the contrary, during his own trial, Manning made more detailed reference to himself and Williams digging the hole in the side of a gully. It is likely that the reference during the Williams trial is one of the very few instances in which Manning's memory failed him, or it could be an error by the newspaper reporter. The reference is not found in the incomplete records of the Williams trial.

Page 46: "near a house on Huland Williams's property": Testimony of Clyde Manning, *The State of Georgia v. John S. Williams*, April 5, 1921. He testified to the same fact in his own trial.

## Chapter 6

Page 50: "run afoul of the Williams family some years before": Testimony of Claude Freeman, *The State of Georgia v. Clyde Manning*, May 31, 1921. It is possible that John Singleton is, in fact, Iron John, the black man whose body was thrown in a pond on the plantation in Chapter 2. Iron John's real name is not known, and there is little information concerning who John Singleton was or the circumstances of his death. There is clear evidence, however, that Iron John's body was securely tied to heavy logs before being sunk in the pond. That seems to make it unlikely that the body would float freely to the surface. On the other hand, some of the bodies that were securely weighted with chains and rocks also surfaced, proving that the weights do not necessarily keep the body from floating later. Since John is a common name, and since many of the men who passed through the Williams plantation shared remarkably similar names, it is not certain that both anecdotes concern the same man.

Page 50: "take some hogs down to John S. Williams's house": Testimony of Clyde Manning, *The State of Georgia v. Clyde Manning*, May 31, 1921.

Page 51: "go anywhere you want to go": Testimony of Clyde Manning, *The State of Georgia v. John S. Williams*, April 5, 1921.

Page 53: "stop putting up such a fuss": Ibid.

Page 55: "knock me in the head first": *Atlanta Constitution*, April 3, 1921, p. 1A.

Page 55: "fell in tandem into the darkness": There is another version of the final moments on the bridge that is substantially different, but most likely apocryphal. (*National Detective Reporter*, September 1933, p. 1.) In this version, John Brown falls to his knees and begs Williams not to throw him off the bridge. The farmer replies by telling Brown that he will be released if he pushes Benson off the bridge. The story goes that Brown was so dimwitted that he accepted the deal, pushed Benson off the bridge and was surprised when he was pulled over the railing by the chains that bound the two men. Such a cruel joke would not be beyond Williams, but the manner in which the men were tied together makes it quite unlikely that anyone could fall for it, even if Brown was not very bright. It is more likely that the tale amounts to a racist joke that was told in the years after the murders.

Another version has Benson being induced to push Brown over the railing, on the pretext that they are only going to scare Brown. (*New York Times*, April 7, 1921, p. 4A.) Benson is then pushed over. This version almost certainly is an error by the newspaper reporter quoting Manning, or (less likely) an error in Manning's recall. The men are not even chained together in this version, and court records clearly indicate that Manning recalled the "we're only going to scare him" ruse being used before the men were chained together.

## Chapter 7

Page 57: "go on down with you": Testimony of Clyde Manning, motion for new trial in *The State of Georgia v. John S. Williams.*

Page 59: "when I swing at *you* with it": U.S. Bureau of Investigation. Summary of John S. Williams peonage investigation, October 27, 1932: p. 10.

Page 60: "take my shotgun and do the same to you": U.S. Bureau of Investigation, p. 10.

Page 62: "teach you a lesson": Ibid., p. 16.

Page 62: "I know what you said": Manning testimony.

Page 62: "Better go get another big one": U.S. Bureau of Investigation, p. 16.

Page 63: "turned around and drove back across the bridge": Ibid., p. 17.

Page 63: "you'll end up the same if you tell anybody": Ibid.

Page 63: "carrying a double-barreled shotgun": Manning testimony.

Page 64: "I'll know where it come from": Ibid.

## Chapter 8

Page 66: "a foot sticking out of the water": Testimony of Carl Wheeler, *The State of Georgia v. Clyde Manning*, May 31, 1921.

Page 67: "ten feet deep—deep enough to drown": Testimony of B. L. Johnson, *The State of Georgia v. Clyde Manning*, May 31, 1921.

Page 68: "front page news in nearby Covington:" *Covington News*, March 17, 1921, p.1.

Page 68: "make an investigation move forward": Ibid., p. 3.

Page 68: "long arm of John S. Williams": Ibid.

Page 69: "unnaturally protruding tongues and eyeballs": Testimony of C. T. Hardeman, *The State of Georgia v. Clyde Manning*, May 31, 1921.

Page 73: "'well-known citizens' of Jasper County": *Covington News*, March 24, 1921, p. 1.

Page 73: "told his story all over again": Ibid.

Page 74: "National Pencil Factory in Atlanta": Dinnerstein, L. *The Leo Frank Case.* Athens, Georgia: University of Georgia Press; 1966: 1.

Page 76: "another high-profile defeat": Ibid., p. 19.

Page 76: "fiendish degenerate": Frey, R. S., Thompson-Frey, N. *The Silent and the Damned: The Murder of Mary Phagan and the Lynching of Leo Frank.* Lanham, Maryland: Madison Books; 1988: 49.

Page 76: "that Frank was homosexual": Dinnerstein, pp. 17–18, 54.

Page 77: "run with innocent blood": Frey, p. 50.

Page 77: "criminal assault and perversion": Ibid., p. 71.

Page 77: "rejected Frank's plea on April 9, 1915": Ibid.

Page 77: "commuted to life imprisonment": Dinnerstein, p. 123.

Page 77: "finest representatives of Marietta": Ibid., p. 139.

Page 78: "originally been dictated by the court": Ibid., p. 141.

Page 79: "members of that race as persecution": Frey, pp. 135–136.

Page 79: "many agreed with him": Dinnerstein, p. 78.

Page 79: "crucial information before the jury": Ibid., p. 154.

Page 79: "very murder of justice itself": Ibid., p. 85.

Page 79: "the judge supposedly told Slaton": Ibid., p. 159.

Page 79: "knew beforehand that he had no case": Ibid., pp. 47–48.

Page 83: "he told the entire story": U.S. Bureau of Investigation, p. 16.

## Chapter 9

Page 85: "obtain men from local jails": *Atlanta Constitution*, April 3, 1921, p. 8A. The newspaper article actually quotes Manning as saying "negroes" instead of "niggers." Based on other documents quoting Manning at the time, it is almost certain that he actually said "niggers" before the grand jury. It is documented in the later trial transcripts that Manning, Williams, attorneys, the judge, and other black witnesses used the word *nigger* in open court as a casual, unremarkable term. The protocol of the day called for cleaning up the quotes to the more polite *negro* for publication in the newspaper, but it should be noted that *nigger* was commonly used among blacks in 1921. The same word, of course, also was used pejoratively, as a slur by whites.

Page 86: "whippings and other forms of abuse": Ibid., p. 1A.

Page 86: "charged with any crime": Ibid., p. 8A. The newspaper article also quotes Williams as saying "negroes" instead of "niggers." It is possible that he actually did clean up his language before the grand jury, but it is more likely that he did not. A white man speaking before a white grand jury in the rural South in 1921 probably saw no reason not to use the common word for blacks. Unlike the same situation seventy-five years later, use of the word *nigger* would not necessarily be seen as pejorative, at least not by other whites.

Page 87: "purchase of some land": Ibid., p. 1A.

Page 87: "insignificant negro": *Atlanta Constitution*, April 10, 1921, p. 1A.

Page 88: "80 percent of them were black": Raper, A. F. *The Tragedy of Lynching*. Chapel Hill, North Carolina: University of North Carolina Press; 1933: 1.

Page 89: "jail where they were being held": Dinnerstein, p. 15.

Page 91: "remark he had made at the coroner's inquest": Ibid., p. 18.

Page 91: "never gave his captors any trouble": Ibid. At one point, Manning misspoke and told the investigators that only he and Williams had killed Lindsey Peterson, Willie Preston, and Harry Price by throwing them off bridges. He later explained that he forgot to mention that Charlie Chisolm was present because, since Chisolm was dead by then, Manning was thinking only of himself and Williams—the two who still could be charged with the murder. The inconsistency is unusual enough for the investigators to highlight it. On the whole, the investigators reported that Manning's confession was remarkably consistent and well supported by the evidence.

Page 91: "one of the best I ever saw": Johnson testimony.

Page 91: "he wanted her protected": *Atlanta Constitution*, April 3, 1921, p. 2A.

Page 92: "no desire to see him persecuted": Ibid.

Page 93: "a bunch of honeysuckles": Statement of Floyd Johnson, filed with the Superior Court of Newton County, Georgia; March 30, 1921.

Page 95: "things were sort of bad on the Williams place": Ibid.

Page 97: "wholesale murder of negroes in Jasper and Newton Counties": *Atlanta Constitution*, April 6, 1921, p. 8.

Page 98: "as the people of any other part of the country can be": *Atlanta Constitution*, April 3, 1921, p. 8A.

Page 98: "nullified the great emancipation work of Abraham Lincoln": *Atlanta Constitution*, April 9, 1921, p. 8A.

Page 99: "the Reverend J. M. Winburn": Ibid.

Page 100: "that justice was accomplished in Newton County": Ibid., p. 2A.

Page 100: "the Williams family and others in Jasper County": *Atlanta Constitution*, April 5, 1921, p. 2.

## Chapter 10

Page 101: "marked by 'perfect order'": *Atlanta Journal*, April 5, 1921, p. 1.

Page 101: "accommodate all the visitors": *Atlanta Journal*, April 6, 1921, p. 3.

Page 103: "you'll see them scatter": *Atlanta Constitution*, April 6, 1921, p. 1.

Page 104: "Don't you worry": Ibid.

Page 104: "she would be arriving soon": *Atlanta Journal*, April 5, 1921, p. 1.

Page 105: "Williams appeared bored": Ibid., p. 2.

Page 105: "defendant's wife made her entrance": Ibid.

Page 106: "court will tolerate no more of this": Ibid.

Page 107: "how worried she was for him": Ibid., p. 1.

Page 108: "'Lessons We Can Learn from the Old South'": *Atlanta Journal Magazine*, May 8, 1921, p. 2.

Page 109: "shaking the defendant's hand": *Atlanta Journal*, April 6, 1921, p. 3.

Page 110: "not seen a single employee abused": *Atlanta Constitution*, April 6, 1921, p. 1.

Page 110: "hotel where he was staying": *Atlanta Journal*, April 6, 1921, p. 3.

Page 111: "names of thirteen fallen soldiers": *Atlanta Constitution*, April 7, 1921, p. 1.

Page 111: "expect they will be here today": *Atlanta Journal*, April 6, 1921, p. 2.

Page 112: "answered 'present' in a shaky voice": Ibid.

Page 114: "little boy curled up and fell asleep": Ibid.

Page 114: "negro carrying a gun": *Atlanta Constitution*, April 7, 1921, p. 2.

Page 117: "plotted to kill negroes by the wholesale": *Atlanta Journal*, April 6, 1921, p. 2.

Page 119: "wasn't a bothering me": *New York Times*, April 7, 1921, p. 1.

Page 120: "after the government officers had been there": *Atlanta Constitution*, April 7, 1921, p. 2.

Page 120: "nobody knows it better than Manning himself": Ibid., p. 1.

Page 120: "perfect order prevailed": *Atlanta Journal*, April 6, 1921, p. 2.

## Chapter 11

Page 121: "wore a heavy black veil": *Atlanta Journal*, April 7, 1921, p. 1.

Page 122: "They're dead now": Ibid.

Page 122: "as fast as they were discovered": Ibid., p. 12.

Page 123: "I am uncomfortably dry": Ibid.

Page 123: "without any cross-examination": Daniel, P. *The Shadow of Slavery: Peonage in the South, 1901–1969.* Urbana, Illinois: University of Illinois Press; 1972:125.

Page 123: "Well, gentlemen": Testimony of John S. Williams, *The State of Georgia v. John S. Williams*, April 5, 1921. Also, *Atlanta Journal*, April 7, 1921, p. 1. The version of Williams's statement to the court depicted here is not exactly the account found in either the court transcript or the newspaper article. In comparing the two, it is apparent that the newspaper article is not a verbatim report and is more likely an approximation based on the reporter's notes and memory. The court transcript is more reliable but also may not represent an exact version, since the defendant's statement rambled on nonstop for some time and the court reporter was taking notes by hand. The account used here is a summary based on both versions, relying more heavily on the court transcript. The meaning of the statement and key points were the same in both versions and are reflected accurately.

Page 127: Closing arguments by attorneys Howard and Johnson: *Atlanta Journal*, April 8, 1921, pp. 1–2; *Atlanta Constitution*, April 9, 1921, pp. 1–2; *The State of Georgia v. John S. Williams*, April 8, 1921. The closing arguments depicted here are summaries based on the reports of two newspapers and the transcript from the trial itself. All of the quoted statements in the closing arguments were reported in at least one of the sources, and usually all three. "That's the kind of nigger Atlanta seems to want" was spoken by an assistant to the defense attorney who presented a small portion of the closing argument.

Page 129: "Let me talk to Mama": *Atlanta Journal*, April 8, 1921, p. 1.

Page 129: "Absolutely I do": *Atlanta Journal*, April 8, 1921, p. 1.

Page 130: "before he could leave the courthouse": *Atlanta Journal*, April 8, 1921, p. 2.

Page 130: "I believe we whipped 'em": Ibid.

Page 135: "We, the jury, find the defendant": Jury verdict form, *The State of Georgia v. John S. Williams*, April 9, 1921.

Page 135: "began to sob openly": *Atlanta Journal*, April 9, 1921, p. 1.

Page 135: "My God, Daddy! I can't stand this!": Ibid.

Page 136: "I am innocent of this charge": Ibid.

Page 137: "whether to break his neck": *Atlanta Constitution*, April 10, 1921, p. 2A.

## Chapter 12

Page 139: "reach a verdict no matter what": *Atlanta Constitution*, April 10, 1921, p. 2A.

Page 140: "another white man was convicted in 1966": Daniel, P. *The Shadow of Slavery: Peonage in the South, 1901–1969*. Urbana, Illinois: University of Illinois Press; 1972:126.

Page 140: "before which this case was tried": *Atlanta Constitution*, April 10, 1921, p. 8A.

Page 140: "may it ever be lifted up": *Atlanta Journal*, April 10, 1921, p. 8A.

Page 141: "as we owe it to no one else": *Atlanta Journal*, April 9, 1921, p. 6.

Page 141: "will clean up the county": *New York Times*, April 10, 1921, p. 1A.

Page 141: "prove that what I say is true": *Atlanta Constitution*, April 10, 1921, p. 1A.

Page 141: "Manning rushed back to his cell": Ibid.

Page 142: "responsible for many more killings": *Atlanta Constitution*, April 12, 1921, p. 2.

Page 142: "hiding out in Mexico": *Atlanta Constitution*, April 10, 1921, p. 1A.

Page 143: "long fur coat and black veil": *Atlanta Journal*, April 12, 1921, p. 2.

Page 143: "driven out by organized lawlessness": Dorsey, H. M. *A Statement from Governor Hugh M. Dorsey as to the Negro in Georgia*. Atlanta; 1921.

Page 144: "the civilized world has long ago agreed to abandon": *Atlanta Journal Magazine*, June 10, 1921, p. 2.

Page 144: "Sunday sermon in May": *Atlanta Constitution*, May 16, 1921, p. 1.

Page 146: "soon after the Williams trial": *Messenger*, March 1921, p. 210.

## Chapter 13

Page 150: "concerning their relationship to Williams": *Atlanta Journal*, May 30, 1921, p. 1.

Page 152: "how the bodies of Peterson and Preston had been found in the river": Testimony of Carl Wheeler, *State of Georgia v. Clyde Manning*, May 30, 1921.

Page 152: "that Manning had identified the bodies": Testimony of B. L. Johnson, *State of Georgia v. Clyde Manning*, May 30, 1921.

Page 155: "Agent A. J. Wismer of the Bureau of Investigation": Testimony of A. J. Wismer, *State of Georgia v. Clyde Manning*, May 30, 1921.

Page 158: "more points before letting the agent leave the stand": *Atlanta Journal*, May 30, 1921, p. 11.

Page 158: "told Underwood he could proceed with that line of questioning": *Atlanta Constitution*, May 31, 1921, p. 2.

Page 159: "all evidence should be limited to that one murder": Ibid.

Page 159: "Howard rose to deliver it.": Ibid.

## Chapter 14

Page 161: "Underwood began to ask about specific incidents": Testimony of Clyde Freeman, *State of Georgia v. Clyde Manning*, May 30, 1921.

Page 162: "sometimes carried pistols": There is some confusion in the records as to who the second farm overseer, or "boss," was in addition to Manning. Claude Freeman apparently was the second farm boss, but even those involved in the trial seemed confused at points, as when Brand at one point asks Clyde Freeman if he carried a pistol and is surprised when the witness says no. The confusion probably can be traced to the very similar names among people who were related and also the number of nicknames that also were very similar.

Page 164: "too scared not to": *Atlanta Constitution*, May 31, 1921, p. 2.

Page 166: "did nothing to intervene": Testimony of B. B. Bohannon, *State of Georgia v. Clyde Manning*, May 31, 1921.

Page 167: "not been there since last Thanksgiving": Testimony of Gus Chapman, *State of Georgia v. Clyde Manning*, May 30, 1921.

Page 168: "vicious hands of the Williams men": Testimony of Frank Dozier, *State of Georgia v. Clyde Manning*, May 30, 1921.

Page 169: "no indications of excitement or disorder": *Atlanta Journal*, May 31, 1921, p. 1.

Page 169: "with his hands folded and began to speak to the jury": Ibid.

Page 169: "I am not guilty of murder": Statement of Clyde Manning, *State of Georgia v. Clyde Manning*, May 31, 1921.

Page 172: "returned to the defense table": *Atlanta Journal*, May 31, 1921, p. 1.

Page 173: "should be meted out the same punishment": *Atlanta Constitution*, June 1, 1921, p. 15.

Page 173: "under threats and menaces and under coercion": Charge to the jury, *State of Georgia v. Clyde Manning*, May 31, 1921.

Page 174: "when the jury began returning to the courtroom": *Atlanta Constitution*, June 1, 1921, p. 1.

Page 175: "Have a seat": *Atlanta Constitution*, June 1, 1921, p. 1.

## Epilogue

Page 177: "spent the whole time in Florida": *Atlanta Journal*, February 16, 1927, p. 1.

Page 177: "mother, Emma, married his uncle Rufus": U.S. Bureau of Investigation. Report by Agent C. E. Argetright, November 12, 1928: p. 2.

Page 178: "eventful years 1917–1921.": *Atlanta Journal*, June 13, 1948, p. 8B.

Page 178: "national recognition as Frank's prosecutor": *Atlanta Constitution*, June 12, 1948, p. 1.

## Conclusion

Page 182: "broke his will to resist": Blassingame, John W. *The Slave Community: Plantation Life in the Antebellum South*. New York: Oxford University Press; 1979.